THE
DOVER
PATROL
1914–18

*Day by day contemplate your
country's power till you grow
full of passionate love for her.
And when you realise her greatness,
remember that it was the
dead who won it for you.*

Thucydides

THE
DOVER
PATROL
1914–18

Roy Humphreys

SUTTON PUBLISHING

First published in 1998 by
Sutton Publishing Limited · Phoenix Mill
Thrupp · Stroud · Gloucestershire · GL5 2BU

British Library Cataloguing in Publication Data
A catalogue record for this book is available from the British Library

ISBN 0 7509 1967 1

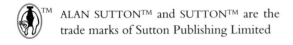
ALAN SUTTON™ and SUTTON™ are the
trade marks of Sutton Publishing Limited

Typeset in 10/12pt Bembo.
Typesetting and origination by
Sutton Publishing Limited.
Printed in Great Britain by
WBC Limited, Bridgend.

Contents

Acknowledgements

Contributors to this reappraisal of a naval command that captivated the imagination of the public are hereby acknowledged with sincere gratitude.

I am particularly indebted to Lord Keyes of Zeebrugge and Dover who not only allowed me access to a copy of Bernard Gribble's painting, used for the jacket, but more especially for his generosity to let me quote freely from his father's *The Naval Memoirs*. David G. Collyer was especially helpful, as ever, in supplying some illustrations from his extensive collection. I would also like to thank the Trustees of the Imperial War Museum, London, for permission to use pictures from their archive; the staff of the Heritage Section of the Folkestone Library; John Iveson of the Dover Museum for allowing me the privilege to sort through their picture library; E.F. Cheesman; A. Moore; John Croft; John T. Williams, and a special thank you to R.W.J. 'Bob' McNae, who discovered an old photo album in his loft.

Preface

This history of the Dover Patrol during the First World War seems barely adequate after researching the whole complexity of Dover Command. It is a vast subject, bigger than I at first anticipated, and in the final analysis I realize I have scarcely scratched the surface of it. Much of the admiration you, the reader, might feel about the men who served in the Dover Patrol, after the narrative unfolds to the conclusion, must inevitably derive from the existing records.

I have given it a new lease of life, for nothing has been written about it since the 1930s. Through the narrative, photographs, maps and memorabilia, this book will, despite some variations in recorded data, reveal the extent of the Dover Patrol's achievements in the First World War.

From its early beginnings the Dover Patrol grew to become one of the most important naval commands during that war, performing several duties simultaneously as the war developed. You will read of anti-submarine patrols, the continuous escorting of merchantmen, hospital ships and troop ships, guarding the southernmost waters of the North Sea, the laying and daily maintenance of anti-submarine nets, sweeping up German minefields and laying minefields in the Dover Strait and – not least – the bombardment of enemy positions on the Belgian coast.

Dover Command, of which the Dover Patrol was a part, assembled cruisers, destroyers, monitors, armed trawlers and drifters, paddle minesweepers, motor launches and coastal motor boats and submarines. In addition the Royal Naval Air Service, attached to Dover Command, possessed fighter aircraft, bomber aircraft, reconnaissance aircraft, airships and flying boats.

Unbidden, perhaps, the sensation is brought back to those times and to those who have experienced the trauma of war at sea, and who might, even now, shiver in the instant recall of the sound of explosives and the reek of burning cordite and even the awful sight of men being killed.

But the reader of this appraisal is not allowed to forget the supreme sacrifice of the men who manned the little drifters and trawlers. Neither must it be forgotten that the principal credit for the U-boat losses in the vast complex of the Folkestone/Gris Nez minefield, from January to September 1918, must inevitably go to Vice-Admiral Bacon. It was he, after all, who originated and worked out every detail and through his untiring, dedicated self-determination caused more than a dozen U-boats to founder. It was to his bitter humiliation that he was relieved of his command and did not see the fruits of his Herculean labours.

The Dover Patrol never faltered during its arduous duties and many acts of heroism and bravery went unrecorded. After the celebrated blockade operations upon Zeebrugge and Ostend in April 1918, its reputation was assured and was held in high esteem by the Allied powers.

CHAPTER ONE

'A Miniature Tin God'

There is, in the Dover Strait – and especially in summer – an almost ethereal quality about the sea at dawn. The water can be velvet smooth as if in a Mediterranean guise, with a paper-like surface wrinkled only by a light breeze. Eventually the water takes on a bluish colour as the light strengthens from the east but beyond this display of tints, a golden hue lies low on the horizon, spilling pastel shades of blue and green upon the wavelets. As the sun rises above the horizon the whole sea changes in colour until a shimmering golden path stretches from eye to skyline.

In this clear morning light the 6th Destroyer Flotilla, in three ordered columns of four ships each, slid smoothly towards its destination. The passage of the ships through the water set a slight breeze to moan low in the rigging. The masts carried the signal halliards and wireless aerials, which gently undulated to the rise and fall of the ship. The only sound was from the white, phosphorescent turmoil thrust upwards from the stern by the turning screws.

The Tribal class destroyers kept perfect station with each other as though it were an indivisible unit. Occasionally a string of gaily coloured bunting would quickly slide up the leaders' signal halliards. Hardly had the flags blown out clear before every other vessel would be flying the white and red answering pendant. It was July 1914, and Lieutenant H.D. Adair Hall, in command of *Mohawk*, was leading the dozen Tribals to Dover to join the '30-knotters' already at anchor in the harbour.

The so-called 30-knotters were incapable of exceeding 25 knots at full speed even with a strong stern wind, as most of them had been built in 1896 and were in poor shape. Many hours were spent on patching up dented platework and their black painted hulls were now covered with grey. Their only saving grace was the highly polished brass windvanes on the masthead and other brass fittings that gleamed in the blackest of nights. No one dared paint them for it was one of the captain's punishments to 'clean brasses'. Captains, officers and men, however, were justly proud of their floating homes. Matelots to a man put up with every inconvenience, not least the dreadful accommodation in dark, ill-ventilated compartments officially designated mess decks. Only two things stood out in their favour – freedom from the big-ship discipline and the sixpence per day increase to their meagre wages.

The immediate cause of the First World War, which so suddenly burst upon an apprehensive Europe in the autumn of 1914, was the unfettered brashness of Imperial Germany. Nursed in the Prussian tradition their statesmen had angered most of their neighbours. It was as if the people had been taught that war was their national function. By the summer of 1914 they had threatened once too often and then realized, when it was too late, they were unable to stop the avalanche they had started.

While Admiral Penrose-Fitzgerald and others were convinced that Germany intended war with France, and perhaps to invade Britain, generally speaking the British just smiled and thought the Admiral one of the eccentrics of their time. But neither did they attach any credence to the sudden assassination of the heir to the Austrian throne, Archduke Franz Ferdinand, and his wife, at Sarajevo on 28 June. Would it be the reason for Germany's campaign for world power? On the contrary, it was the excuse.

Germany's pre-war industrial output had quadrupled. Her whole economic structure depended largely on her ability to secure rapidly expanding markets, markets that could only be accelerated to keep ahead of bankruptcy. Most of the industrialized world was heading in that same direction, following Britain's fine example and attempting to equal her success. Fostering their new industries the businessmen of every large nation in Europe, helped by state subsidies and a bogus system of credit, struggled to undercut their rivals. The world became a huge field of exploitation, everyone competing with one another for new customers and raw materials.

Envying Britain's vast empire, the Continental industrial powers vied with each other to found their own empires in the still largely unexploited territories where cheap raw materials could be procured. For these and many other reasons, beyond the remit of this work, the Germans and the British were rivals. The Germans envied, secretly admired but probably disliked the British, for they were seeking the empire they had long possessed and would not use for themselves in hegemony.

By the turn of the century Germany had the largest and most highly organized army in the modern world and was often recognized as invincible. Although the British were somewhat reluctant to concern themselves in Europe's affairs, they did actually reject Germany's attempts to rule Europe.

There were psychological differences, too. When the Germans could not quite reach omnipotence they gave themselves a certain *modus vivendi*. The British just laughed at them, which did not help, for it cut their vanity to the quick. German statesmen, diplomats and merchants, with hardly any exceptions, held a grudge against Britain which was to astonish the people in 1914.

Perhaps the most serious difference, however, despite the rivalry of commerce, was the blue ribbon of sea power. A deep-sea fleet came to be regarded as a national necessity on both sides. Lord Palmerston, when answering a question in the House as early as July 1863, said, 'There is no disguising the fact that what is at the bottom of the whole German design . . . is the dream of a German fleet and the wish to get Kiel as a German seaport'.

The first German Navy Act of 1898 set out to develop the High Seas Fleet within ten years, a race for supremacy and command of the high seas that quite upset Britain. However, there was something incongruous in the idea that German naval ambitions should be treated seriously. After the Boer War, Britain began to wake up to the fact that a European power was actually challenging command of the high seas. At the close of King Edward VII's brief reign and the beginning of King George V's, Britain's attentions were drawn towards the disquieting spectacle of German dreadnoughts swiftly gliding down the slips at Kiel and Wilhelmshaven into the waters of the Baltic and North Seas.

Admiral Sir Percy Scott's visionary letter to *The Times*, in July 1914, said:

All war is, of course, barbarous, but in war the purpose of the enemy is to crush his foe; to arrive at this he will attack where the foe is most vulnerable. Our most vulnerable point is our food and oil supply. The submarine has introduced a new method of attacking these supplies. Will feelings of humanity restrain our enemy from using it?

Twenty years before Sir Percy's clear observations of the inevitable, the design and construction of submarines was going on apace throughout Europe. Admiral von Tirpitz had said in a Reichstag speech in 1901, 'Germany has no need of submarines'. But the Imperial German Navy, later to become Europe's largest builder of submarines, completed its first *unterseeboot* in December 1906.

The first practical submarine anywhere in the world was built by the Dutchman Cornelis Drebbel, which was demonstrated on the Thames in 1620. But 150 years passed before the American David Bushnell designed the next. His *Turtle* actually attacked the British frigate *Eagle* while she lay off New York in 1776. Bushnell's craft was replaced by his countryman Robert Fulton's *Nautilus*, launched in July 1800.

Admiral von Tirpitz had misled the world, as the Bavarian inventor Wilhelm Bauer launched his *Der Brandtacher* in 1850. It was fully submersible and was Germany's first *unterseeboot*. Improved designs and construction techniques continued and the development of the *unterseeboot* never looked back. The first vessel, the *V1*, was completed by the Krupp-Germania works at Kiel in December 1906. By 1914 Germany had twenty-three available.

The British were not taking a back seat, despite the Revd G.W. Garrett's unfortunate private venture: his steam-driven *Resurgam*, sank off Birkenhead on her maiden voyage in 1878. British submarines can trace their ancestry back to John P. Holland, an Irish Republican who built the first practical craft in America with funds provided by Republican sympathizers, who intended to use it against the British. He sold it to the American Navy who promptly sold it to Britain. The first British submarine built by Vickers, *Holland 1*, was launched in October 1901.

It was not, however, accepted with any enthusiasm by the Admiralty who remarked at the time, 'What the future value of these boats may be in naval warfare can only be a matter of conjecture'. Be that as it may, significant improvements in design and construction gave the Royal Navy a lead by 1914, with a total of ninety-eight submarines either built or in the process of being built.

The Kaiser was quick to assure the British that there was no truth in the assumption that the German Navy Bill was meant as a challenge to British naval supremacy. But the sea was Britain's lifeline. While the British populace was struggling for a better and happier existence a young Winston Churchill, now First Sea Lord, boldly laid down two ship's keels to Germany's one. Churchill's appointment at the Admiralty put into motion the creation of a new outlook in the navy upon the sea warfare to come. The fighting of the future was to be upon the high seas, or blue water as it was often called. The enemy was not going to be encouraged to bottle up his dreadnoughts in harbours but to be tempted out for a fight and destruction, wrought by superior speed and heavier armament.

It was the educated minority rather than the majority who soon grasped the overall

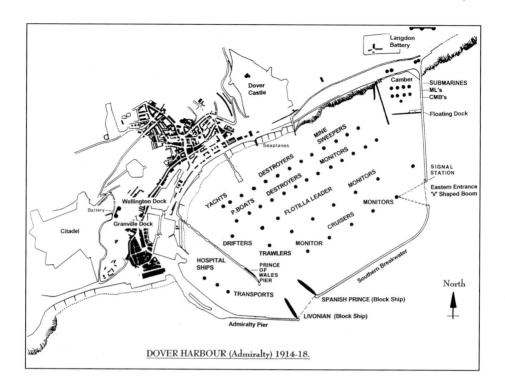

DOVER HARBOUR (Admiralty) 1914-18.

significance of what was actually happening when, through an agreement, the French were given the task of policing the Mediterranean and the British were given the responsibility for the defence of the English Channel and Atlantic coasts.

When the First Sea Lord was inspecting some new shipbuilding on the Clyde, and having heard of the Kaiser's speech announcing a large increase in Germany's shipbuilding programme, he declared, 'for us a great fleet is a necessity, for Germany a luxury. It is existence for us, it is expansion for them'.

It only needed a small spark to set off the politically explosive material. At Germany's head – though far from exercising a controlling influence over politicians or his vast military machine – was the Kaiser, an intelligent, garrulous and quite undisciplined man. The official Teutonic policy of the High Seas Fleet, however, was to hold back until the margin of Britain's sea power had been worn down by either raid, mine or submarine, then risk all upon an sea battle in blue water.

The British statesmen close to world affairs knew that the conflict that had prevailed before was considered child's play in comparison with what they now recognized would happen it the most powerful empires in the world faced each other in a deadly battle. At the time Britain knew enough of Germany to know that she would fight with desperation, that her plans had been well laid and that she had left nothing to chance.

But then it all happened rather suddenly. The British fleet had been reviewed by George V at Spithead in the middle of July and afterwards certain exercises were carried out in lieu of the usual summer manoeuvres. These did not last very long, however, for in the last week of July ships of the Home Fleet returned to their respective home ports to effect repairs and take on fuel and ammunition. Four days' leave was granted to the crews. But their leave was short-lived as each matelot received a small orange envelope, a telegram, which succinctly stated, 'Rejoin your ship at once'.

British Foreign Secretary Sir Edward Grey had done his utmost to confine hostilities to the Balkans and so prevent the outbreak of a general European war. He had urged for a European Conference to decide the questions at issue. Germany, however, refused point-blank to cooperate. On 31 July Grey had sent to both France and Germany asking for an assurance that Belgian neutrality would be respected. France gave her promise, but Germany refused. This then was the decisive issue for Britain. On 4 August Grey demanded an explicit pledge from Germany on the subject. At 1400 hrs news reached him that Germany had already invaded Belgium.

The British people were suddenly aware they were involved in another European war. Beyond the knowledge that Britain had promised to maintain Belgian integrity and her neutrality, scarcely anyone realized that an invasion was a distinct possibility. More importantly, an overcrowded and quite unprepared island could not feed itself for more than a few weeks at the most. Britain was dependent on imported food. The people – even after four generations of *laissez-faire* thinking – flung themselves as one man into the fray. Patriotism was a peculiar concern of each state in Europe, taught in schools and stamped upon the mind and body of every citizen. But in Britain it was and is so different. The British seemed not to teach patriotism with any fervour. If the individual chose to be patriotic, that was his affair. Quite wrongly the Germans had assumed the British to have a casualness that evoked no love for their country, and assumed also that they lacked any fighting spirit of self-sacrifice, discipline and *esprit de corps*. How wrong they were.

With their long history the British retained a stronger consciousness and underlying unity than probably any other people in the world. Usually late in the practice of modern warfare, once they got the hang of it, they set their minds to it and soon caught up with the material accomplishments of their antagonists.

At Dover on 4 August 1914 dinner in ships' wardrooms had been over for some time, the long tables in the apartments had been cleared. The mess, although it was nearing 2200 hrs, seemed full of officers, far more crowded than any other evening. Even the dress was noticeably different as most wore the 'monkey jacket', the eight-buttoned reefer coat usually seen only during the daytime, instead of the customary mess jacket, low waistcoat and starched white shirt.

There was a distinct air of expectancy. On the larger ships lying at anchor, the gun casemate, which usually served as an officers' smoking room, was now cleared of furniture and replaced with shells, instantly converted back to the legitimate function of an armoured gun position. The air in the wardroom was blue with tobacco smoke as the occupants sat in the well-worn armchairs or on sofas. In the cramped mess decks of the smaller destroyers, the officers were reading the daily newspapers. During most of the day, additional to the normal harbour routine, pictures had vanished from bulkhead walls and carpets and other non-essential items had disappeared. Cabins, too, were short of their comforts, such as they were: curtains, pictures, rugs and photographs had been sent ashore.

There was a sense of urgency as the officers packed away exquisite striped shirts, suits of plain clothes, uniform dress, frock coats and mess jackets. Afterwards, they were left with a shallow bath, the drawers under the bed, a small bookcase containing a copy of King's Regulations and Admiralty Instruction, and a washstand.

The atmosphere in the wardrooms was by no means gloomy, everyone seemed in good spirits except that perhaps the bubbling conversation and usual hilarity was a trifle forced. But no other signs associated with the eve of hostilities were evident. Deep in their subconscious, however, they knew that they were about to take part in a great struggle of arms. It was just a matter of time.

Germany was at war with Russia, her troops violated the neutrality of Luxembourg and Belgium and had crossed the French frontier at various points. Urgent wireless messages in cypher – the contents of which was only known to senior officers – had been pouring in all day. Steam had been raised in the battleships, cruisers and destroyers in every British naval port and they were ready to slip their cables at an instant's notice.

It was a little after 2300 hrs – all wardrooms had closed for the night and officers had retired to their quite bare cabins – when the sound of cheering broke out. Within minutes every commanding officer was reading a copy of a message sent by the king to Sir John Jellicoe, the Commander-in-Chief of the Home Fleet.

The *Mohawk*'s crew, not to be outdone, left their hammocks *en masse*, crowded the upper deck and gave vent to their feelings.

At this grave moment in our national history I send to you, and through you to the officers and men of the fleet of which you have assumed command, the assurance of my confidence that under your direction they will revive and renew the glories of the Royal Navy, and prove once again the sure shield of Britain and her Empire in her hour of trial.

The 6th Destroyer Flotilla, commanded by Captain C.D. Johnson, RN, and officially known as Captain (D), was considered by many to be a miniature Admiral, his flotilla of boats a miniature fleet, and the officers in charge of their own division of four boats were known as the commanders in all naval signals. Lieutenant-Commander Evans once said of them, 'It would not be inaccurate to describe each destroyer captain as a miniature "Tin God"'. He went on to say that they were mostly young men, full of independent opinion and initiative, commanding respect and most often the affection of their command.

The four light cruisers attached to the Dover Command were not regarded as modern ships. Whatever plans the Germans had regarding Dover and the adjacent French coast as easy pickings, it might be said that the 6th Flotilla was eager to get to grips with its enemy. When yeoman signallers handed to their respective captains the message, 'Commence hostilities against Germany', there was an immediate response from the ships' companies which spread like wildfire. The *Mohawk*'s crew – not to be outdone – left their hammocks *en masse*, crowded the upper deck and gave vent to their pent-up feelings. Wondering what all the fuss was about, the rest of the destroyers enthusiastically joined in. Armed to the teeth with mess kettles and any other utensils they could find handy, they marched round the decks creating pandemonium and noise. They were demonstrating a patriotism that the Germans never knew existed, a patriotism that lies dormant in a Briton's heart.

CHAPTER TWO

'Van Tromp, Old Dear'

In hindsight it cannot be said with any conviction that, as the only naval base at the southernmost end of the North Sea, Dover was at all prepared for any warlike activity. The naval harbour had been completed just five years previously and during the intervening period it had been dredged as deep as was possible. In the north-east corner of the harbour, a camber had been made to shelter submarines, motor launches (MLs) and coastal motor boats (CMBs), and several oil tanks had been built into the cliff face. The Admiralty had decided to build an enclosed harbour in 1897. The work was completed and formally opened in 1907 by the then Prince of Wales, later King George V.

The enclosed harbour of 1914 was intended to accommodate battleships as well as destroyers and submarines. The entrances, however, so badly designed, had not been improved and the boom defences made specifically to protect them were, even before the war, known to be quite useless. The calmest seas and even a flood tide carried them away like flotsam. The currents at these two entrances – east and west – at certain states of the tide, were found to be extremely dangerous to negotiate.

When the British sea antagonist had changed from France to Germany, the Royal Navy battle squadrons were sent further north. The occupation of the Belgian coast by German forces had never entered into the equation of a war with that country. Even when the war seemed imminent, British eyes were largely focused on the Elbe and not on Ostend and Zeebrugge. So Dover was not considered a base of particular naval importance, either by the politicians or the Admiralty.

Therefore, at the outbreak of war, the original Dover Patrol formed part of the East Coast Command under Rear-Admiral G.A. Ballard, who made his headquarters at Harwich. The chief function of its operations was initially to prevent German ships breaking through the British lines of defence and sailing down the Channel to the Atlantic. All German homeward-bound ships were to be intercepted by the Dover Patrol, while all neutral ships were examined to see if they carried contraband materials of war. As a consequence all vessels of every sort and tonnage, whether British or neutral, were made to anchor in the Downs off Deal and were examined while they rode at anchor. To prevent any ships slipping through the wide expanse of water between the treacherous Goodwin Sands and the French coast a large minefield was eventually laid, closing off most, if not all, of the relevant sea, leaving a closely guarded channel open near the French coast from Calais to Dunkirk.

The waters in which the Dover Patrol worked extended from the Scheldt to the North Foreland and from Beachy Head due south to the French coast. It formed an area of water of about 4,000 square miles. The vital front that needed protection was 55 miles long, with Nieuport and the Allied lines on the extreme right, then 20 miles of trade route to Calais; there was then a further 20 miles of the mouth of the English Channel, through which commerce ships, raiders and destroyers might pass. On the extreme left was the Downs anchorage with its north and south entrances, between which eighty to one hundred ships could lay anchor by both day or night. Ostend and Zeebrugge were only 62 and 72 miles away respectively from Dover, the nearest point to the English coast, and Dunkirk, a satellite of Dover Command, only 23 miles from enemy-held Ostend.

Despite the well-laid plans of the Admiralty, it was soon apparent that the Dover Strait was destined to become just as important as the east coast. The subsequent rapid advance of German troops towards Paris and the consequent capture of a large part of Belgium, with the utmost need to keep British lines of communication open with the British Expeditionary Force (BEF) in France, coupled with the detection and interception of enemy submarines, all pointed to the strategic importance of Dover's naval complex. The First Sea Lord of the Admiralty, Winston Churchill, was already firmly convinced of the aeroplane's future as a military weapon and so, by 1 July 1914, the RNAS had been formed. A number of seaplane stations were established along the east and south-east coast of England and among the first was Dover's seaplane station adjacent to the Marine Parade.

When the Kaiser's troops moved westward the Dover Patrol became a separate command under the tutelage of Rear Admiral the Honourable Horace Hood. Among the complexities of the new command were the twenty or so drifters from the northern fishing fleets, hurriedly fitted out at either Yarmouth or Lowestoft. The Auxiliary Service – as the drifters and trawlers became known – was not fully operational until February 1915. However, under the command of Captain H.E. Grace, they were originally put to work with the quite bizarre idea of entangling enemy submarines in their drift nets, much the same as they would in catching fish. When the trawlers arrived soon afterwards both drifters and trawlers, based at either Dover or Ramsgate, swept up enemy mines and regulated shipping traffic in and around the Downs anchorage for the next four years.

The sea mine became recognized as an aggressive weapon from the early 1800s, especially after the Danish brig *Dorothy* was sunk by a primitive mine off Walmer Castle by the American inventor Robert Fulton in 1805. It was an experiment to impress William Pitt just before Trafalgar but the year before, Lord Keith had used barrels of black powder against French ships off Boulogne. Various mine devices were used in the American Civil War; the Russians had used them to defend the ports of Sebastopol and Kronstadt during the Crimean War; and they were used in the Russo-Japanese War of 1904.

The British Admiralty, however, seemed unimpressed by these experiments, some of which had successfully sunk ships, whereas the Germans were noticeably quick to learn lessons from such practices. They carried out elaborate experiments and laid plans for the use of mines in war. But still the Admiralty had not foreseen the possibility of submersibles laying mines around the coasts of England. It was Admiral Lord Charles Beresford, Commander-in-Chief, Home Fleet who, in 1907, foresaw the need to protect naval ships against mine warfare. It was Beresford who first suggested the use of Grimsby trawlers for minesweeping duties in time of war.

At the outbreak of war in 1914, Germany was laying mines off the Suffolk coast. They were either spherical or pear-shaped, containing about 350 lb of guncotton, trinitrotoluene (TNT), or amatol. This explosive, together with batteries, took up half the space, while the remainder was filled with air to give buoyancy. About half-a-dozen horns were fixed to the upper half of the mine, each having a glass tube within its structure containing a chemical mixture. When a ship's hull struck a horn, the glass would break allowing the release of chemical liquid to activate the battery which fired the detonator.

Mines were attached to a sinker and when laid would sink to the bottom of the sea. After a short interval the mine was automatically released and shot to the surface unreeling a mooring wire, while the sinker – to which the wire was attached – remained on the bottom. A hydrostat system gripped the wire when the mine had reached the required height, usually just below the surface of the water.

The task of sweeping up mines was fraught with difficulties, not least the atrocious weather conditions in which the trawlers worked. The Admiralty boffins came up with a serrated cable called a sweep wire, which was towed between two trawlers and which was held beneath the water surface by a heavy kite system. In 1917 a fish-shaped paravane was invented that was used by warships and merchantmen for their own protection. One to port and one to starboard, they were extended at an angle from the ship's bows on cables which cut through mine wires very effectively. The paravane system of mine cutting was, it has been suggested, a secret that was kept from the Germans.

Regarded by the Admiralty as an 'expensive luxury', Captain Dorling wrote in 1935, the British sea mine was badly designed and cost a mere £40 each. During trials only one third exploded on impact with a target. There were just 4,000 available when war broke out in 1914. It was not until September 1917 that a new design evolved – the H2 – which, incidentally, was almost certainly based on the superior German example.

Captain W. Vansittard RN, whose yacht *Diane* operated patrols, was appointed Traffic Manager for the Dover Strait. Captain G.N. Tomlin RN, became the Senior Naval Officer Ramsgate, in charge of the Downs anchorage.

With a compliment of armed boarding steamers based at Ramsgate, the Examination Service was established and was assisted by a small fleet of semi-armed drifters operating in the defence of the Downs anchorage against a surprise enemy attack. There is little doubt that the presence of this quite small flotilla of ships went some way to checking German sea movements along the English coast; their intention probably being to eventually seize the Channel ports prior to an invasion.

In any event, shortly after the receipt of the 'hostilities' signal, the sleek-hulled destroyers of the 6th Flotilla were observed slipping their cables. The weather was fine, clear and warm. The signal lamps blinked in the darkness between the leader and the port war signal station as each ship glided through the eastern entrance of the harbour on their first war patrol. This little flotilla of ships was the nucleus from which the Dover Patrol afterwards evolved. They had passed the camber in which lay the submarine tender ship *Hazard*, with her seven C class submarines tucked in beside her like ducklings, Close by lay the old Atlantic Fleet second-class cruiser *Arrogant* – now gutted and simply a hulk full of stores and naval gadgetry. She was to serve as the

The F class Tribal destroyer *Zulu*, built in 1909 and commanded by Lieutenant-Commander L.D'O. Bignall, was mined in October 1916 in the Dover Strait.

stationary flagship of Rear Admiral Hood, Vice-Admiral Bacon and lastly, Vice-Admiral Keyes.

On the eve of hostilities it had been a Bank Holiday Monday. At midday crowds had assembled on the cliffs to observe the French cruiser squadron of six vessels steaming up and down the Channel. The 6th Flotilla had been brought up to war strength with crews who had arrived by special train from Portsmouth. The destroyers had remained in harbour and, with full steam up, their oil-stoked boilers poured out a dense black smoke over the town. The powerful smell of oil and paraffin mixture from the funnels of *Afridi*, *Amazon*, *Cossack*, *Gurkha*, *Mohawk*, *Tartar*, *Saracen*, *Maori*, *Nubian*, *Viking* and *Zulu* pervaded the nostrils and was to linger in the memory of all those assembled on the cliffs.

Adding to the excitement, that same afternoon saw the first aeroplanes of the Royal Flying Corps arrive at Swingate Downs, above the harbour. As night fell, the London Electrical Engineers switched on their powerful searchlights from the breakwater and swept the harbour entrances continuously.

In the first few months of the war, the German fleet had been given credit for enterprise that it never actually showed. No one – least of all the destroyer crews of the Dover Patrol – expected for one moment that two years would elapse before the enemy showed itself in the Strait of Dover in any comparable force.

The 6th Flotilla maintained its patrol vigil from the onset and took charge of half the English Channel while the French took on the other half, a line being taken from Goodwin Sands across to Dunkirk. For some months the French laboured with the

Zulu seized the four-masted German barque *Perkoe* on 5 August 1914. *Perkoe*'s master cheerily invited *Zulu*'s captain on board for a drink.

British at the somewhat uninteresting work of intercepting all vessels attempting to pass through the Dover Strait. The Examination Service personnel were a collection of officers and men with merchant service experience, who shrewdly sized up fools from rogues and separated the wheat from the chaff. Destroyer captains were constantly on the bridge and, at night especially, experienced great difficulty with vessels who tried hard to evade examination. Some of them were clever in evasion tactics and, inevitably, some got through.

HMS *Zulu* was the first destroyer to seize and bring to Dover a beautiful four-masted German barque called *Perkoe*. Her captain spoke English well but knew nothing of the war. He cheerily invited the *Zulu*'s commander on board and asked him down for a drink. He broke down when he heard the news and was near to tears when he realized that *Zulu* had actually captured him. The SS *Franz Horn* from Lubeck was the next ship to be seized.

The destroyers had three days in harbour out of four and three nights at sea out of four. It was soon found unnecessary to patrol so closely during the daylight hours, for the patrol could hold the Strait with just five destroyers, whereas at night the number doubled.

The Royal Navy discovered that Dutch and Swedish vessels ignored the patrol signals to heave to and only succumbed to Admiralty orders after a shot was fired across their bows. Politeness through the megaphone was often ignored which resorted to such familiarities as described by Evans: 'Van Tromp, old dear, you'll never see Rotterdam, Schedam or Amsterdam again unless you take your damn ship through the Downs!'

The Dutch liner *Tubantia* was made to drop anchor off Folkestone. She had several Germans aboard but the Admiralty had issued orders not to arrest Germans travelling on neutral ships. Later on in the war, the Germans torpedoed and sank her themselves. Ordinary patrolling was a pleasure to begin with, despite some tension, but the destroyer captains began to grow envious when news reached them of sporadic sea actions. One such action concerned destroyers with the light cruiser *Amphion*, when the German minelayer *Köningen Luise* was sunk by destroyers *Lance* and *Landrail*. These same destroyers rescued the survivors of the *Amphion* the following day after she struck a mine in the Thames Estuary, laid by her original victim. *Amphion* lost 150 men. Five days later the Admiralty was justly proud to be able to claim first naval laurels when Admiral Beatty made a daring raid into Heligoland Bight and wiped out three enemy cruisers and a destroyer, with the loss to the enemy of 700 men.

Seven minelayers, the *Andromanche, Intrepid, Latonia, Thetis, Apollo, Iphigenia* and *Naiad*, crept into Dover Harbour and tied up to their buoys. They remained idle for some weeks as they were refused permission to lay mines to protect the Strait during the embarkation of the BEF to France. The Admiralty was so far pleased with their transporting of the army to France; over 240 transport ships had made their journeys without loss of life. General Sir John French, Commander of the BEF, arrived by special train, embarked on HMS *Sentinel* and was taken across to Boulogne.

So far the Germans had not developed their U–boat warfare and although the English Channel was being swept regularly for mines, there were none found. There was some anxiety in government circles, however, when the Belgian coast was threatened by the rapidly advancing enemy. The Royal Naval Division was sent to Antwerp on 28 August. The 6th Flotilla destroyers escorted the huge transports that conveyed the force to Ostend and Zeebrugge. They moved out of Dover under cover of darkness, the large liners were never subjected to the risk of submarine or mine, The transfer was timed so no moonlight would indicate their movements.

While the Germans advanced towards Paris, the French army suddenly, and without any warning, abandoned the ports of Calais and Boulogne, leaving them open to capture. As a result of this deplorable action the British immediately lost their means of communication. The Admiralty meanwhile were looking for means to defend the Belgian coast and so, on 29 August, there arrived at Dover three river monitors, the *Mersey, Severn* and *Humber*, originally built under contract at the Armstrong yard for Brazil. These small monitors of about 1,260 tons displacement could reach about 12 knots and mounted a pair of 6-in guns in a turret forward, with a 4.7-in gun aft. Their main advantage, however, was their shallow draft which only required a fathom or so of water to manoeuvre in: this made them eminently suitable for close inshore gunnery.

Having been rushed into service at short notice the monitors took on stores. Innocent-looking lighters and barges, crammed to the hatches with shells, cases of cordite and cartridges, came alongside before the crews had finished tying up to their respective buoys. The variety of ammunition was awe-inspiring. Some shells had bright yellow bodies with red bands painted round their middles and sundry stencil marks on their sides. These were the Lyddite high-explosive shells that burst into thousands of minute fragments on impact, designed primarily to kill personnel. Then there were the common shells with black painted bodies and red and white bands round their noses. They, too, were deadly, but not quite so deadly as the Lyddite, since they were only filled with black powder.

The armour-piercing shells were also painted black and had white-red-white bands round their noses. These had very thin steel walls and specially-toughened noses, designed to penetrate through an enemy's armour then explode. Then came the shrapnel shell for the lighter guns, with their red tips and red bands; they possessed a small bursting charge, were filled with bullets and had time fuses so they would burst in the air sending their bullets flying in all directions. The practice projectiles were black, with yellow bands painted round their middles and white tips. Made of cast iron, these were comparatively harmless (at least to handle), had no charge inside to explode, but could inflict serious damage to any delicate structure on an enemy ship in an emergency.It was quite late in the evening by the time all the ammunition had been transferred, stowed in their respective magazines and shellrooms.

On the following day they began loading provisions from the victualling stores. This time the decks were strewn with bundles of cloth, sacking, bags of flour, boxes and cases containing biscuits, condensed milk, tea, coffee, chocolate, jams and a multitude of other items. To this was added casks of rum, vinegar and sugar. Sailors worked like Trojans to store everything in its proper place.

Much to the dismay of the Admiralty, the enemy appeared on the Belgian coast. Zeebrugge and Ostend were taken and the enemy advance crept ever westward until they met the French naval division at Dixmude. Enemy naval forces were now within a few hours of steaming into view of the British coast and, more importantly, could easily threaten the busy sea route to the Continent.

The three monitors slipped their anchors on 31 August, to sail for Dunkirk in preparation for their first bombardment of the Belgian coast. As they steamed out into the swell, they passed the *Jan Breydel* packet boat carrying the queen of Belgium and her children to England. Destined for London, the Belgian state archives and gold reserves were also on board.

Meanwhile, the bluejackets at Ostend had been withdrawn soon after they had occupied the town. All naval depots by this time were overflowing with recruits who were not yet required to man vessels. These surplus men were to form naval brigades used for fighting on land. Equipment was sadly lacking in any quantity and only a rifle was issued to each man. Ammunition was at a premium and only blanks were used in training and when their call to action came more than half had received no training at all. It was a shocking oversight. The Royal Marines marched into Dover on Saturday, 19 September and embarked on two transports at the Prince of Wales Pier destined for Dunkirk. Soon after their departure, German submarines suddenly appeared in the eastern approaches of the English Channel.

Three days later, on 22 September 1914, *U9*, commanded by Kapitänleutnant Otto Weddigen, rose to the surface after spending the night submerged in order to avoid a violent storm off the Dutch coast. The early morning sun spread over the calm sea, while a stiff breeze decreased to a mere whisper. The horizon was sharp and clear. It was *U9*'s second-in-command, Johann Speiss who first noticed three wisps of smoke curling above the horizon.

Soon, much to the dismay of the Admiralty, German forces appeared on the Belgian coast, occupying Zeebrugge, Ostend and Bruges. Here, German troops march into Bruges.

Weddigen dived to a depth of about 10 m and looked through the periscope. The unsuspecting British cruisers *Aboukir*, *Hogue* and *Cressy* had no inkling of impending danger. Torpedoes were made ready while Weddigen raised and lowered the periscope at intervals to carefully observe his prey. The cruisers remained on course and they proceeded in an ominous direction towards point-blank range. *Aboukir's* huge bulk almost filled the periscope lens. Weddigen gave the order, 'Fire number one tube!' The torpedo ran straight and true towards its target. *Aboukir* shuddered as she was struck on the starboard beam below the waterline. Officers and men of the *Hogue* and *Cressy*, heard the muffled explosion and saw the huge water spout rise up against the vessel's superstructure. Everyone believed *Aboukir* had struck a mine. She began to heel over as water gushed through her damaged hull. Still unaware of *U9* lurking at depth nearby, both *Hogue* and *Cressy* changed course to assist the crippled ship and take off survivors.

Aboukir's bow was pointed skywards, high above the surface, while her stern was fully submerged. Lowering lifeboats crammed with sailors was almost an impossibility. Amid the confusion *U9* silently approached her next victim − *Hogue*. Weddigen carefully positioned his submarine so that his forward-facing torpedo tubes were pointing at his quarry. Perfectly positioned, *U9's* pair of torpedoes sped towards their target at less than 300 yards distance. Weddigen, fearing he would ram the cruiser, as he was so close to the target, ordered reverse engines.

Both torpedoes struck *Hogue* just as *U9*, her bow considerably lightened by the discharge of two missiles, suddenly broke surface. *Hogue's* guns immediately opened fire on her adversary as the submarine lay exposed for a few seconds before regaining control and submerging. The cruiser's gunfire was lamentably inaccurate and shells plopped into the seething white foam around the fast-disappearing submarine.

Hundreds of sailors were swimming in the turbulent water as *Aboukir* slipped beneath the surface. Above her last resting place, half-empty lifeboats bobbed about in the disturbed swell. *Hogue* settled gracefully on an even keel until her quarterdeck was fully awash, then she rolled over and sank to the bottom.

Otto Weddigen surveyed the scene through his periscope. What he had achieved seemed more like a dream than reality. Even so, despite the fact that *U9's* batteries were almost discharged and stale air and a lack of oxygen was proving a hazard to his own crew and engines, he relentlessly pursued the third and remaining cruiser. *U9* pivoted on her axis until she was stern first to her next and final target. *Cressy* was on full alert but it made very little difference to the outcome. Weddigen was already giving orders to fire numbers three and four tubes. *Cressy's* lookouts saw the menacing foaming missile wakes as they streaked towards their ship. She altered course but it was too late to avoid the torpedoes. The first torpedo missed its target by just a few feet but the second struck the cruiser's starboard side. The warship shuddered under the weight of the explosion. Her guns opened fire directly at the periscope when it broke surface. Weddigen had already loaded his last remaining torpedo in one of the bow tubes. He swung *U9* round 180 degrees to fire it into the stricken cruiser.

HMS *Cressy* − Clyde-built in 1901 − her four funnels belching out white-hot steam, slowly turned turtle, just as if in a slow-motion film. The crew, in sheer desperation, clambered up her sides to eventually congregate on her broad, slippery keel. With no chance of survival, they huddled together in frightened, ashen-faced groups, waiting for death. Releasing huge bubbles of steam, their ship sank beneath them in a turbulent sea. *U9* edged away from the horrific scene, her task completed. Otto Weddigen had sunk three British armoured cruisers with a total tonnage of over 36,000, had caused 1,460 men to lose their lives and, in consequence received the Kaiser's personal award of the Iron Cross.

When the truth of the incident reached the Lords of the Admiralty, pandemonium broke out in the corridors of naval power. But, when the initial shock had subsided, they reluctantly acknowledged Weddigen's success. The official statement, later issued by the Secretary of the Board, stated:

> The loss of nearly 60 officers and 1,400 men would not have been grudged if it had been brought by gunfire in an open action but it is particularly distressing under the conditions that prevailed.

First Sea Lord Winston Churchill became aware of the serious inadequacies of the cruiser squadron. Afterwards he wrote:

> The Bacchantes ought not to continue on this beat. The risk to such ships is not justified by any service they can render. The Narrow Seas, being the nearest point to the enemy, should be kept by a small number of good modern ships.

One thing was clear, however: naval warfare would not be the same after the September fiasco and, more importantly, the Admiralty would need to seriously consider the U-boat threat in a new light. The potential for error was unquestionable.

From late September the U-boat commanders confidently patrolled the English Channel in broad daylight seeking out new targets but although hundreds of merchantmen were sighted each day on the busy coastal routes, not one had so far been attacked. At this stage in the war, Germany was concentrating on the Royal Navy, an omission they were soon to remedy with devastating results.

The British blockade which the Admiralty quickly enforced soon gave problems to German economy, a stranglehold on the enemy carried with a certain expertise gained from centuries of experience. The British enforcement of rights of search and examination frequently brought friction with neutral countries who made their objections known through diplomatic circles. Such an effective blockade sealing off all the sea exits from Germany's main ports swung the battle of attrition towards using U-boats against the merchant ships. The most suitable vehicle of retaliation was undoubtedly the submarine. International law in 1914 permitted certain war materials to be seized or confiscated by a belligerent power, providing they were going to help the enemy. In a nutshell, the sinking of merchant ships was considered 'fair game', provided that both passengers and crew were given the opportunity to abandon ship in safety.

The blockade actually started in November 1914, when the British declared the whole of the North Sea as a military zone. The result was that all neutral shipping going to and from their various ports in Norway, Holland, and the Baltic were forced to take the English Channel route and, by doing so, came under the Admiralty's search and examination structure. In the event the German government exercised extreme skill in

The dazzle-painted troopship SS *Victoria*, belonging to the South East & Chatham Railway Company, leaves Folkestone *en route* to Boulogne.

justifying her submarine campaign to sink Allied shipping *en route* to and from the British Isles.

Euphoric at their recent success in sinking three British cruisers, German U-boats chose the Dover Strait and in particular the rest of the English Channel as their first battleground. It was not, therefore, surprising to find *U18* submerged close to Dover's white cliffs on 27 September. That its position was undoubtedly an impertinence compounded by Kapitänleutnant von Hennig, when he fired a single torpedo at the cruiser *Attentive*. Luckily for Captain Johnson it missed but only because he was able to steer clear of the missile after it was spotted. Almost at once this incident relegated cruisers to a less active role in the area. U-boats had already influenced the war at sea and yet they had scarcely begun their profound and unprecedented operational strategy. But it also gave the necessary impetus to an Admiralty decision to lay the first minefield between the East Goodwin Sands and Ostend. *U18*, incidentally, was rammed by a trawler off Scapa Flow on 23 November and her crew captured.

When Ostend had been taken over on 15 October, shiploads of Belgian refugees and British wounded were landed at Dover. In many cases the wounded soldiers had not received any kind of treatment until they disembarked at Admiralty pier. As a result, chaos reigned for some days afterwards as no provision had been made to deal with them. Being the closest port to the Continent, Dover became the first to accept

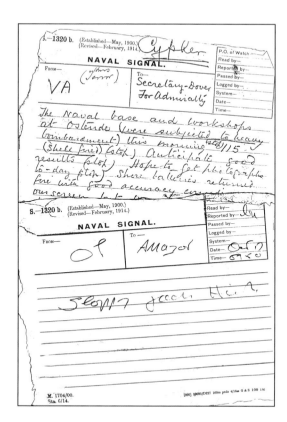

Message-pad signals found stuck
between the pages of an old book.

wounded men who had been transported from France in a number of cross-Channel
steamers, hastily converted to hospital ships.

The first offensive operation made by the Dover Patrol under Rear Admiral Hood
commenced on 17 October 1914. His flagship, the old cruiser *Attentive*, together with
the river monitors *Severn*, *Humber* and *Mersey*, and the light cruiser *Foresight* with several
destroyers escorting, had already arrived and anchored off Nieuport pier on the French
coast. The following day the Germans had advanced sufficiently to take the coastal town
of Westende and the flotilla moved out to a position where the bombardment would be
more effective. Once in position they opened fire with shrapnel shell but this did not
deter the Germans from mounting heavy artillery along the sand dunes that fringe that
part of the coast.

'The flotilla', Commander Evans said, 'cut a sorry figure', when he compared it with
the larger monitors used in subsequent bombardments. Fortunately the German shore
batteries seemed rather awkward in their aiming techniques, despite the slow-moving
targets offered to them. But to the lone signalman, put on the end of Nieuport pier, it
soon became blindingly obvious that it would be a miracle if he survived. As soon as the
bombardment began he was flashing Morse code seawards and semaphore landwards,
passing messages as to the fall of shot from army observation posts back to the Admiral

in *Attentive*. At the start his signals were done in impeccable style and in true naval fashion, until the enemy spotted his position. He then came under fierce gunfire. Large sections of the pier were being systematically shot away until he was completely cut off from the land. That he had stood it for so long was a major achievement. The obstinate matelot stuck to his job nevertheless. When *Amazon*'s flag-lieutenant, Lieutenant J.B. Adams, read the last signal, which said 'Sloppy Jack High', he thought it was time to rescue the man before sanity eluded him. While *Amazon* closed on the pier head she received an armour-piercing shell and had to retire for immediate repairs.

Several other vessels suffered damage from shrapnel shells, especially the destroyers, which began dashing about like frenzied sharks. It was difficult to imagine that these fast-moving targets were being hit while the river monitors remained stationary at anchor in the shoals. The matelots seemed not unduly worried by the enormous splashes the enemy shells made around them; this was their baptism of fire. But whatever damage these small monitors and gunboats did was not immediately apparent, even though their untiring efforts and their plucky obstinacy was total. The ships took many long hours getting into position but, once they were in range of enemy guns, they stopped there until the ammunition was gone or the day had come to an end. It was only then that they ploughed homeward to their anchorage to take on more shells and provisions. The crews worked through the night to avoid missing the action and excitement the next day. Early next morning these 'toy' ships weighed anchor, and at about 5 knots set course for the Belgian coast.

Perhaps the most absurd feature of those early operations was the use of the two 'Flat Iron' gunboats *Excellent* and *Bustard*. They were even smaller than the Thames ferries and literally crawled about the sea like tortoises, getting into position with much to-ing and fro-ing, then firing off their 9.2-in or 6-in breech-loaders. To make matters worse both ships continually drifted off their marker buoys in the tideway and had to grope back in laborious slow motion before being able to resume firing. That they were quite unfit for ordinary sea fighting was borne out by an Admiralty report which stated, 'as of no naval value'.

When the bombardment force had left, a night division of destroyers patrolled the Belgian coast and, closing with the shore, their crews had a splendid view of burning houses and bursting shells as the two opposing armies fought continuously. After a few hours, however, a sadness crept over them when they realized they were watching the complete destruction of the Flanders seaside resorts. It was, for most of them, the first real war they had ever experienced. The red-hot flashes of exploding shells and the uncanny flames that licked through the houses showed through the shattered windows of the Belgian villas at Westende and Middelkerk.

During the latter half of October, the Germans brought up some heavier 8-in naval guns. With typical military thoroughness they soon had the guns installed and the British bombardment force was outranged and outmatched. On 28 October, Lieutenant H.O. Wanton lost his life. He was the first 6th Flotilla captain killed in the war. His ship, *Falcon*, was struck by one of those 8-in shells, which accounted for twenty-four of the sixty men on board. The 375-ton obsolete destroyer was taken out of action by her second-in-command. She fired back with her puny armament of one 12-pounder and the five 6-pounder guns, until the shots no longer reached the shore.

Lieutenant H.O. Wanton, captain of *Falcon*, lost his life when his ship was struck by an 8-in shell on 28 October 1914.

Both *Syren* and *Mohawk* stood over to assist *Falcon* at full speed but suddenly the *Syren* ran up on to one of the shallow sandbanks. *Mohawk* reduced speed and sharply came about so as not to tempt the same fate. *Falcon* got clear of the enemy shells while *Syren* threw up a huge wave with her propellers as she worked in the shallows. She came off the sandbank unhurt by the shells exploding round her, but her propellers were badly bent.

There were a number of obsolete ships drawn into the bombardment force, among them *Vestal*, *Rinaldo*, *Wildfire*, and *Brilliant*. In addition, five French torpedo destroyers were also placed under Admiral Hood's orders. On one occasion he flew his flag in the French destroyer *Intrépide*, leading the flotilla into action off Lombartzyde.

The old pre-dreadnought battleship *Revenge* made a brief visit to the offshore squadron. Built in 1892 her four 13.5-in guns were re-lined and reduced to 12-in. Spotting for fall of shot was not the elaborate system that later evolved. Captain Hughes-Onslow RN commanded her and once or twice she received slight damage, but could not have been sunk easily for the water depth was not great in the West Deep, from where she operated. Her gun range of 16,000 yards was increased by heeling her over to assist elevation.

A rather less outmoded battleship also made a visit, the London class *Venerable*, a

This Short (Admiralty) 830 type seaplane served at Dover and Dunkirk. No. 1335 was lost in
March 1916, after being fitted with heavy bomb racks and a Lewis machine-gun.

deep-draught vessel, that kept well out to sea where the enemy submarines lurked.
Commanded by Captain V.H.G. Bernard RN, the *Venerable* escaped any punishment
although she bombarded the Belgian coast with her 12-in guns from the Nieuport
Roads. During the three-week-long bombardment the German heavy 8-in guns
managed to disable the *Mersey*, *Wildfire* and *Vestral* with direct hits, while the *Brilliant*
and *Rinaldo* sustained casualties because of bursting shrapnel shell.

The first recorded attempt to sink a passenger vessel was made on 25 October.
Admiral Gauteaume, carrying 2,500 refugees from Lille, Arras, via Dunkirk, to a French
port lower down the English Channel, was struck amidships by a torpedo. The cross-
Channel steamer *Queen* went to her assistance and, except for the few who had jumped
into the sea in panic, she managed to take off the rest of the crew. Kapitänleutnant
Rudulf Schneider, captain of *U24*, fired one torpedo into the French steamer without
giving any preliminary warning. He had claimed later that it was a case of mistaken
identity, as he thought the steamer was a troopship.

War had come upon the British when its air force was by no means ready. Both the
Royal Flying Corps and the RNAS would soon fight and bomb with zeal and
enthusiasm but they were not then much advanced in the science of warfare, as they
later became. The Dover Patrol personnel, however, soon learned to appreciate the
enormous possibilities that there were in flying and in particular the assistance offered to
them by the RNAS in various operations.

The Admiralty proposed as early as 1913 that Dover should have a hydro aeroplane
station. A purpose-built base was constructed adjacent to the town's skating rink on
Marine Parade and quite soon afterwards it accommodated the Seaplane Training
School. A year later a base was established at Dunkirk under the command of Wing
Commander Samson RN and was made up of three squadrons, two at Antwerp and
one at Manbeuge. They were used mainly for bombing attacks upon the Zeppelin sheds

in Germany and Belgium. The whole force was protected by a Royal Marine armoured car unit. By November 1914, the enemy had occupied Bruges and Ostend and a seaplane base was consequently established at Dunkirk. Bombing enemy positions in those days was carried out using the 10-lb and 20-lb bombs, dropped over the side of the cockpit by the co-pilot.

In early 1915 the RNAS squadrons were formed using landplanes to work closely with the Dover Patrol. Initially there were about a dozen aircraft at Dunkirk with a similar number at Guston Road aerodrome above Dover. The seaplane station on Marine Parade was then equipped with just six seaplanes, although a couple of experimental airships were held there until the airship station was constructed at Capel le Ferne, between Folkestone and Dover. In the harbour there was the seaplane carrier *Riviera*, also attached to Dover Command.

Difficulties associated with flying in those early days were many. For one thing the aircraft were extremely frail in construction and the engines were mostly unreliable, and for another, they carried no defensive armament to speak of. The rapid development of aircraft and equipment, however, was remarkably efficient and it was realized early in the conflict that command of the air was so essential. Soon after the first bombardment of the Belgian coast the Admiralty concluded that complete accuracy of artillery demanded an improvement in aerial observation techniques.

With the rapid advance of the German army, Belgian and French refugees flocked into the port of Dunkirk almost continuously. They were crammed into steamers sent there to transport them over to England. These unfortunate people, among them wistful-looking children, bent old men and indignant women, had fled their homes before they were overrun. Pushing and pulling rickety handcarts, barrows and perambulators overloaded with household goods, they were a pathetic spectacle of dejected humanity.

Tough matelots, leaning over the handrails of their ships, watched with curiosity at first, then, overcome with a sense of heartfelt generosity, they exploded into action. A pitiful, hungry-looking line of people slowly shuffled past *Mohawk* one evening. A sailor handed a piece of cake to a wild-eyed child. Lieutenant-Commander Evans wrote, 'and in a matter of seconds the mess decks were bereft of jam pots, tins of sardines, oranges, apples and biscuits. Even the wardroom steward cleared everything out of his larder.'

The U-boat campaign increased during the winter months of 1914 to 1915, and Dover Command was hard-pressed to counter this menace with the antiquated weapons at its disposal. The Flanders submarine flotilla was not officially recognized until 29 March 1915. Before that date U-boats used to put in at Zeebrugge for supplies and maintenance. The first boats to use the newly captured port in 1914 were *U5, U8, U11, U12* and *U24*. British light cruisers had continuously patrolled as support vessels for the destroyers to fall back on if suddenly overwhelmed by German surface craft. *Hermes*, formerly a second class cruiser, was now a seaplane carrier plying between Dover and Dunkirk (not to be confused with the modern aircraft carrier), and was torpedoed mid-Channel on 31 October. She was near the Ruytingen Shoal when *U27*, commanded by Kapitänleutnant B. Wegener, launched two torpedoes at her. She remained afloat for about forty-five minutes before sinking, taking twenty-two men with her. Vessels of every description went immediately to her assistance but most were turned away for fear of another attack. The survivors – who naturally had an account to settle – soon learned that Wegener and his *U27* was eventually destroyed by the Q-ship *Baralong* on 19 August 1915, off the Scilly Isles.

In 1914 there was no effective means of attacking submarines which were, by their nature, usually submerged deep enough to avoid being rammed. This was before the days of the depth charge and the only means available to sink them was either the gun, torpedo or to ram them; the latter technique was quite often carried out before the ship's bow was strengthened enough to sustain the enormous shock. Someone had thought of the enterprising improvisation of an explosive charge of guncotton which, when thrown overboard, was then fired either by means of a Bickford fuse or by an electrical circuit attached to a strong piece of wire towed from the stern.

The Admiralty were fast acknowledging their deplorable inexperience in the detection techniques of submerged submarines. The ill-equipped 1892-built gunboat *Niger* was anchored off Deal pier and was hopelessly outclassed when a torpedo fired by *U12* struck her amidships on 11 November. Incidentally *U12* was the first U-boat to enter Zeebrugge on 9 November and was commanded by Kapitänleutnant Walther Forstmann, who was to become a submarine ace. The huge columns of smoke which rose above the water off Deal seemed to emphasize the terrible inadequacy of the navy's defence against enemy submarines to the hundreds of civilians crowding the seashore to see the spectacle. Orders were soon afterwards received from the Admiralty that no vessel, except a destroyer at full speed, was to cross the Channel during the daylight hours. Patrolling cruisers were withdrawn and the destroyers were required to patrol the area previously watched over by the four cruisers.

Everyone began to see submarines after the *Niger* episode. The fins of black fish, rorquals and anything vertical sticking out of flotsam and wreckage immediately became a periscope and a rapid signal was sent. Depending where the patrol vessel was at the time destroyers, either at Dover or Dunkirk, resting or taking on oil or coal, would immediately slip their moorings and shoot out of the harbour at full speed. This was all very patriotic and certainly exciting to the many observers who watched the destroyers plunging their bows into a high swell, taking on sheets of green water, shaking themselves free before the next plunge, but it was ultimately a waste of time.

The submarine hunts were considered most unsatisfactory during the winter months of 1914–15, for all the advantages were with the enemy. The U-boats had not yet begun their ruthless campaign, although they were freely using the English Channel without a care in the world. Even so, the submarines were not immune to the catastrophic events of war. *U11*, commanded by Kapitänleutnant F. von Suchodoletz, struck a British mine off Zeebrugge on 9 December and was followed nine days later by *U5* at almost the same spot. Both submarines were lost with all their hands. Within five months of the war starting a total of five U-boats had been lost. By the end of the year Germany possessed twenty submarines. A new building programme would not alleviate the problem until about April 1916, although by methods of mass production the smaller UB and UC class were soon built in large numbers. As for the British sea mine it was not so deadly as the German mine and neither did the British have sufficient mines or the minelaying capability to block the Dover Strait completely.

The 6th Flotilla's arduous duties continued unabated, however, performing as escorts of troop-carrying transports and carrying out submarine hunts and dreary patrols both by day and night. But there was a limit to destroyer endurance – of both ship and crew. A 'stand off' system was introduced whereby after about eleven days' operational duties, each boat was granted three days' stand-off ashore, if it could be arranged. While the crews were allowed ashore they were required to keep within the boundary of the port. Public houses close to the dockyard did not complain.

The unprepared state of Dover, both as a fortress and a naval base, was well known, despite vigorous efforts to provide all the necessities vital to meet a war situation. Even so, a small floating dock had been seen as a necessity and was built large enough to take a destroyer. It had arrived in the autumn of 1914 and was located in the camber opposite the East Cliff dockyard, where the repairs of destroyers and other vessels, including submarines, was attended to. Behind this dockyard a safe storage for explosives and ammunition and shells was provided using caves cut into the chalk cliff face. The repair staff cleaned boilers, tinkered with engines, riveted new plates to hulls and were often known as the 'sticking plaster brigade'.

Anyone who has any knowledge of Dover Harbour, even if only from the shore, will soon realize that it is a harbour in name only. The tidal streams are so variable and strong that when the wind blows in gale force, there is scant protection for ships lying at anchor. Oilers and colliers attending the ships at times lie athwart the wind and the destroyers especially would bump their light steel sides against the heavier iron plating of the supply vessels. Fenders were considered useless, even those of the heaviest pattern were chafed into a pulp while the supporting chains snapped almost continuously.

In complete contrast the port of Dunkirk was the better of the two and destroyer commanders appreciated the protection of the smaller French harbour. Despite being cramped for room, three monitors could be berthed alongside the main jetty and in fine weather two of them could lay abreast giving an increase in accommodation. Additionally, there was room for a dozen destroyers, twenty drifters, two small monitors of the M-class and four paddle minesweepers. One complete destroyer division was usually kept in Dunkirk to act in conjunction with the French Navy as a cutting-off force. A German destroyer raid in the Dover Strait was always a possibility. These vessels, like their counterparts at Dover, usually made coastal reconnaissance patrols by day and night, sailed on escort duties to transports and made daily trips with the mail. During the dark winter months with a howling gale blowing the crews often turned in, snugly secure from the perils of the open sea and the awful discomfort at Dover.

CHAPTER THREE

'Where Have You Been?'

That the 6th Flotilla and all their ancillary vessels were in considerable danger, was only realized when an enemy submarine attack was thought to have taken place in the early hours of 11 December 1914.

An alert coastguard reported seeing three periscopes approaching the western entrance of Dover harbour at about 0530 hrs. There was a lot of commotion, not only from the defending breakwater guns, but from the local residents who were suddenly and quite unexpectedly aroused from their beds by the sound of gunfire. Searchlights had snapped on and their beams began to sweep both entrances and along the complete length of the breakwater. To the inquisitive civilians it was a wonderful sight as the shells sent up huge plumes of spray brilliantly lit by the searchlight beams. But there were no tell-tale signs of submarines, or anything else for that matter.

Then, at about midday on 20 December, two German aircraft dropped a couple of small calibre bombs close to the Admiralty pier. Their presence was not detected by any mechanical means and that they were reported at all was due to the vigilance of coastguards who saw the slow-moving raiders flying out to sea towards France. But four days later, shortly before 1100 hrs on Christmas Eve, a single German aircraft dropped a bomb in the garden of a house in Leyburne Road, Dover. This was recorded as the first bomb dropped by an enemy anywhere in the British Isles.

When Christmas Day arrived, Dover Command quite expected the Germans to make a special effort to disrupt their celebrations. Over half the flotilla was on stand-off while a division of volunteers elected to perform the ritual of daily patrol duties. Those in harbour derived some satisfaction in realizing that the civilians in the town were taking an interest in their welfare. While officers made merry at the Burlington Hotel, their less fortunate chums shivered on their frail bridges and drew what comfort they could from an occasional glimpse of the South Goodwin lightship or the slow, jerking beams of the Dover and Calais searchlights.

But it was a relief to everyone that the weather remained fine. The sun shone on Christmas Day. Ships' companies, seventy or so men in each destroyer, mustered aft at 1000 hrs to listen to their respective captains who were impersonating the parish vicar. When the short divine service was over, the men mustered to the bosun's pipe. The coxswain called each man by name and, cap in hand, he would step forward to receive the small but welcome gift from the Princess Mary's Christmas Fund.

Officers visited the decorated mess decks, where each was adorned in a way that left no doubt as to the general spirit of the ship's company. At each masthead there hung a small Christmas tree. Unknown benefactors had sent boxes and tins of food. Wives, mothers, aunts and female relatives of every description, sweethearts and lady friends, seemed to be consoling themselves for the absence of their men at sea. They had sent hand-knitted woollen mufflers, balaclavas, mittens, gloves, jerseys and numerous pairs of socks. The mail office on the quayside was filled to capacity with parcels containing thousands of cigarettes, pipes and tobacco, bars of chocolate and cakes. Canvas mailbags were impregnated with the smell of disintegrating food, brown paper and soggy string.

The alleged periscope incident, however, provided the necessary impetus to improve the two boom defences in the harbour. Until now the booms were constantly broken up by heavy tidal seas and it was decided to sink block-ships at the western entrance. The scheme was to provide a long bottleneck approach into the harbour so that a small boom system could be activated in just a few minutes at the inshore end. At the eastern entrance a new 'V' boom was designed to float on the inside of the two pier heads clear of the tidal seas.

There have always been two different seas that wash into Dover harbour, a rather peculiar phenomenon which Lieutenant-Commander Stanley Coxon RNVR explained in some detail after the war. One comes from the North Sea (in the east), while the other comes from the Atlantic Ocean (in the west). During the flow of the flood tide they both work up on either side until, at a point just west of Dover, there is a slow expiring stream which turns suddenly into a strong flood tide that drives in the opposite direction. At spring tides, and with a south-westerly gale blowing, this frequently reaches a speed of anything from 3 to 5 knots and often more.

The first action of this released tide sweeps with a rush into the western entrance and at the same time swirls along the outside of the breakwater, where it seeks a fresh inlet at the eastern entrance. These two streams of water – one from the east and one from the west, also meet inside the harbour, to the detriment of vessels seeking their moorings. It is bad enough in daylight but at night it often resulted in bumps and collisions between ships. One example, to give credence to Coxon's view, is to relate what happened to Lieutenant-Commander John Brooks, who took two and a half hours in an attempt to reach his particular mooring. Brooks abandoned his attempt to seek shelter in the Downs off Deal.

Two block-ships were selected from the Thames, the Atlantic liners SS *Montrose* and the SS *Livonian*. The former had the infamous Dr Crippen and his lady friend among her passengers in 1910. As fate had taken a hand in the detection and eventual arrest of the murderer, so it was to deny the vessel's use as a defence block-ship.

Both liners had been gutted of everything, cut down to the main decking, and in place of the masts, funnels and superstructure, they were fitted with large iron gantries upon which the wire anti-torpedo nets were to be hung. On 20 December *Montrose* was completed and had been moored alongside the extreme end of Admiralty pier, in readiness for her sinking in the appropriate position the following day. She was moored with several 6-in steel wire hawsers fore and aft and twenty strong coir ropes and chain cables at bow and stern.

It was about 1800 hrs when a severe south-westerly gale suddenly blew up, accompanied by a tremendous sea, the force of which broke over the pier, overturned

To replace the lost *Montrose*, wrecked on the Goodwin Sands, the *Spanish Prince* was brought to Dover and used as a blockship in the western entrance of the harbour.

loaded railway wagons, and fell in large volume on to the deck of the *Montrose*. A heavy swell came through the western entrance which set the old liner to tug at her moorings at an alarming rate. By 2230 hrs she had set her bow into the western entrance. She rocked to the scend of the swell which beat afresh into the harbour through the entrance with a rising tide. Suddenly the cables snapped in flashing sparks and the ropes tore apart like pieces of string. *Montrose* was free, and halfway through the entrance an enormous wave flung her back into the harbour. She rode the wave like a huge shuttlecock, all the while scraping the sides of the breakwater.

How the runaway vessel managed to drift along the inside of the harbour walls without colliding with cruisers, destroyers, drifters and trawlers riding at anchor, remains to this day one of those unexplained mysteries. Everyone was powerless to stop her progress. *Montrose* somehow negotiated the eastern entrance on a fast-running tide, without scraping either pier-head, and eventually slipped out of the harbour to go aground on the East Goodwin Sands. Despite many attempts to effect a salvage she remained stuck fast in the sands until all hope was abandoned. She was left to her fate.

To replace the lost *Montrose*, SS *Spanish Prince*, an old cargo vessel lying in the Thames, was brought to Dover. Sinking these concrete-filled hulks was a highly skilled operation but in the event both block-ships were sunk within a few feet of their designated positions; *Livonian* gurgled her way to the sea bed shortly after *Montrose* had left in such a spectacular fashion, followed by *Spanish Prince* in March 1915.

People began to expect many more air raids before the year was out. Enemy aircraft had already bombed Calais and Boulogne but so far Zeppelins had not violated British shores, although one or two had been seen over the Channel. Perhaps the more serious observation was the German announcement that they would sink without giving notice any neutral or Allied vessels in the English Channel. The steamer *Durward* was stopped off the Dutch coast on 21 January 1915 by a German submarine. The *U19*'s captain ordered the crew to abandon ship then placed a timed explosive charge in her engine room. On the following day, Otto Hersing took his *U21* through the Channel defences. He found it easier than expected as the marker buoys, used to indicate the net barrage, enabled him to avoid them and the mines floating close to the surface off Deal were easily spotted. Once clear of Dover the U-boat moved off down the Channel without further hindrance.

The new German submarine bases in Flanders were causing some concern to the British. As a result the air arm of Dover Command, the RNAS squadrons based near Dunkirk, launched its first ever bombing raid on Zeebrugge on 23 January. It was a clear indication that the War Office had realized the vital necessity of using aircraft to combat the submarine. Further raids were made with increased frequency. On 12 February thirty-four aircraft were used in just one attack; four days later, forty-eight machines were being used. Following severe damage to *U14* at Zeebrugge, the German High Command ordered the remaining U-boats to quickly withdraw from Flanders until their anti-aircraft defences were strengthened.

Further steps had already been taken by the Admiralty to combat the U-boat and this was made evident by the arrival at Dover and Ramsgate of the small force of drifters sent in February from the north-east fishing ports. These drifters were mostly made of wood and in the very early stages of their patrol work were unarmed except for one American Winchester rifle. The drift nets and associated gear were offloaded at Dover and their crews and other ratings of the RNR immediately began to construct large-meshed wire nets. The nets were originally designed to entangle submarines and cause them to surface. Later, new methods of running mines down to a certain depth were introduced. It was the commencement of what was to become known as the Dover Barrage.

The development of the Auxiliary Patrol was composed of two sections, the Trawler Patrol and the Drifter Patrol. The former was under the control of Captain W. Vansittard Howard, who was also in charge of the Dover minelaying section. When they were eventually sufficiently armed, the trawlers worked a patrol system which was unsuitable for the destroyers. Slow-moving by comparison, they were usually employed close in to the shore and between the shoals, and could be given the task of both minelaying and minesweeping.

The drifter *Crescent Moon* at anchor in Dover harbour. In the first year of the war the drifters would 'shoot' their anti-submarine nets from the Goodwin Sands to the Ruytingen Shoal.

The Dover Drifter Patrol established a unit that was different to those drifters protecting shipping off Ramsgate and the Downs. They were originally under the command of Captain Humphrey Bowring, who was later superseded by Captain F. Bird. By June 1915, the drifters had reached a maximum strength of 132 vessels, including 3 yachts, and was manned by about 1,500 officers and men.

This system of anti-submarine operations was an entirely new concept in naval work. The whole idea of submarine hunting was that a submarine should be caught in a net system much the same as a fish. The nets were made of a thin, galvanized steel wire, the size of the mesh roughly 10 to 12 ft square. Each net was 100 yards long and the depth varied from between 30 and 120 ft, depending on the depth of the water in which they were used. Each drifter stowed ten nets, which equalled 1,000 yards in length.

After many experiments with all sorts of devices to 'float' the nets on the surface of the water, a solution was found in the hollow glass ball. These balls were put in net bags secured at the head of each net, so that a 100-yard-long net at a depth of 30 feet required about 150 glass balls to float it successfully. Of all the insurmountable difficulties associated with the anti-submarine nets – and there were many – one of the main problems was how to devise a buoy or float which could be attached to the net to indicate its position. Hundreds of designs and suggestions were received, tried out and abandoned; no solution was ever considered foolproof.

Day after day, night after night, the drifters would 'shoot' their nets in the Dover

After many experiments to float anti-submarine nets on the water the final solution was found in the hollow glass ball. These drifter crews are fitting glass balls into net bags.

Strait on a line between Goodwin Sands and the Ruytingen when the tide was running westward, and would drift down slowly with them until near Folkestone and Cap Gris Nez. Then the nets were hauled in, re-shot on the east-going tide and the whole gamut of nets were drifted back again to where they had started. There were occasions when a net got fouled up, which brought out destroyers to hunt for a suspect submarine. These incidents were frequent, and often they were false alarms, but they were moments of excitement which helped pass the time in one of the most depressing jobs of the Dover Patrol. But without doubt, the most successful invention was the 'net mine' invented by Admiral of the Fleet Sir A.K. Wilson VC. This electrically fired mine completely revolutionized the method of net employment.

A study of the tides was essential but on the whole it became quite easy to place these nets in such a fashion that a continuous line reached across the Strait. There were about half a dozen drifters in each division, and each division had an RNR Sub-Lieutenant or Lieutenant in charge. An armed yacht, usually commanded by a naval officer, attended the drifters, taking full responsibility for the whole operation while at sea.

On the occasion when a U-boat attempted to pass through the nets, the net line would contract and speed away up or down the Channel and the drifter would standby to attack with a bomb-lance, a sort of giant hand grenade, which was the precursor of

Local women were employed to maintain the earlier type mine nets designed to entangle submarines and cause them to surface.

Securing a net barrage so that it remained in position irrespective of weather or tides was overcome by using large metal buoys.

the more efficient depth charge. At the same time a wireless signal was sent out for destroyer assistance.

This was the theory but in practice it did not yield any great results. Although the scheme was an excellent one, the long run of bad weather often made it extremely difficult to keep the nets in more than just an approximate position. German submarines took to passing through by night with just their periscopes awash, but always ready to dive if they were attacked. They seldom, if ever, attacked the drifters, as they would have given their positions away. They were after bigger game. A U-boat commander once remarked after capture that he would keep his torpedoes for a 1,000-ton merchantman in preference to sinking a warship, let alone a mere drifter, He went on to say that British warships were so numerous and the loss of just one or two would not matter to Britain, but the loss of merchant tonnage was undoubtedly the more serious.

Dover's harbour was becoming more congested. It was so full of ships, both large and small, that in bad weather collisions were not infrequent. The Auxiliary Patrol skippers of the trawlers and drifters, together with their crews, came from all parts of the British Isles; places like Hull, Aberdeen and even the Shetland Isles, and some of them, denied a formal education, found it extremely difficult to read the most simple orders posted up on notice-boards. But whatever their educational drawbacks, every man was a seaman through and through.

Discipline was, however, difficult to enforce in the Auxiliary Patrol, for naval punishments could not be fairly applied to willing fishermen who worked their fingers to the bone for king and country, and who were loyal and immensely courageous. Therefore it came as no surprise when a couple of deckhands of the drifter *Girl Annie*, came up before the local magistrate having acquired a barrel of beer. Handed over to the naval authorities, the presiding captain remarked, 'The civilian authorities should know better than to leave casks of beer unattended. Case dismissed. On caps, right turn, quick march!'

There were other, slightly more complex, difficulties especially when auxiliary vessels were not in their correct positions. On those occasions destroyer captains usually laid the blame, fairly and squarely, on the auxiliary skippers. There was one particular occasion worth mentioning, when a destroyer had suddenly appeared in the midst of a cluster of drifters. The destroyer was challenged in the normal way but, for whatever reason, she failed to acknowledged the signal. The senior skipper of the drifters insisted on a reply but none was forthcoming, and so he took a megaphone and shouted angrily, 'What destroyer is that?' The sharp reply was not one that he had expected. In his report of the incident submitted to Admiral Hood, the skipper wrote, 'the language used convinced me that I was talking to friend.'

Food was more expensive and became scarce when a number of coastal merchantmen were diverted away from the danger zone. The auxiliary boats, however, were able to provide a plentiful flow of fresh fish. Throughout February the U-boats were active, sinking merchantmen in the lower reaches of the English Channel and the North Sea. On 19 February *U16* severely damaged the Norwegian tanker *Belridge*, which was carrying oil from America to Holland. Just four nights before the same submarine had sunk the steamer *Dulwich*. Being neutral *Belridge* was showing all her lights and it was a simple matter for the U-boat commander to launch a torpedo. The ailing tanker was

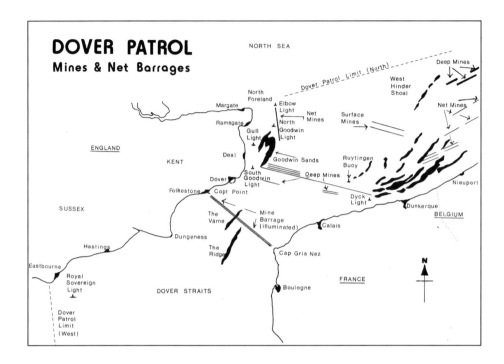

brought into Dover by the tug *Lady Brassey*, which was promptly given the 'denied entry' signal as she approached the eastern entrance. The port war signal station was sticking to Admiralty orders with surprising inflexibility but the tug's skipper ignored the signal and held his course, risking a 6-in shell fired across the bow.

Another Norwegian ship, the *Regin*, was sunk off the North Goodwin Sands that same day, the crew being rescued by a patrolling destroyer. Kapitänleutnant Alfred Stoss, commanding *U8*, made a successful attempt to negotiate the defence nets the day before, but not without the fearful risk involved. The net barrage was considered quite dangerous and some submarine commanders chose not to attempt the passage through the Dover Strait. For two years, the larger, ocean-going submarines, operating out of Wilhelmshaven, would make their way round Scotland.

Stoss took a chance but because his Korting kerosene engine gave off a tell-tale black exhaust smoke when running on the surface, he had decided to take his boat deeply submerged and to run under the net barrage, rather than give his position away. *U8*'s progress, however, was suddenly and forcibly impeded when her bow ploughed into the net system. The indicator buoys, attached to the nets, bobbed about like corks as the submarine thrashed about beneath them in an attempt to free herself. Drifters moved in for the kill.

U8 backed away from the net, then made another rush to break through. Stoss was successful on this second attempt and moved away slowly, clearing the remainder of the barrage to eventually arrive off Beachy Head, a favourite inshore haunt for U-boats.

Stoss claimed later that he then dispatched five steamers without giving any warning, as each vessel was not carrying flags of identity. It must be said the British use of neutral flags as a means of misidentification was a well-known ploy used by U-boat commanders to lend justification to attacking any ship.

U6 was lying in wait at the same spot on 28 February, submerged, with just the tip of her periscope above water. Heading towards her was the 500-ton coaster *Thordis*. Captain Bell saw the periscope just as the U-boat moved across his bow ready to attack. Oberleutnant Reinhold Lepsius fired a torpedo but Captain Bell had already swung his ship towards his assailant, intending to ram.

U6 was too slow in her dive and was unable to avoid *Thordis* who smashed the periscopes and severely damaged the conning tower. Helped by the tremendous impact, U6 rolled over to disappear in the turbulent waters: she was not seen again. Traces of oil and debris came to the surface and were evidence enough for the jubilant John Bell to set course for Plymouth. Bell became the toast of the town and a local newspaper awarded him £500, saying he was the first merchantman to have destroyed a U-boat. The story does not end there however, for Lepsius succeeded in renegotiating the Dover net barrage, in spite of steering difficulties and returned home to Wilhelmshaven.

On 4 March the weather had deteriorated into a blanket of dense fog. Visibility was so poor when *Viking* was on patrol that it was quite impossible to make out where sea and sky met. But an alert Sub-Lieutenant Young-Husband saw the sinister grey form of

'As *Viking* bore down upon U8 with the intention to ram, she was firing her 4-in guns, but with seconds to spare the submarine dived.'

a submarine about half a mile distant. *Viking*'s captain's rang down for full speed but the increase from 15 knots to 30 or more took some time to build up. As *Viking* bore down on *U8* with the intention to ram, she was also firing her 4-in gun but with just seconds to spare, the submarine managed to dive. Lieutenant-Commander Evans was furious with his gun-layer, although he had observed his fall of shot very close to the target. Rolling into a high swell at full speed were not the ideal conditions for gunnery. *Viking* steamed around and around, just north-east of the Varne Shoal where the submarine was last seen, all the while sending wireless signals to call up more destroyers.

Maori was first to arrive and took command of the search. The drifter *Roburn* signalled that she had seen an indicator buoy bobbing about in a frenzy. The search continued for a few hours, during which time the U-boat fired a torpedo. It ran rather badly and missed the destroyers. *Gurkha*'s anti-submarine sweep encountered an obstruction almost immediately. The contact switch on the detonator closed and the explosion shot *U8* up to the surface like a champagne cork. *Gurkha* and *Maori* opened fire almost at once, hitting the submarine's conning tower with their first salvo, just as Alfred Stoss appeared at the hatch. The destroyers closed in to lower boats when the U-boat's crew had gathered on the decking. Stoss, four officers and twenty-five crew were saved. The 600-ton *U8*, built in 1911, was taken in tow by the River class destroyer *Ure*, which was of equal tonnage. Unbeknown to *Ure's* skipper, Lieutenant-Commander H.B.L. Scrivener, Stoss had arranged for the seacocks to be opened, with the result that Scrivener's prize began to sink rather rapidly and eventually settled in six fathoms of water.

Once they disembarked at Dover, Stoss and his officers were taken on board the *Arrogant*, the parent ship of Dover's submarine flotilla, laying in the Camber. That night they were given the hospitality of the Dover submariners, not unlike the well-intentioned social affairs synonymous with German pilots brought down behind British lines on the Western Front. But the rest of *U8*'s crew, the lower ranks, were marched through Dover's streets surrounded by armed bluejackets and placed under guard at the castle to await transfer to Chatham.

The captains of *Gurkha* and *Maori* were awarded the DSO, while several DSMs were awarded to certain crew members. Lieutenant-Commander E.R.G.R. Evans recalled that the man who pressed the firing button and blew up *U8* deserved his DSM. The new modified sweep fitted to the larger destroyers was, in point of fact, the first anti-submarine device with which they were officially equipped. But being the first of its kind, it was often thought the worst. This particular modification consisted of a double line of high explosive charges, towed at different depths. The charges were made buoyant by wooden floats attached to them and the whole contraption was adjusted to maintain a certain depth by means of deploying a kite. The sweep was put over the stern and towed about in the vicinity of the hunt. In practice it was able to reach anything from the surface to a depth of about 10 fathoms, where it could be fired electrically at will.

Towards the end of March the sixteen U-boats on anti-shipping patrols around the British Isles had sunk a total of 28,000 tons. This figure was miniscule compared to the peak sinkings which occurred two years later but it served as a warning to the Admiralty and to the British government of the submarines' ability to successfully blockade the island.

The sixteen U-boats on anti-shipping patrols had sunk a total of 28,000 tons by the end of March 1915. It served as a warning to the Admiralty of the U-boats' ability to successfully blockade the British Isles.

There was no sign either that the German campaign was any nearer to bringing Britain to heel. On the contrary, in spite of merchant shipping losses, the majority were still capable of sailing undisturbed. The cost to Germany was another three U-boat losses, including her leading ace Weddigen, of *U29* fame, who was rammed by the battleship *Dreadnought* off the Pentland Firth on 18 March.

Details of U-boat losses were no longer made public by the British government, a suggestion made by Admiral Jellicoe after the loss of *U29*. The U-boats were now subjected to an insidious war of nerves as their comrades-in-arms vanished from the face of the earth with no explanation as to how they had met their fate. This cloak of silence quite unnerved the German High Command; they believed the Dover mine barrage was now a formidable defence and that no submarine could pass through it unscathed. This theory was further enhanced by the reports of U-boat commanders returning through the Dover Strait. *U35* had been been trapped in the nets for several hours before wrenching herself free, while *U32* had experienced the same difficulties. When *U37* had failed to return after an explosion in the Strait, orders were issued forbidding U-boats to use that route. Even so, U-boats increased their terror tactics to frighten the merchantmen.

On 28 March *U28,* commanded by Freiherr von Forstner, sent the Dutch steamer *Medea* to the bottom. She was flying her national flag and had her name and port of origin painted in large white letters on her sides. She was carrying oranges and tangerines from Valencia to London when she was intercepted off Beachy Head. Forstner allowed the captain and crew to abandon ship before sinking the vessel with his 4.1-in gun. This was the first recorded sinking of a merchantmen by gunfire. More interestingly, Forstner towed *Medea's* lifeboats for over two hours before leaving them to their fate. It was a lucky chance, however, when the Dutch crew, none the worse for their experience, were found by the destroyer *Teviot* and were brought in to Dover.

The ensuing row between the Dutch and German governments over the legality of the sinking of a neutral vessel, an argument soundly based on maritime law, came to nothing. The rights of neutrals were further prejudiced when the British government reminded her merchant skippers that using false colours was an accepted disguise and, further, a definite instruction was also issued to fly the American flag, especially in the English Channel. The more neutral flags were exploited the more likely it became that U-boats would sink any vessel they came across. The result was a deplorable propaganda exercise.

In spite of the assurance, outlined in the German directive to take effect on 22 February 1915, which stated, 'Ships belonging to the Belgian Relief Commission are likewise to be spared', the 5,940-ton steamer *Harpalyce* was torpedoed on 10 April, without any warning. She was flying a white flag and had the words 'Commission for Belgian Relief' painted on her sides. Seventeen crew went down with the ship.

In April there was a flag change, when Rear-Admiral R.H.S. Bacon DSO was appointed to command the Dover Patrol. Admiral Hood was transferred to a sea-going command and subsequently hoisted his flag in the battle cruiser *Invincible*, as Rear Admiral of the 3rd Battle Cruiser Squadron. It was to everyone's lasting regret in the Dover Patrol that they heard of his death in the Battle of Jutland a year later.

Rear-Admiral Bacon was to face even greater difficulties than his predecessor, for the Germans were now launching submarines at an alarming rate. Bacon had retired from the navy some time before the war started and had taken the post of Director of the Coventry Ordnance Works, a new armament firm. Immediately on the outbreak of war he at once volunteered for active service, was accepted and given command of the Royal Marine heavy batteries in Flanders. His speciality, however, was largely connected with submarines and adapting new scientific methods to naval use. He was no slouch, on the contrary, he threw himself into his new command with boyish enthusiasm, always ready to try new ideas to deny Germany access through the Dover Strait. Quite naturally, there were a few dissenters among the officers of the Dover Patrol when he took command. It is a human condition to resist change and everyone was aware that Admiral Hood, with the very poor resources at his disposal, had managed to keep the enemy guessing as to the strength of his command.

But it was not long before Bacon sent his first signal to the Admiralty, asking for better facilities, weapons and, more especially, wireless apparatus. Before April was out, he had visited every unit under his command. Totally committed and ingeniously inventive, he designed equipment that actually worked, drew up plans and charts, and sent off messages to the Admiralty with monotonous regularity. Telephone wires hummed between his office and various depots, insisting on the fast delivery of equipment ordered. He pounded the corridors of the Admiralty, knocking on doors to persuade – even threaten – some minor official whose lackadaisical mannerisms annoyed him immensely.

One of Bacon's first priorities was to ensure a rapid communication system between ships at sea and his signal staff. When the drifters and trawlers arrived they were not fitted with any wireless apparatus at all. By the end of the year, however, one vessel in every six had been fitted with a transmitter. For defence purposes each trawler became armed with a 6-pounder high-angle gun, a 7.5-in howitzer and two depth charge traps, one on each quarter with as many depth charges as the boat could conveniently stow. There was little doubt that the 7.5-in, with a range of 2,000 yards, was considered the best weapon against a surfaced submarine. The trawlers also received hydrophones, the device through which an operator could detect noises transmitted through the water. Unlike modern-day sonar units, the one drawback of the hydrophone system was that the operator could not 'fix' a distance from his ship close to the source. In bad weather, and if the trawler was wallowing about in a noisy sea swell, the apparatus was quite useless. To detect a submarine's engines it was imperative that the trawlers' engines were stopped. The hydrophone had many disadvantages but it served a purpose and was also considered useful in the hands of an experienced operator.

During April the Royal Marines, who had been used on drifters as a crude defence measure, each man having a rifle, were discharged from the vessels and sent back to their depot. They were immediately replaced by forty Canadians and twenty Newfoundlanders who were to remain with the Auxiliary Patrol for more than six months under training, before being sent back to Canada.

New U-boats began operating from Zeebrugge and the other Flemish ports. The UBs were small craft, only 92 feet long with a displacement of just 127 tons on the surface, and were particularly suited for the shallow waters such as the Thames Estuary and the Dover Strait. The prefabricated submarines were assembled at the coastal ports, carried two 18-in torpedo tubes and were quite successful in their designated role. Similar in size were the minelaying UC types, fitted with six minecarriers with an overall compliment of twelve mines. The latter carried neither gun nor torpedo, but proved successful in sowing mines in areas previously regarded as safe. Both the UB and UC types were regarded by the Admiralty as a serious and quite unforeseen threat, which upset the formal defence arrangements of nets, explosive sweeps, moored mines, guns and ramming tactics.

The drifter *Lord Claud Hamilton* was on a heading for Ramsgate with survivors of the SS *Cathay* which had been sunk by a mine on 7 May, when the Dover Patrol lost its first destroyer. *Crusader* and *Maori* had been sent to inspect moored nets off Ostend and *Maori's* captain, Commander B.W. Barrow, had been instructed to approach Zeebrugge to sketch salient marks ashore to assist Admiral Bacon in his preparation for his first bombardment of the Flanders coast by monitors. *Maori* was edging closer to the shore at near low tide and within about 1,000 yards she struck a rogue mine. The Tribal class destroyer was a sitting duck when the German shore batteries immediately opened fire with considerable accuracy. *Maori's* thin hull splintered in a dozen places as the enemy shells found their target. She was soon listing heavily and surrounded by fuel oil. The order was given to abandon ship. Her lifeboats, crammed with sailors, tried valiantly to pull towards *Crusader* but after an hour they had to abandon their efforts because of the strong tide. Seven officers and eighty-eight men were eventually taken prisoner by a German trawler. Lieutenant-Commander T.K. Maxwell in *Crusader* was furious to

The 290-ton UB class U-boat was particularly suited for shallow waters in the English Channel, and carried two torpedo tubes in the bow with a 3.4-in gun forward of the conning tower.

The UC type U-boat carried an overall complement of twelve mines. *UC5* was captured off Harwich in April 1916: she was responsible for the loss of the hospital ship *Anglia*.

An aerial view of the RNAS Capel le Ferne air station that was part of the Dover Patrol complex of operations.

receive a signal to 'hold off'. Bacon was not going to lose another destroyer to the German guns.

It was in May 1915 when the airship station at Capel le Ferne was ready to receive the first lighter-than-air craft, attached to the Dover Command. At about 2000 hrs on Friday 7 May, men of the RNAS were awaiting the arrival of the SS-Type (Submarine Scout). Designed and built at the Royal Naval Airship Station at Kingsnorth, it was one of the most spectacular arrivals at the newly built station on the cliff edge above Folkestone.

Flight-Sub-Lieutenant R.S. Booth, seated in a modified cockpit of a BE2c fuselage, suspended beneath the envelope, was becoming rather anxious as it was his first cross-country flight. A white canvas arrow had been laid out on the ground to indicate wind direction. The coastline was directly ahead of the craft as Booth steered towards the single large hangar, which was no more than a stone's throw from the cliff edge at Abbott's Cliff.

When the SS.10 fell into the water in September 1915, the destroyer *Myrmidon* was close by to rescue the two-man crew.

The light was already fading when Booth reduced speed and gas and descended towards the ground. Thankful that men were waiting to catch the trailing ropes dangling from the enveloped, he was unaware that he had misread the white arrow system. His approach was opposite to the wind indicator but, more crucial to a perfect landing, the wind was sufficiently brisk to carry the airship beyond the landing ground. Instead of settling on the grass, the SS1 careered through the lines of men and made for the main Folkestone–Dover road. Booth and his observer crouched in their seats as the fuselage passed between two telegraph poles beside the road, The cut telephone wires produced sparks of electricity and they touched and rubbed alongside the envelope, filled with 75,000 cubic feet of highly inflammable hydrogen.

Escaping gas from the punctured envelope caught alight instantly and within a few seconds the envelope was a blazing inferno. The rapidly deflating airship crossed the road and struck another pole just a few yards from the cliff edge. The ground crew had sprung into action by now, and reached the blazing wreckage half expecting to see two severely burned bodies. However, to their astonishment, Booth and his companion were standing just a few feet away in smouldering leather jackets and melted goggles.

The SS1 had arrived, ostensibly to mark the opening ceremony of the station, the commissioning of which was performed on the following day. The burned-out wreckage at the cliff's edge served as a reminder to everyone present of the precarious nature of their work. But despite the ignominious arrival of the SS1, several other

Airship duties were anti-submarine and observation patrols. Here, C23A is being released from Capel for an anti-submarine patrol in 1917.

airships were delivered to Capel le Ferne, some by air, while others arrived crated by rail to be assembled in the hangar.

The first commanding officer at Capel le Ferne, Commander A.D. Cunningham RN ran a 'tight ship', to use a naval term, and personally supervised every department, even initiating Sunday morning inspections to check that all airships were fit to fly and were, more importantly, gas-tight. The word 'blimp' – now a colloquialism – has been attributed to Cunningham who, while carrying out his Sunday inspections, used to flick the airships' envelopes with his fingers which gave a sound not unlike 'blimp' indicating the correct gas pressure. He went so far as to imitate the sound, saying 'blimp' as he passed from one airship to another. From that time onwards, it has been suggested the word blimp has always been associated with non-rigid airships.

The airship duties within Dover Command were two-fold – anti-submarine and observation patrols. However, the first designs, in terms of speed and their carrying capacity of the bombs, flares and smoke canisters, were totally inadequate. Winston Churchill's prediction that, 'these airships will only tease the U-boats', was to prove correct in numerous sightings. Ponderously slow, the airship was considered a 'toy' by the U-boat captains, who usually submerged long before the airship came within range to make an attack. When they were fitted with wireless transmitters and had a reasonable height advantage, they were able to signal the submarine's position and allow surface craft to take up the hunt.

It was in May that the first successful interception of a Zeppelin was made. A whole squadron of RNAS aircraft set off to attack it as it reached a position about 10 miles off La Panne. The Zeppelin was returning from a bombing raid on Ramsgate and gained height much faster than the aircraft could manage. Flight Lieutenant-Commander Bigsworth was the only one able to get above it. He dropped four 20-lb bombs along its back while the airship was over Ostend, which reduced its height so that other pilots could get in to attack. Intelligence reported that it made an emergency landing between Brussels and Ghent.

The Zeppelin sheds at Gontrode were attacked on 25 May by Flight Sub-Lieutenant Warneford, who dropped six bombs from about 3,000 feet. Flight Lieutenant Wilson similarly bombed a Zeppelin shed at Evere, north of Brussels, on 7 June, which burst into flames. Warneford was chasing another Zeppelin at about 6,000 feet over Ghent and was so close to it as it exploded and fell to the ground in flames that his aircraft turned upside down. He made a forced landing in enemy-held territory, restarted his engine and took off again. He was awarded the VC for his tenacious exploit. Sadly, Warneford was accidentally killed in a Henry Farman machine just ten days later, on 17 June, after the award ceremony in Paris that day.

When the small and mostly isolated minefields suddenly appeared overnight along the Kent and Essex coasts, they had baffled the Admiralty who assumed, quite wrongly, that they had been laid there by neutral fishing vessels. It was not until *UC2* was sent to the bottom on 2 July, having been rammed by SS *Cottingham* off Yarmouth, that salvage revealed the source of these mysterious mines.

Preventing U-boats from passing through the Dover Strait and into the English Channel proved a formidable task for the Royal Navy, which was due to the lack of suitable materials and modern equipment. The ocean-going submarines based at Wilhelmshaven would lose about one week's effective time out of each cruise, especially if they were obliged to take the route round Scotland. To induce this course the Dover Strait would have to be blocked somehow. So a mine net barrage was constructed between Folkestone and Cap Gris Nez in July, which provided a quick barrier against U-boats attempting the passage. Strong winds and tides, however, played havoc with the barrier and quite often mines became a menace to merchant shipping.

Admiralty intelligence received reports of a Zeppelin with a broken back sitting on the water just outside Ostend on the morning of 10 August. L. 12 was one of five Zeppelins ordered to make an attack on London the night before. Led by Commander Strasser in L. 10 they ran into foul weather after leaving the rendezvous point at Borkum and each one had navigational difficulties. Commanded by Oberleutnant Werner Peterson, L. 12 arrived over Dover just after midnight, with Peterson under the impression he was over Harwich. The ominous black shape was immediately illuminated by the searchlights and the guns opened fire. It was the accurately aimed shells from the Langdon battery on the East Cliff that eventually struck home. Informed of the damage to the rudder section Peterson immediately released his bomb load of explosives and incendiaries over the harbour. Losing gas fast, Peterson offloaded the water ballast and set course for home. But L. 12 was well down by the stern and Peterson had no alternative but to jettison everything that could be spared, including his wireless equipment. Unable to cross the North Sea, and losing altitude rapidly, he set

Zeppelin L. 12, ordered to attack London on 9 August 1915, was later seriously damaged over Dover, and was seen sitting on the water off Ostend with a broken back.

course for the Belgian coast but was forced to alight on the water before reaching his destination.

As dawn broke the crippled Zeppelin was seen by a German TBD, which secured a wire hawser to the Zeppelin's nose ring and towed her into Ostend. Inevitably the RNAS put in an appearance for the *coup de grace*, but their bombs failed to damage her further. Flight-Commander Smyth-Pigot returned after releasing his bombs and hand grenades to report that L. 12 had broken its back. In fact, L. 12 had broken its back long before it was towed into Ostend, and this was probably the cause of its demise after being hit by Dover's anti-aircraft guns. Beyond repair, L. 12 was later dismantled.

Attacking submarines from the air was always extremely difficult as the intended victim quickly dived out of harm's way when approached. The Vice-Admiral was already aware that his enthusiastic pilots would often interpret their U-boat attacks in the most favourable light. Bacon was not unsympathetic but insisted that to claim a submarine as a 'kill' he would require irrefutable evidence of wreckage, bodies or oil observed floating on the surface after the craft had disappeared below water level.

In the summer of 1915 the Dover Command commenced the harassment of enemy shore positions from the sea using specially designed monitors, which had been built during the winter months. As they did not become available until July, the enemy were free to fortify their artillery positions on the Belgian coast, from the Dutch frontier to Nieuport.

Vice-Admiral Bacon thought the monitors had been roughly and hurriedly

One of several unforgettable images at Capel, when the twin-engined C23A with its four-man crew was being released for anti-submarine patrol.

assembled, using gun turrets taken from old battleships of the Majestic class. They fell far short of his expectations. But there was no shortage in finding suitable commanders for them, as junior officers were anxious to participate in any action. Six monitors were delivered and each mounted a couple of 12-in guns as their main armament, with a few smaller calibre guns for anti-aircraft or anti-destroyer purposes.

The first three monitors to arrive were *Sir John Moore*, *Prince Rupert* and *Lord Clive*. Their speed was little more than about 6 knots, although some enthusiastic commanders boasted they could manage about 8 knots in a fair wind. The displacement was roughly about the 6,000 ton mark, their length approximately 335 feet, with a beam almost approaching 90 feet. Each had been fitted with anti-torpedo bulges, but their greatest advantage was that they only drew about ten feet of water. They were, in fact, larger versions of shallow-draught river gunboats, simply designed for the support of military operations on land. 'Monitor captains,' Evans wrote, 'were always conscious of the absurd appearance of their vessels as, generally speaking, they seemed to waddle about like giant ducks.'

They were sent, after stowing hundreds of shells and cordite cases, to anchor together in a channel called the Middle Deep among the shoals and sandbanks which lie in the Thames Estuary. Here, away from prying eyes, their crews began to practise with the

A collage showing the specially built monitors of the Dover Patrol's bombardment force that shelled German-held positions on the Belgian coast.

gun turrets and the awkward ancillary equipment. By a process of elimination, the numerous defects were made good and the guns actually fired.

Bacon knew from experience that it was not of the slightest use firing guns unless each shot found its target. He knew that it was not an exact science, for however accurately the gun was aimed, certain variations occurred in every round fired. Among the many variables, the exact weight and composition of the cordite charge was essential; the exact weight of the shell and wear and tear on vital parts of the barrel and its breach all affected its velocity when it left the muzzle. After leaving the muzzle, the shell experiences an uncertain path to its target. The wind force, density of air and its temperature all influenced the projectile's flight path.

Bacon's next problem was the accurate spotting of the fall of shot and as far as he was concerned no accurate or reliable method existed. He first considered the promising use of seaplanes but when they were tried in the Thames Estuary it was a dismal failure, largely due to the primitive wireless equipment which could only send messages. It was frustrating, to say the least, when the seaplane pilots could not understand what was required of them. And then the early seaplane types available were quite inadequate and could only rise from reasonably calm waters. Their poor endurance and mechanical reliability were also an uncertainty.

The Vice-Admiral looked elsewhere for a solution to his spotting problem and came up with the idea of erecting observation islands fixed on the sea bed. Quite undeterred by numerous unkind remarks made by his contemporaries – some said it was a hare-brained scheme – he nevertheless designed and constructed four tripods made from rail

Admiral Bacon's observation platform that was fixed to the sea bed off the Belgian coast and used to observe the fall of shot.

track, each weighing about 5 tons, with an equilateral triangle style of construction with a height of just 44 feet. The platform area on the top was wide enough to accommodate two officers and two rating signalmen, who would use observation instruments and an oxy-acetylene signal lamp, which could be seen for at least 5 miles, even in daylight.

Bacon selected the 37-knot Tribal class destroyer *Viking*, as his *modus operandi*. She was a fast six-funnelled ship and was the only one of its kind in the Royal Navy. Surprisingly, Bacon was often seen, at either Sheerness or Chatham, carrying pieces of piping or tube or some other piece of gun-turret mechanism to make a repair or alteration. He exuded such obstinate energy and firmness of purpose that everyone else felt obliged to help. Along with his previously sceptical colleagues, Bacon was more than pleased when the monitors were ready for action.

To avoid being seen by enemy reconnaissance aircraft, or, indeed, enemy agents, who were known to operate in the naval dockyard areas, the bombardment force had assembled at different places: the monitors with *Cossack*; *Crusader* and *Saracen* were anchored in the Swin area of the Thames Estuary; the tripod vessels *Curran* and *Gransha*, each with a drifter to tow just in case the tripod crews needed rescuing in a hurry, were anchored off Margate with the destroyers *Amazon* and *Ure*, while the *Viking*, *Gurkha*, *Tartar* and *Mermaid* were moored at Dover. The slow steaming squadron left their respective positions on 15 August and was to bring off a surprise action.

Admiral Bacon's first bombardment was directed against military defences, ammunition factories, harbour installations and the lock gates at Zeebrugge. The procession of monitors and their escorts left the anchorage in time to ensure they were in position for bombarding by daylight. They slowly crossed from the Thames Estuary, through the Galloper Shoal, and made a long detour northward so as to avoid the British minefields. The times of sailing for all these vessels were arranged so that each section would meet at Galloper Light just before it was dark. The whole force, consisting of about 100 vessels of every kind, eventually steered for the North Hinder lightship. Adherence to the strict planning was accomplished without fault. The mine net drifters assembled two miles east of Kentish Knock with the yacht *Sanda* and the ordinary drift-net boats just one mile off.

A more extraordinary flotilla had surely never been seen before. The Admiral flew his flag on the monitor *Sir John Moore*, then came the *Lord Clive* and *Prince Rupert*, surrounded by destroyers, drifters, yachts and minesweepers, followed by four large steam lighters, *Bickford*, *Lewis*, *Gransha* and *Curran*. In no time at all, just as the flotilla was settling into a speed of about 6 knots, the minesweepers, old paddle-wheel pleasure boats, pushed ahead to sweep in the path of the squadron. Destroyers scouted on the flanks, zig-zagged this way and that in the darkness, ahead and astern, at between 12 and 15 knots, which must have put the fear of God in the minds of the drifter skippers because of the poor visibility. They were steaming in two lines to port and starboard of the monitors, keeping station with immaculate perseverance and creditable expertise. Unaccustomed to alter course *en masse* in the dark, the drifter skippers were a little apprehensive of the sudden appearance of a destroyer bearing down on them. Time and again, they saw a dark shape heel over suddenly to starboard and stay there pressed hard down as it turned to port. There were no collisions and the drifters pushed on, their crews comforted by the sights and sounds of the Royal Navy in close proximity.

'Unaccustomed to alter course *en masse* in the dark, the drifter skippers were apprehensive of the sudden appearance of a destroyer bearing down on them at great speed.'

Commander H.G.L. Oliphant's *Amazon*, with *Ure* and the east tripod ship, altered course for their position off Zeebrugge. Lieutenant-Commander R. Viney in torpedo boat No. 24 set course for Thornton Ridge, to sound and mark the south-west and north-east ends of the shoal with light buoys. The weather stayed fine and so, far from interfering with the Vice-Admiral's plans, the German navy might not have existed. The destroyer escort was not really strong enough to combat a well-organized German attack that could have caused havoc among the drifters and minesweepers. Had they done so, the monitors could not have used their 12-in guns, and they possessed a negligible secondary armament to speak of. So the defence relied heavily upon the half-dozen Tribals and a couple of 30-knotters which, although poorly armed, might have put up some kind of resistance had an attack materialized.

Before daybreak the four tripod carriers had taken up their respective positions and lowered the tripods on to the pre-selected shoals. To seaward, a dark sky made the tripod carriers quite invisible to the enemy shore guns, while the buildings and other prominent objects on the land side were boldly silhouetted against the bright morning light in the east. It was no mean feat, to have every vessel in position, on time, with the anti-submarine nets run out, and then to carry out a three-hour bombardment only ten miles from a port infested with enemy submarines and destroyers, not to mention the long-range guns supporting them. The only protection the force had was the sixteen miles of nets, laid by the drifters on three sides.

As day broke on 23 August, it found the monitors in line abreast, in perfect position for the bombardment. When each ship was ready, *Sir John Moore* fired her first salvo to within a second or two of the scheduled time of 0530 hrs. The observers, perched precariously on the tripod platforms, and only about three feet above sea level, carefully noted the fall of shot and almost immediately flashed the result back out to sea with their oxyacetylene lamp. Two sets of observers were necessary and once the signals were received by the monitors, the shots were quickly plotted on a chart and gun barrels corrected on to the target. The attendant carrier vessels, with two drifters, stood off about half a mile away. They could be seen by the enemy, albeit indistinctly, and so a number of shells were fired at them. The monitors, however, remained out of sight and no shells fell anywhere near them. The drifters spread their nets even wider around the monitors as an anti-torpedo precaution. But they might have been fishing for herring, for no one took any notice of the shells plopping into the sea around them. The division of destroyers were split into two, one dashed about between the nets shoreward of the drifters, while the other seemed casually to patrol seaward.

The chill moist morning air did little to alleviate the unpleasantness of damp clothing, or the heavy eyelids caused by the night's vigil. The only source of amusement was the spectacle which presented itself when occasionally a drifter rapidly altered course to avoid a 30-knotter bearing down on it without a care in the world. As the sun rose higher in the sky, the wind fell away to a thin bitter draught, which mourned about the worked spaces of the air. But the shoreline showed up more distinctly, and the chimneys of the Solvaye submarine factory stood out clear against the shimmering dawn. Intelligence sources later confirmed that the factory was hit many times.

Once all the shells had been used, the signal to conclude was given. The ahead flag appeared at the signal halliard of *Sir John Moore*. It was time to go home. The monitors waddled their unwieldy bulk to form a single file ahead, the minesweepers moved into position ahead of them and the tripods were once more approached. The volunteer observers re-embarked and the tall trellis-work structures were overturned on the sandbanks. Little wisps of smoke lazily ascended towards the bright sky, revealing that the sleek destroyers had joined the procession. Everyone seemed satisfied with the results, except the captains of *Sir John Moore* and *Prince Rupert*, both monitors had developed defects in their gun turrets and were unable to fire their intended rounds.

Considerable patience was needed when the September morning mists interfered with subsequent bombardments. After several vain attempts at shelling targets close to Ostend, the weather changed for the better and a composite force, very similar to the original, set out on the morning tide of 7 September. Spotting conditions were, however, abysmal, and although everything was ready and in position, the squadron was reluctantly forced to abandon because of low-lying mists. Even the lighthouse, used as an aiming mark at zero point, was hidden on that occasion. Several targets had been selected for that particular day but it was most disappointing to observe the flotilla crawl back to their anchorage off Dunkirk without firing a shot.

They had no sooner anchored when a German aircraft suddenly appeared. Bombing, until then, had not been taken seriously by the Dover Command but the circling Albatross machines proceeded to drop bombs of various sizes. One bomb actually exploded on the deck of *Attentive*, killing two crew and injuring seven others. A 4-in

Joining the bombardment force was the old pre-dreadnought battleship *Revenge*, relegated to fire her 12-in guns from the West Deep.

gun was completely disabled but, as luck would have it, no other successes were recorded. Strange to relate, officers and men were calmly eating their midday meal while bombs fell around the ship.

Soon afterwards the mists dispersed and the ships slipped their anchors on the afternoon tide. Joining them was the old pre-dreadnought battleship *Revenge*, now fitted with anti-torpedo bulges and renamed *Redoubtable*. As she drew a great deal of water, she was relegated to fire her 13.5-in guns from as far back as the West Deep. When the mists had cleared sufficiently the tripod observation platforms were seen by the enemy.

The 12-in monitors came into position and opened fire on their targets. Unfortunately, the first salvo knocked over the lighthouse. The observers were not at all pleased, for when they glanced through their telescopes to line up with their zero mark, it was nowhere to be seen. During the delay which followed this calamity, the German shore batteries opened fire on the monitors. Two shells struck *Lord Clive,* neither of them exploding, but then Commander Bickford's tripod was hit below the water level. Bickford had left the navy before the war but, like many others, offered his services in whatever capacity. Vice-Admiral Bacon had found him unloading howitzers in Le Havre. After his tripod had almost collapsed into the water, he and his two signalmen were left perched on what was left of it like soaked sparrows. The tripod began to sink into the soft sand and,

One of the German heavy artillery pieces on the Belgian coast that straddled Admiral Bacon's bombardment force with accurate shooting.

with a rising tide, the water was within a few inches of the top of it. Frantically signalling for assistance they were somehow forgotten when the bombardment force returned to Dunkirk for the night. It was about fourteen hours later when the *Viking* made a successful rescue. There is no record of Bickford's reply when he was asked by *Viking*'s captain, 'Where have you been?' While *Tartar* stood off *Viking* had moved in slowly to the tripod but, owing to a strong tide, bumped rather heavily against the frail trellis-work knocking it over. The two signalmen jumped to *Viking*'s deck but Lieutenant-Commander Lewin dived into the water to avoid being crushed. Unceremoniously dragged out with a boat hook he lay on the deck gasping for breath and heard the *Viking*'s captain congratulate him on being 'the only Englishman to bathe in public off Ostend'.

A fortnight later the bombardment force reappeared off the Belgian coast with something they thought would out-gun the Germans. The monitors had been practising with smokescreens and gunnery to perfect their skills, but even more important was the newly built *Marshal Ney* monitor that had joined them. She was a curious looking floating fort of about 6,670 tons, propelled by unreliable diesel engines. Her only assets were the two modern 15-in guns. As no one could see through the smokescreens, the spotting was achieved by using aircraft from No. 1 Wing RNAS, who had joined Dover Command in August.

The next bombardment was on 20 September and this time the spotting was done by the shore observation platforms and a French-built Cacqot balloon, tethered to the stern of a P-boat. Lieutenant Coxon first saw the new balloon in Dover harbour: 'I saw coming out of the bowels of a ship a huge inflated mass which appeared at first sight to be in pain and struggling. Gradually it took shape and evolved, and then floated aloft as a huge spotting balloon.' There was an air of excitement too when *Marshal Ney* cocked her huge guns skyward to belch thick black cordite smoke. Such excitement, however, soon paled when she was ordered closer inshore off La Panne. There was a narrow passage leading from La Panne into the West Deep area. *Viking* led the way hoisting flags on either side to indicate the depth in feet. Reaching her allotted position the monitor began firing but her engines became unmanageable and she was soon drifting towards the shore.

Almost immediately the German batteries had got her range, and shells whistled and shrieked over her mast with frightening regularity. To stop drifting, she dropped anchor. *Viking* smartly made a smokescreen which effectively hid the ailing monitor from the enemy's view. Under the cover of the black oily smoke, the destroyer steamed quickly alongside, took a towing hawser on board and gently moving ahead turned the monitor's bow westward. 'With the most delicate of speed', Evans recounted, '*Viking* got the enormous bulk going towards Dunkirk, and because of the monitor's shallow draught, she towed quite easily at about 8 knots.'

Attentive was anxious to know where *Viking* was, when someone looked out of a porthole to discover the monitor actually passing them. A semaphore signal was sent, 'They don't believe it!' Evans replied, 'Tell the monkeys to look out of their cage at the zebra and the giraffe!' *Viking* was painted in a striped camouflage at the time, the *Marshal Ney*, with its single huge tripod mast, towering above the small destroyer, had an awkward giraffe-like appearance.

The failure of the new monitor to remain on station, without having her engines ticking over continuously, for fear they would never start again, relegated her to the dockyard soon afterwards. She was given a second chance on a later bombardment but afterwards was used as a floating fort off the Downs, sporting nothing more fearful than some 6-in guns and some pom-poms in an anti-aircraft mode.

On the evening of 24 September the bombardment force was assisting the C-in-C of the BEF, Sir John French, to launch spoof attacks upon the port of Zeebrugge and the Middelkerke and Westende sectors simultaneously. Keeping the attack going for at least several days, the force was split into two squadrons. *Prince Eugene* and *General Crauford*, with five destroyers, two paddle minesweepers, one division of drifters, and the yacht *Sanda*, under the command of Captain E. Wigram, left to bombard Zeebrugge. On the following day the Vice-Admiral took the remainder of the monitors, including the ailing *Marshal Ney*, to West Deep, to open fire on Middelkerke and Westende.

Sadly the Zeebrugge force lost the *Sanda* when it was hit by an 8-in shell and was sunk. All her executive officers perished, including Lieutenant-Commander Gartside-Tipping, the oldest naval officer serving at sea: he was over seventy years of age at the outbreak of war. The drifter *Fearless* rescued some survivors as did *Hyacinth*, which was being heavily shelled. The skipper and crew continued to haul in their nets. Skipper Lawrence Scarlett received the DSC and his First Mate, J. Prior was awarded the DSM, for their perseverance and gallantry under fire.

Hundreds of closely packed khaki-clad bodies were jammed into troopships. Escorted by destroyers of the Dover Patrol, they had carried 16 million troops without mishap.

It became increasingly obvious to the Vice-Admiral that bombardment of the Belgian coast under the most modern heavy gunfire the Germans had, was, perhaps, acceptable in theory but in practice was quite useless. The Admiralty, however, did not share his view and the bombardments continued.

Sir John Moore and *Prince Eugene* again shelled Middelkerke and Westende on 26 and 27 September. When the monitors went in to shell the German gun batteries on 2 October, *Lord Clive* came under a bombing attack. In the following month a feasibility study was made to ascertain if troops could be successfully landed near Ostend.

This, the second winter of the war, seemed to have set in rather more severely than the first, snow flurries sprinkled the decks of patrolling ships, while the white cliffs and the sky were the same dead colour. The air was bitingly cold for most of the time and there was not a breath of wind at sea level. Higher up, the pale ranks of stratus cloud moved very slowly from the east, then winds would suddenly surge from a southerly direction bringing cold rain and sleet. It dampened everyone's spirits.

Although the monitors fired the occasional shot, they spent much of their time at anchor and since the destroyers were not needed as escorts, they returned to patrolling

The troopship SS *Victoria* leaving Boulogne on her return journey, with destroyer escort, in May 1918.

duties. In addition, some of their time was spent escorting troop transports running between Folkestone and Boulogne in fog, gales and very high seas. The transports stuck rigidly to their high-speed timetables, always punctual, while the destroyers stuck rigidly to the transports. Hundreds of closely packed khaki-clad figures were jammed into each vessel, uncomfortable and unsheltered from the wintry spray which crashed over the bows with depressing constancy. In spite of the canvas windshields, erected on both sides of the decks, the soldiers were inevitably soaked to the skin before their vessel had reached mid-Channel. The only redeeming feature was their fast journey. But for many it was their last sea voyage before death in the trenches.

Destroyer captains secretly admired the transport captains, whose only anxiety was to help win the war. The careful and skilful way they handled their ships was borne out by the thousands of crossings they made without a collision. They frequently navigated at about 20 knots, without any lights showing and with other ships in close company, but no record exists of transports colliding with each other. It would have been a major achievement if no collisions had occurred at all. The old 30-knot turtle-back *Myrmidon* sank after colliding with the SS *Hamborn* steamer on 26 March 1917. A year later, the old A class *Boxer* destroyer was sunk after a collision with SS *Patrick* in February 1918. Two minor bumps involved the destroyers *Leven* and *Cossack*, although neither boat was sunk in the incident.

CHAPTER FOUR

'It's Like Fred Karno's Navy'

On the occasion *Leven* collided, it was a dreadfully dark winter's night. A rather plaintive wireless signal was intercepted. The nearest destroyers went at once to assist a transport in difficulties which, in her heavily laden state, would need urgent attention, having upwards of 2,000 troops on board. *Viking* altered course and, when about two miles from the transport, came across the 1889-built *Leven*. Searchlights were switched on and a pathetic sight greeted *Viking*'s crew. The bow of the old destroyer appeared flattened out of all recognition and resembled crumpled papier mâché. 'She was drifting broadside to a heavy swell, rolling about in the wave troughs and likely to make even the most hardened sailor feel seasick,' Evans said. *Viking* immediately pumped oil over the sea until there was a chance to get alongside her. Seriously damaged, the *Leven* was unable to make any headway and, to cap it all, she was drifting towards the French coast off Boulogne. Commander Evans decided to tow *Leven* stern first and remarked, 'it would be child's play after the *Marshal Ney* episode'.

A wire cable was passed to the stricken ship and soon the two destroyers were gently moving away from the coast. But then the tow parted. *Tartar* meanwhile had arrived and stood by while *Viking* moved alongside *Leven* once again. Protected by her fenders, *Viking* got herself thoroughly tied to the old destroyer, using every available hawser from both vessels. By daybreak, they were met by the tug *Lady Crundall*, which eventually manoeuvred the pair of them into Dover harbour.

It was, perhaps, not so surprising, after being involved with salvage operations, that Evans should receive a signal on 13 December 1915 which said simply, 'Take charge of salvage operations'. *Viking* was taking her turn at Dunkirk with the destroyer division based there when the transport steamer *Southgarth*, loaded with trench gear, had run on to the Traepegeer Bank. The commodore of Dunkirk, had already moved out in *Attentive* to take charge while most of the steamer's crew had abandoned ship. The impatient Evans, having received his order to salvage, lost no time in wrapping the two vessels together and, waiting for high tide, pulled *Southgarth* clear of the sandbank.

A week later Commander Evans was ordered to change places with the captain of *Crusader*, Commander F.C.H. Williams. Evans, who always carried a penguin mascot nailed to the mast (a relic from his days with Captain Scott's ill-fated Antarctic Expedition), took the mascot with him. While the officers were at lunch in *Viking*'s tiny wardroom, she struck a mine off Boulogne. Her stern was blown in by the explosion, killing all the officers. It was a severe blow to Evans, who had grown to like every one

When transferred to *Crusader*, Commander Evans took with him his penguin mascot and nailed it to the foremast.

of them. Even more tragic was the fuel oil that spilled itself around the vessel from her ruptured tanks. It caught alight with disastrous results, consuming sailors who had been blown into the water, including her skipper, Commander Williams.

When help arrived *Viking* was on fire. Fortunately it was confined to a patch of oil in the stern. The crippled destroyer was then towed to Dover. Vice-Admiral Bacon boarded her at once and discovered her aft magazine had exploded. He was astounded to see the stern only connected to the rest of the ship by the propeller shaft. He said afterwards, 'it was just as if a giant had seized her round the wardroom and scrunched her through his grip'. *Crusader*'s First Lieutenant said, 'Evans should be nailed to the mast instead of his mascot.' Both *Mohawk* and *Viking* had struck mines soon after Evans left them.

Vice-Admiral Bacon looked through his monthly reports, while his secretary looked on, apprehensively expecting a broadside if something had not been attended to. Bacon read

'2 June: enemy submarine sighted near Elbow Buoy – one other near Downs Gate. 3 June: hostile seaplane attacked drifters off the Goodwin Sands. Bombs dropped. Several reports of submarines sighted near North and South Goodwins and Downs

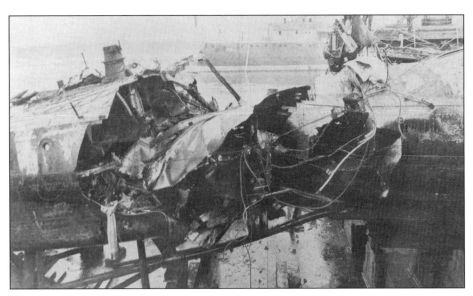

Viking had struck a mine. Admiral Bacon said, 'it was as if a giant had seized her round the wardroom and scrunched her through his grip.'

Gate. 6 July: *Campanula* on weighing at Gate, found a mine attached to anchor. Mine later picked up by Lieutenant Stephenson in *City of Glasgow* and brought to Ramsgate. 29 July: *Lord Claud Hamilton* brought crew of SS *Salicia* (mined) back to Ramsgate. 1 August: *Corona* attacked by enemy seaplanes near Elbow Buoy. Ten bombs dropped. *Corona* exploded German mine by rifle fire at distance of 20 yards, causing large volume of water to fall on deck with fragments of mine. 19 August: *City of Liverpool* towed into Ramsgate an abandoned Admiralty lighter. 7 October: *Feasible* being fitted with wireless telegraphy. 12 October: *Frons Oliviae* blown up by mine near Elbow Buoy, Lieutenant T.R. Rogers RNR (skipper) and nine men lost, two survivors. 15 October: *Lord Claud Hamilton* brought crew of SS *Salerna* into Ramsgate. 1 November: *Lord Claud Hamilton* went aground on Sandwich Flats. 3 November: *Corona* picked up one survivor from SS *Sigrun* (Norwegian). Rest of crew taken off by drifters. Lieutenant Irvine RNR (*Corona*) and three men spent night on board trimming vessel, which was later towed into Ramsgate the following morning by *Corona* and *Rooke*. £2,000 salvage was awarded. 8 November: *Lord Claud Hamilton* was refloated. 17 November: loss of hospital ship *Anglia*. 27 November: *Arcady* brought into Ramsgate crew of Norwegian ship SS *Klar*.

Towards the end of 1915 over 150 German mines had been laid off Dover, with a further 108 near the Isle of Sheppey, 306 off Lowestoft and a dozen or more off Grimsby. Many ships had fallen victim to the new minefields, trawlers, drifters, merchantmen and destroyers – but perhaps the saddest of all the incidents during that

Showing nothing but the faintest flicker to betray her furious movement, the hospital ship *Anglia* slipped to her final resting place.

year was the loss of the hospital ship *Anglia* which struck a mine near No. 8 buoy on 17 November. The *Anglia*, which belonged to the London and North West Railway Company, had been requisitioned and converted into a hospital ship in May 1915.

On the day of her demise she was lying in Boulogne harbour with wounded soldiers on board and sailed at 1100 hours. The day was fine and clear and the journey to Folkestone to disembark her human cargo was just routine. The master, Captain Manning, had just reached the bridge when the explosion occurred, throwing him violently to the deck below. He at once went to the wireless cabin intending to send the customary SOS signal. Unfortunately the shock of the explosion had rendered the fragile apparatus worthless. He ran to the telegraph system to stop the ship but found everything damaged. The engines were still going ahead. The ship was soon very much down by the head and the starboard propeller was still turning while clear of the water. Manning, together with his Chief Officer, was able to launch No. 2 lifeboat over the side, where they were able to get about fifty people into it. Other lifeboats had also been successfully launched before the ship began to list, but one of them sank soon afterwards having been overloaded. Manning remained on deck to see the lifeboat pull clear of the sinking vessel, then threw life-jackets into the water.

Ure, an E class destroyer captained by Lieutenant Commander H.B.L. Scrivener RN, manoeuvred alongside *Anglia* while she was still moving ahead and all the while turning in circles owing to the list, as her engine room men had been driven out by the rush of the water. Scrivener steered *Ure* right over *Anglia*'s bow and he managed to save many lives. *Hazard*, too large a vessel to get in close, stood off to receive the bulk of those saved.

The German mines that had been laid around No. 8 buoy during the night claimed another victim. The steam collier *Luisatania*, on hearing the explosion, had altered course towards the crippled hospital ship and immediately launched her lifeboats. *Anglia*'s No. 2 lifeboat slowly moved towards the collier but, just as the first man began to climb up the rope ladder dangling over her side, there was another explosion. *Luisatania* had had the misfortune to strike a mine and began to sink before the hospital ship had actually settled on the bottom.

Captain Manning was on *Anglia*'s lower bridge at the time the collier foundered. He had entered B Ward to find that the nursing staff had already evacuated the wounded to the upper deck. The forecastle head was at that time under water, so Manning simply let go of the rail he was holding on to and slipped into the sea. He swam away from the sinking vessel for fear of being sucked down with her. He did not have a life-jacket as he had thrown them all overboard. Completely exhausted, he lay on his back to rest his aching arms. Overhead he could see where the sky was apparently still, showing nothing but the faintest flicker to betray the furious movement as *Anglia* slipped to her final resting place. His next conscious observation was waking up in the doctor's cabin on *Hazard*.

Had *Anglia*'s engines been stopped, the nursing orderlies, who had elected to stay with their cot patients, would have been saved. There were no less than 200 helpless cot cases and about 100 walking wounded and it is all the more surprising that the loss of life was later estimated in the region of 150, considering the suddenness of the catastrophe.

There was no denying the fact that the Germans had deliberately laid mines in the path of a hospital ship, a route which had been purposely organized with specially lit buoys and on which no other ships were allowed to travel. It was at the last buoy round which *Anglia* had to pass on her homeward journey that the trap was laid.

It was *Anglia* that had brought King George V back to England on 1 November, after he suffered an accident while visiting troops in France. In appreciation for his treatment on the ship by Matron M.S. Mitchell, the king had sent her a brooch from London. Mrs Mitchell had survived the sinking incident but had lost all her possessions including the brooch. On hearing about this loss, the king lost no time in replacing it but he was also informed of her devotion to duty during the sinking. She had been found by Lieutenant Bennett, an RAMC officer, up to her waist in water and at a time when the ship was about to sink. She was struggling to rescue a patient from a cot. With his help they succeeded in saving the patient. Lieutenant Bennett, however, had to forcibly restrain the matron from re-entering B Ward to effect another rescue.

The trawler *Falmouth III* was already sweeping for mines in the area and struck one of them which blew her in half. Lieutenant H. Beedle, the skipper, actually went down with his stricken vessel but came up to the surface and was rescued. Both the *Luisatania* and *Falmouth III* sank almost on top of the *Anglia*.

Soon afterwards all hospital ships were painted a slate grey colour so as not to exhibit their distinguishing marks in daytime and their illuminated Red Cross at night. It was this change in colour that caused the Germans to consider all transports as fair game.

They voiced their opinion in print, stating that the hospital ships were being used for military purposes, carrying munitions and weapons to France, and were armed. Of course there was no truth in the allegations. The regulations of the Hague Convention had never been contravened.

The Transport Staff at Dover, led by a Divisional Naval Officer with four transport officers under him, were responsible for the movement of ships in and out of the harbour. It was a colossal task which required management skills beyond those taught at any naval college of the time. Lieutenant Commander Stanley Coxon RNVR, the junior transport officer, said at the time, 'we were all men long past the first flush of youth'. The building of the South East and Chatham railway station at the Western Dock was not sufficiently advanced to accept the first wounded from France in October 1914. The disembarkation occurred at the Admiralty pier extension, which caused unforeseen berthing difficulties for other ships. The biggest problem was getting stretcher cases across the decks of other ships lying beside the pier and on to the quayside. So for a while, and until the Marine Station was completed, wounded men were sent to Southampton. But the shortest route to France was the most convenient and the first hospital ships arrived at Dover to disembark their wounded at the Marine Station terminus on 2 January 1915.

The nucleus of the fleet of hospital ships were *St David*, *St Andrew*, *St Denis*, and *St Patrick*, vessels which had been requisitioned from the Fishguard to Rosslare route between Britain and Ireland. Strange as it may seem, naval casualties, as distinct from military casualties, used Lord Tredegar's yacht *Liberty*, Lord Dunraven's yacht *Grainaigh*, the aviator Graham White's *Paulina* and the *Queen Alexandra*. Under the Hague Convention, hospital ships were painted white, with yellow funnels and a broad green band painted round the hull, with a row of green lights to show at night. The naval yachts, however, had a red band painted on their hull, with a row of red lights illuminated at night. Both classes of vessel displayed the large Geneva Red Cross, which was also illuminated at night.

In addition to berthing transports and small cargo vessels carrying every conceivable calibre of ammunition, shells and weaponry and also the colossal tonnage of food and stores of every description, the transport staff were especially involved with the hospital ships. The RAMC staff were solely responsible for the disembarkation of the stretcher cases and walking wounded, both of which received medical attention before being put on special trains at the Marine Station. It was a formidable task, as more than 12,000 men could either disembark or embark each day.

The fleet of hospital ships was gradually increased as the war got into its stride and was to include *Cambria*, *Anglia*, *Dieppe*, *Brighton*, *Newhaven* and the two Belgian vessels *Stad Antwerpen* and *Jan Breydell*. From June 1915 there were regular daily services between Boulogne–Calais and Dunkirk–Dieppe. The port of Dunkirk, usually entirely confined to naval casualties, was sufficiently monitored by the yachts, while all other military casualties used the other three ports. The intense activity from these ports was an infallible barometer to the severity of the fighting on the Western Fronts.

But despite the submarine menace and the far greater danger of indiscriminate mines, ships proceeding either up or down the Channel or crossing it could number over 150 each day. Nevertheless, hardly a month passed during which some vessel would fail to reach its destination without some mishap. No fewer than seven ships

The powerful sea-going tug *Lady Brassey*, belonging to the Dover Harbour Board, was responsible for saving lives during both world wars.

had been sunk within sight of Dover. Those ships that had foundered on the French side of the Channel were still Dover Command's responsibility. Take for example the 10,000-ton steamer *SS Surrey*, carrying frozen meat to the BEF, mined off Dunkirk in February. Commander Bevan had volunteered to make a rescue attempt and set off with two salvage tugs *Lady Brassey* and *Lady Crundall*. Bevan arrived to find the *Surrey* at anchor with her bow high in the air and her stern very low in the water. Avoiding floating mines the volunteer rescuers boarded the vessel, placed one tug alongside to pump out the water, while the other proceeded to tow. Although the ship was visibly sinking she was eventually beached in soft sand north of Deal pier. More than half her valuable cargo was recovered and *Surrey* was salved and repaired to sail another day.

Not all beached ships were so obliging. When the *SS Karanja*, an oil tanker, was beached to the east of Dover Harbour, her 8,000 tons of crude oil had to be released before she could be lifted and towed. Just 1 mile from the eastern entrance, the state of the harbour for months was indescribable. The heavy black slime covered ropes, cables, landing stages and every bit of clothing, not to mention the beach areas and the small packet boats which plied between ships and shore. Only a series of south-westerly gales finally washed and cleansed the harbour until the filth had disappeared.

With over 12,000 men to look after in the drifter section of the Dover Patrol, it was essential to have some form of physical exercise. Before too long, under Captain G.W. Venn DSO, RNR, everybody under twenty-five years of age was required to attend physical exercises on the Prince of Wales pier each morning, and this led to football, boxing and tug of war sessions.

When the Admiralty insisted that the drifters should recruit signalmen from within their own ranks, there was no shortage of volunteers as each successful candidate would receive 2d extra per day. But it was not a simple task; the greatest difficulty was to find seamen whose spelling was of an acceptable standard. Surgeon Bailey, in his spare time, devoted incalculable hours holding spelling lessons on the Prince of Wales pier, surrounded by classes of twenty or more fishermen whose only attribute was that they were all willing to learn. He found the Scotsmen were the most keen to learn. After passing the rudiments of spelling, successful candidates were then selected to attend the Wireless School at Crystal Palace.

The instruction in wireless telegraphy was carried out under the Flag Lieutenant Llewellyn Morgan, who was ultimately responsible for all signals, both on shore and sea. About twenty wireless ratings would arrive back from Crystal Palace every two months. The enthusiasm of the newly trained signalmen in the most modern science of the day inevitably created competition between trawlers and drifters, whose skippers delighted in being the first to signal their area 'Clear of Mines'. They made mistakes of course. One of them concerned a man with acute rheumatism. Seen by a doctor he was ordered to hospital and the skipper was left instructions to signal for an ambulance. The man did not arrive. The irate doctor revisited the ship and was informed by the skipper that a police sergeant had refused to allow the man ashore, and further, if he did then he (the skipper) would be fined £100. Neither the signalman nor the skipper could spell rheumatism so they had signalled 'smallpox'.

The British shipbuilding industry was furiously engaged in making up the mercantile marine losses. A total of 362 steamers, small cargo boats and even fishing vessels had succumbed to either gunfire, mines or torpedoes. Both the Admiralty and the German High Command had gained invaluable experience during 1915. For Britain it was time to consider the design and construction of new methods of anti-submarine weaponry, for the Germans would build U-boats in far greater numbers.

While the Germans were shrewdly laying lethal mines at strategic positions in the Dover Strait and the English Channel especially, Vice-Admiral Bacon was perfecting a traffic route system for merchantmen starting at Beachy Head and ending at Margate, where the Nore vessels took over to escort the boats to the Thames and beyond. His system succeeded so brilliantly that, after a comparatively short time, navigation became reasonably safe for merchantmen, provided that they kept to the designated route without straying outside of it.

Minesweeping became one of the most important duties of the Dover Patrol. Large areas were declared dangerous and navigation charts were often covered with circles denoting 'Caution Mines' or symbols showing 'Wrecks'. The whole of the shipping traffic was marshalled into lanes marked by buoys and wreck-marking vessels, while trawlers were working along the route, guiding merchantmen passing up and down the Channel. But despite this highly organized system, losses were still experienced from mines, rarely by torpedoes.

Dover Command's aircraft were noticeably thin in certain areas over the Channel but, even so, the first enemy machine shot down by an RNAS pilot occurred in 1915. Flight-Sub-Lieutenant Ferrand, with his observer, Oldfield, approached four enemy seaplanes escorting a German destroyer to Ostend. Oldfield fired his machine-gun at the

Merchantmen were marshalled into mine-swept lanes by armed trawlers and escorted to the Downs anchorage off Deal.

nearest and was delighted when it fell into the sea. It must have been beginner's luck, as Oldfield wrote in his report that the distance between aircraft was about 100 yards.

Flight-Sub-Lieutenant Viney, with Lieutenant Commander Comte de Sincey as his observer, took off with a couple of 65-lb bombs on 28 November, to look for a U-boat spotted off Zeebrugge. Six miles off Middelkerke they saw two submarines, one completely stationary on the surface, while the other was underway. Viney made his approach on the stationary submarine as the other had quickly dived, and from about 1,000 feet released his bombs. One of them struck the conning tower which produced dense smoke and almost hid the vessel from view. When the smoke cleared the U-boat was sinking with both its stern and bow sticking out of the water, surrounded by an oil slick. The results of this action, however, were never confirmed.

Strong gale-force winds and heavy rains during December 1915 had grounded the RNAS aircraft on most days. However, on 12 December, a merchantman was observed stranded on the Whistle Buoy sandbank and was being bombed by enemy machines. She was a sitting target and quite defenceless. Dover Command aircraft were able to prevent further attacks by patrolling over the ship. She was still stranded two days later, when Flight-Sub Lieutenant Graham, with Sub-Lieutenant Ince as his observer/gunner, chased off an enemy seaplane. Ince fired at it from less than 50 yards range. It burst into flames and dropped almost vertically into the water. Graham's Nieuport developed an engine fault so he was forced to alight on the water where, because of a heavy swell, it turned over on to its back. Upside down in the water Graham had difficulty in releasing his body strap but the paddle minesweeper *Balmoral Castle* was close by and both of the crew were rescued.

So near the coast and in close proximity to Dunkirk harbour, the RNAS depot was vulnerable to enemy attacks. The most concentrated of them was made on 25 September, while other attacks continued through October. The Germans were determined to wipe the depot out once and for all, as it had been a thorn in their side. More than 600 bombs of various calibres were dropped, which resulted in workshops and repair sheds being burned to the ground, while the quite horrendous explosion of a bomb dump devastated the complete area.

There was little doubt that the primitive anti-submarine defences in position in early 1916 were a real danger confronting U-boat commanders. To actually become trapped in a steel mesh net was an experience that few U-boat captains were to forget in a hurry. Kapitänleutnant Wenninger of *UB55* described his particular nightmare to newspaper correspondents in January. A red-painted buoy, one of several that floated attached to the net line, became entangled with his submarine's aft structure and was being pulled along the surface of the water like a rubber duck. Wenninger tried his utmost to rid himself of this tell-tale buoy. He dived, then steered to port and then starboard alternatively, but still the buoy followed his course precisely at the same distance. Even though the submarine was submerged for most of the time, any unexplained movement on the surface of the water would inevitably attract the Dover Patrol lookouts. As expected, destroyers soon gathered at the scene and began to circle the runaway buoy. *UB55* appeared trapped, until Wenninger decided to fill his ballast tanks to capacity. The submarine sank to the bottom like a stone. The buoy broke away and Wenninger tentatively surfaced, only to find a destroyer waiting for him ready to ram. The submarine dived fast and succeeded in its bid for freedom to eventually reach its home base without further incident.

Anxious to avoid any kind of friction with the United States of America, the Kaiser issued orders to his U-boat commanders forbidding them to attack and sink passenger liners. A postscript, however, instructed them that all ships heading for one of the Channel ports at night could be regarded as transports. Inevitably confusion set in when young and inexperienced U-boat officers were to interpret these operational orders to their own advantage. As most of the UB and UC-type submarines were commanded by young officers seeking honour and glory, they were also after promotion to the larger ocean-going U-boats. There was no postscript preventing these officers from laying mines in the traffic routes used by the passenger liners.

The uncertainties of flying are amply illustrated in this report from the archives. Anti-Zeppelin patrols were usually flown before dawn and on 1 February, ten Nieuport aircraft took off from Dunkirk to rendezvous at about 10,000 feet and it was not atypical of many others performed daily.

Reaching the required height at about 0500 hrs, they began their patrol of the coast from ten miles to seaward and about five miles inland. As the sun crept over the horizon a dense mist rose from the ground which hid them from prying eyes. With two and a half hours fuel in their tanks and no reserve tanks fitted, they were told to leave their

This Nieuport Type 10 (3967), served with No. 1 Wing RNAS at St Pol, France, and was used on anti-Zeppelin patrols in 1916.

patrol area at 0730 hrs. The Wing Commander's report states, 'All aircraft were completely lost on coming down to a low altitude but all managed to strike the coast at various points between Gravelines and Cap Gris Nez, with the exception of Flight-Sub Lieutenant Clayton, who missed Cap Griz Nez completely, ran out of petrol, and was finally picked up from the water about twenty miles north of Dieppe.'

The mists persisted and two other pilots only managed to find their aerodrome when aided by hastily erected oil flares on the ground. Flight-Sub-Lieutenant Penley ran out of fuel and was forced down on to the sands where he capsized in a strong crosswind. During the rest of the day Flight Lieutenant Muloch, in a two-seater aircraft and carrying a mechanic and a box of tools, located a further five machines sitting on the sands at the high tide mark.

The Vice-Admiral used aircraft quite often and suggested a night bombing attack upon the Bassin de Leopold in Ostend harbour in February. Reconnaissance cameras had shown several enemy destroyers moored there. The raid was carried out by five Nieuports carrying five 20-lb bombs each, although only three machines actually reached the target. There was a further disappointment due to the many searchlights used over the target area and any damage caused was purely circumstantial. A month later Bacon suggested a Anglo-French-Belgium bombing raid on the German-held Houtave aerodrome. The whole operation, which was made just before daybreak, consisted of bombers and fighters totalling over forty and was most imposing. Damage was reported as 'considerable'. A further raid was made simultaneously on Zeebrugge Mole, by seaplanes operating from their carriers *Vindex* and *Riviera*.

The P&O liner *Maloja* had just passed Dover's Admiralty pier on Sunday 24 February when she struck a rogue mine thought to have been laid by a UC-type submarine. *Maloja* was seriously damaged aft on her starboard side. Being close in-shore, relatively speaking, her captain attempted to beach his vessel. When she had lost sufficient weigh to enable lifeboats to be lowered he ordered stop engines. By this time, however, the engine room was flooded and she continued to go astern at about 8 knots, listing rather dramatically, and only allowing one or two boats to launch over the side. For whatever reason she began to sink rather more quickly than expected, taking a third of her passengers with her to the bottom, all the while blowing her foghorn which could be heard for many miles inland. Every available vessel in the vicinity came to render assistance but even so just over the third of her 441 passengers drowned. The small craft brought in fifty-eight bodies and, once again, the market hall was used as a temporary mortuary. Similar to the sinking of *Anglia*, while the rescue attempts were progressing, the coaster SS *Empress of Fort William* struck a mine in the wake of *Maloja* and sank almost in the same position as the liner.

Lieutenant Coxon was helping to disembark survivors from the small craft. They were taken to the Lord Warden Hotel and Coxon wrote:

> The hotel was simply crammed with them and the dining room reminded one of nothing so much as a scene in a tragedy at the Drury Lane theatre. There they were, men, women and children, all seated at different tables and garbed in every sort of wonderful garbing. Reach-me-downs of all sorts and sizes, dressing gowns, pyjamas of strange and wonderful pattern and hue, a priest's cassock, large warm bath towels, and rugs and blankets were all in evidence, and had the sight not been such a pathetic one it would make a cat laugh.

Throughout March and April 1916 the drifters and trawlers attached to Ramsgate were increasingly active. At 1810 hrs on 1 March the RRS drifter, along with several others, was fired upon by an enemy aircraft returning from a raid on the North Foreland. One seaplane was reported hit by rifle fire and was last seen slowly descending into a minefield. Four days later *City of Glasgow* was machine-gunned east of the Goodwin Sands while she rescued French airmen from their waterlogged machine. Lieutenant Irvine, who was skipper of *Corona*, received a congratulatory letter from the Vice-Admiral for his fine show of seamanship in assisting the mined trawler *Abelard* to reach Dover on 17 March. Sadly Irvine's fine seamanship was not to last. On 23 March *Corona* struck a mine and he and the rest of his crew perished near the South Downs.

But no one knows what happened to the trawler *Flicker*. She had been patrolling along the minefield where *Maloja* had sunk, warning merchantmen to steer clear, when she just disappeared from the face of the earth. No sign of her or any wreckage was ever afterwards seen – except the body of one of her deckhands floating in a lifebelt. *Flicker's* disappearance was recorded on 4 March 1916, then, on 28 March, *Saxon Prince* vanished during a furious south-westerly gale. The Vice-Admiral signed the daily report which said, tersely, 'Disappeared in storm off Dover'. Every incident recorded in the daily summaries failed to mention the acts of extreme bravery and courage which went unnoticed. Risking their lives daily, the minesweeping men often passed into oblivion without anyone being aware of their existence. There is, in truth, something rather heroic, even awesome about the men who suddenly disappeared without trace. Their names appear almost enigmatically on pieces of paper tinted by age, their souls hovering over the Dover Straits searching for recognition. They have no known grave.

Oberleutnant Herbert Pustkuchen, commander of *UB29*, seemed set on defying orders. After leaving his Flanders base at night he successfully negotiated the Dover mine nets with complete confidence, then sank a French steamer at anchor, a Norwegian freighter and a Danish ship. Edging westward on the afternoon of 24 March, he came across the packet boat *Sussex* in mid-Channel between Folkestone and Dieppe. Pustkuchen fired a torpedo at about 14,000 yards range which struck the steamer's bow, instantly killing over fifty men, women and children. *Sussex* was soon down by the head but she refused to sink. An SOS signal was transmitted in haste and brought immediate response from the nearest destroyer *Afridi*. Lieutenant-Commander P.R.P. Percival raced to the last position given, then placed his ship alongside the crippled vessel, rescuing everyone he could find. Of the 386 people on board no less than 97 lost their lives in what was considered a deliberate act of murder by those who knew about it at the time. *Sussex* was eventually towed into Boulogne harbour where salvage experts discovered the torpedo fragments among the wreckage. She was, incidently, the only cross-Channel steamer actually torpedoed in the Dover Strait during the war. Of course Berlin denied all responsibility to begin with until the damning evidence of the torpedo fragments was made public and was then forced to admit that a U-boat had made the attack. Pustkuchen was, however, given the benefit of the doubt after pleading mistaken identity. His plausible defence was hardly justified when he then proceeded to sink the British steamer *Salybia* without warning. But Pustkuchen was to lose his life in *UC 66* when she was depth charged to destruction off the Lizard on 12 June 1917.

The *Sussex* incident was considered a crime and as she was carrying several American citizens, American politicians were soon demanding – indeed almost threatening – to sever diplomatic relations with Germany, and drew a parallel with the *Lusitania*. 'How many more Americans must be killed before President Wilson declares war?', ran the *New York Herald*'s headline. The American threat brought an immediate response from Berlin, although the Germans argued that the British blockade was just as criminal, causing women and children to starve in the Fatherland.

Dutch ships were just as vulnerable to attack from U-boats as other neutral ships. The 13,911-ton Dutch liner *Turbantia* was lost on 16 March, torpedoed off the North Hinder lightship, and bound for Buenos Aires. It was revealed she was carrying German bullion, concealed in cheeses, which was consigned to German banks abroad. The U-boat commander was quite unaware of the nature of her cargo and so by his action had deprived Germany of considerable assets. The Dutch steamer *Medea* was sunk off Beachy Head on 28 March, along with several others, but when *Palembang* and *Eemdijk* went to the bottom there was some suggestion made that German saboteurs, working in New York under their leading agent Kapitän Franz von Rintelen, might have been responsible.

'It's like Fred Karno's Navy', a destroyer captain was heard to remark; vessels of the Dover Patrol at anchor in Dover Harbour.

By early spring an entirely new scheme of patrolling and defensive minelaying was adopted and this change resulted in a less strenuous summer for Dover Command. But even so, the number of vessels in the command had swollen to such an extent, and the types of ships presented so many variations of size, shape and displacement, that one destroyer commander was heard to remark, 'It's like Fred Karno's Navy'.

The drifter *Paramount* rescued twenty-two men from the torpedoed SS *Hollandia* on 1 April. Four days later *Lord Charles Beresford* sent a coded signal saying she had seen a submarine's conning tower at about 2010 hrs off the North Foreland. Then there was a collision near the Elbow buoy between the armed liner *Macedonia* and the Norwegian steamer SS *Correct*. The drifter *Feasible* was soon at the scene and made fast alongside *Correct* and began to tow, albeit in a heavy swell. Unfortunately the tow parted and the crippled vessel sank.

As soon as the German minelaying submarines became active all the traffic routes needed sweeping daily by trawlers. The seas between Beachy Head and the North Foreland, through which merchantmen were guided on a pre-planned course, were divided into sections and swept by a pair of specially fitted trawlers. The maximum number of trawlers based at Dover at any one time was sixty-six, but usually half a dozen were absent due to minor collisions, mine damage, repairs or maintenance. There were twenty-four trawlers stationed one mile south of the traffic route, four units of six boats, one of which was equipped with a wireless transmitter. They remained on their designated positions at either the South Goodwin lightvessel, the Folkestone Gate (a narrow entrance off Folkestone), Dungeness or the Royal Sovereign lightvessel near Beachy Head, for four days and nights. Two other units swept the entrances to Boulogne and Calais harbours every morning.

By the end of March all trawlers with sufficiently strong winches had been converted to minesweepers. Sweeping up mines in an area of one and a half miles radius usually took from two to three days to complete. When first laid, German mines seemed to have been grouped in sixes, then in twelves. Areas designated as 'clean' could only be accepted when either six or twelve mines had been found. Later still, and after several months had passed, enemy UC-type U-boats laid mines indiscriminately, often laying them in ones and twos along the route. Trawlers swept mines in the strongest of weathers, even in gales and fierce winds, and it was to their credit that they never once left their designated positions.

These trawlers were also responsible for escorting either a convoy or a single ship through their particular section, handing over to another along the patrol line. As each ship was passed from one to the other a signal was sent back to Dover reporting a 'safe passage'. It was, nonetheless, a constant anxiety to trawler skippers to arrive at the handing-over position, at, say, Beachy Head, on the western route, only to discover that their relief was not there. Time after time, the escorting trawler was required to continue its journey to either Portland, Portsmouth or Devonport, arriving back at Dover long after they were due for a rest period. After coaling and taking on provisions, they were back at sea. There was no rest for the crew.

Dagon, commanded by Lieutenant E.E. Roberts, was the only trawler torpedoed in the Dover Strait. A destroyer was passing between a U-boat and the trawler just when the former fired its missile. It missed its target, struck *Dagon*, and at one stroke wiped out the whole crew.

The steamer SS *Shenandoah* struck a mine near the Folkestone Gate on 15 March. Lieutenant Barnes, commanding the trawler *Macfarlane*, instructed the master to beach his ship. Unfortunately, damaged bulkheads gave way under the extreme pressure so that the crippled vessel sank by the stern, leaving the section from the bridge to bow afloat. *Macfarlane* immediately began to save the crew and found a capsized lifeboat with three men sitting on it. They said they could hear knocking from inside. The *Returno* arrived, moved alongside the up-turned lifeboat and, using hooks, turned it over. Thoroughly exhausted by their experience, the wireless operator and fireman swam out, from then on believing in miracles.

Etoile Polaire, with Lieutenant Lansley on the bridge, was escorting a vessel to repair a telephone line on the Sunk lightship, when the SS *Volscian* struck a mine close by. Lansley took her in tow, even though the crew refused to go back on board their ship. The princely sum of £75 as salvage payment was awarded to the trawler's crew, when the value of the salved ship was about £10,000!

Lieutenant Lansley was again in reports submitted to Admiral Bacon when the trawler *ST Germain* was mined off Folkestone Gate. The *Strathgairn* came alongside and put a line on the stern of the sinking trawler. Meanwhile, Lansley quickly transferred his confidential papers, ammunition, depth charges and other valuable items to the *Strathgairn* then, with four other volunteers, went back on board his crippled boat to discover sea water gushing through a crack in the foremost bulkhead. Using mats and rugs, and anything they could lay their hands to, they managed to stem the flow. Lansley also discovered that in spite of the influx of water, which had put out the fire under the boilers, there was enough steam to work the pumps. An SOS signal had already been sent and tugs were sent out from Dover to assist but a heavy squall came up and they failed to see her. Although the weather had deteriorated alarmingly, Lansley persisted with his vigil and was able to beach his trawler near Folkestone.

When the trawler *Otello II* struck a mine amidships she was blown in two halves and sank almost immediately. Admiral Bacon learned from the only survivor, a deck boy, that the wheelhouse had been so damaged by the explosion that neither doors nor windows would open sufficiently to allow escape. The skipper, second mate and the helmsman had pushed the deck boy to safety through the only half-open window available. The rest of the crew perished. Acting on this information, Bacon issued instructions to remove all fixed doors of wheelhouses and to substitute them with a light canvas frame, which could easily be removed.

The instinct to survive put Chief Engineer Stark's life in danger when *Electra II* was in collision on 14 April. Standing up to his waist in a flooded engine room he kept the vessel afloat until it reached Dover. The skipper found the water was within six inches of the fire-bars.

In April two trawlers *Osta* and *Ostrich* were taken from normal duties to be fitted out at Sheerness as minelayers, to supplement the four already in service. These six vessels were transferred to Dunkirk. Being of medium draught, they were able to creep in through the sandbanks and lay their mines closer to the Belgian coast than the larger minelayers could manage. They usually operated either at night or in heavy sea mists so that they could avoid detection. They carried out their task for six weeks, despite being spotted more than once when the mists suddenly cleared. On those occasions they were subjected to seaplane attacks.

Vice-Admiral Sir Reginald Bacon, made a KCB in January, had decided that the only way to stop enemy submarines leaving their Flanders bases was to make the waters off the Belgian coast as dangerous as possible. He was not convinced that the monitor bombardments actually deterred the submarines at all, and it was risky to have his ships come under fire from the Ostend Tirpitz battery and the Kaiser Wilhelm battery effectively protecting Zeebrugge.

After many days of planning and construction of nets and buoys, the larger minelayers, *Orvietto*, *Princess Margaret*, *Biarritz* and *Paris*, under the command of Captain F.S. Litchfield-Speer, left their anchorage in the Thames Estuary on the afternoon tide of 23 April. They arrived at the Dyck lightship at 1600 hrs the following day. The destroyers *Zulu* and *Nubian* dropped dan buoys every three miles or so to mark the positions of the light buoys and where the nets were to be laid. Once they were in position the minelayers began laying a double row of mines. The Trinity House vessels *Vestal*, *Argus* and *Alert* followed soon afterwards to lay the light buoys. Where the waters were too shallow the newly fitted trawlers moved in to complete the minefield. The monitors *Prince Eugene* and *General Wolfe* acted in support of the destroyers, the whole surrounded by drifters in a protection role.

The larger minelayers had completed their task by 0730 hrs and left the area but

Before the invention of the depth charge, the Dover Patrol used the bomb lance, a sort of giant hand grenade stuck on a pole.

such a vast undertaking of laying 1,421 mines did not go undetected. Several vessels were attacked by enemy seaplanes, one of them being shot down to explode on hitting the water. Drift-nets put out by *Arndilly Castle* were fouled about noon by a suspect submarine and, although the yacht *Diana* dropped depth charges, *UB10* got clear of further hindrance. The Tirpitz battery opened fire on *General Wolfe* from about 32,000 yards range then, at 1415 hrs, *Gleaner of the Sea* encountered *UB13* in her nets. She attacked the U-boat with bomb lances until the destroyer *Afridi* joined in with her explosive sweeps. Oberleutnant A. Metz died with his crew.

Vice-Admiral Bacon on board *Crusader* had omitted to warn destroyers not to venture too close to the enemy held shore for fear of enemy guns. At 1430 hrs three enemy destroyers were seen off Zeebrugge. The destroyers *Medea*, *Melpomene*, *Murray* and *Milne*, under Commander Gibbs, immediately turned to engage, but when they were about 16,000 yards from the shore they came under accurate fire from the heavy guns. *Melpomene* was the first hit when a shell bored into her engine room without exploding. *Milne* and *Murray* took her in tow just as the enemy destroyers made another attack. They slipped their towing wires and gave chase, helped by the 12-in salvoes

This German torpedo boat destroyer was photographed in the Bassin de Leopold, Ostend, in early 1918.

from the two monitors. The enemy destroyers retreated out of harm's way. *Melpomene* was eventually towed into Dunkirk for repairs.

The skipper of the drifter *Clover Bank* made a serious mistake when, after shooting his nets, he lost his sense of direction by steaming south instead of north, struck a mine and blew up. There were no survivors.

Anxious to telephone the First Sea Lord, Sir H. Jackson, Bacon returned to Dover in *Crusader*, only to find a message waiting for him to withdraw his ships immediately from the Belgian coast, as a large force of enemy ships was reported in the North Sea. The Admiral realized at once that his net barrage, so painstakingly laid, could be investigated by the enemy without interruption.

A withdraw signal was made to each division but it is recorded that the 9th Division of drifters, at anchor off the Raab Bank, failed to receive the message. They remained at their position throughout the night. Under Commander Venn, the 9th Division weighed anchor next morning when they heard gunfire. They saw, through the early morning mists, several German torpedo craft machine-gunning the buoys and mines. Venn collected his drifters and steered north-west. The destroyers gave chase but when the enemy vessels opened fire on them Venn ordered his division to scatter. *Au Fait* had dropped behind the rest and was hit several times. She stopped in a cloud of steam and smoke. A German destroyer went alongside her just as the drifter's crew took to their lifeboat. Venn watched the skipper Charles Bridge and his crew being taken prisoner. The scattered drifters were reassembled when the enemy gave up the chase. Neither Commander Venn or Admiral Bacon quite understood why the Germans failed to pursue the drifters to either capture or destroy them. It was not until 1918, when Skipper Bridge had been released from captivity, that they learned he had told the Germans that a signal had been sent for assistance.

Air reconnaissance later reported a force of eleven enemy destroyers, three small cruisers and a seaplane carrier off Zeebrugge. Bacon was quick to seize the opportunity to make a show of strength. He immediately obtained Admiralty approval to use the Harwich Force and the cooperation of Commodore Tywhitt. On 28 April Bacon met Tywhitt off the Ratel Bank, on the very day another deep minefield was about to be laid. The show of strength consisted of two cruisers, two flotilla leaders, thirty-two destroyers and four monitors, all to arrive at the Hinder light buoy at the same time. Commander Evans recalled, 'There was a pleasurable pride at the sight of this perfectly manoeuvred flotilla steaming at full speed and in full view of the Belgian coast.' German seaplanes watched the whole proceedings, which was exactly what Admiral Bacon had intended.

A double line of mines had been laid which was fifteen miles in length, thirteen miles of mine nets were moored, fourteen large light buoys and several other buoys were put in position while a protection of eighteen miles of drift-nets had also been provided. Reading through his reports later Admiral Bacon discovered that through the whole of the two operations he had lost one officer and seventeen men killed, with two destroyers damaged.

From spring to autumn the mine barrage of nets was laid, rearranged, repaired and maintained, the whole time being watched over by RNAS aircraft and destroyers during the day, while at night the Dover-based submarines patrolled. Severe weather conditions played havoc with the mine nets, which resulted in poor maintenance. It was not always possible to visit them during the hours of darkness either, since the days were shorter. Additionally, it was considered doubtful that the enemy molested the barrage and Dover Command could only operate for seventeen per cent of the day anyway. Taking everything into consideration, they were able to harass the enemy and keep his head down for most of the time. But, true to form, German guns shelled everything in sight and their flying machines learned to appreciate that fast destroyers were difficult to hit, while the slower monitors afforded them a more tempting target.

It was not unusual for enemy aircraft to make bombing attacks upon shipping in Dunkirk harbour on a Sunday. *Crusader* had taken General Sir William Robertson and Admiral Bacon over to the French port on Sunday 30 April and berthed alongside the monitor *Marshal Soult*. German aircraft appeared just after lunch and began to systematically drop their bombs over the whole port area. The first of these fell beside *Crusader* and only caused minor damage but the next hit the monitor's deck, killing five men and wounding many others. The 2-pounder pom-poms were brought into action just as another bomb made a huge hole in one of the monitor's anti-submarine bulges. More German aircraft came into view and the sky resembled bees round a honey pot,

The paddle minesweepers became indispensable in the Dover Patrol, sweeping up German mines ahead of the bombardment force and ships carrying VIPs to and from France.

with bombs exploding among a crowd of motor transport men and their vehicles and French soldiers parading on the quayside. The result was a mass of tangled bodies lying everywhere. As luck would have it, several of *Crusader*'s crew were out on the local sands collecting cockles. They ran for their lives but several were hit by flying pieces of shrapnel.

Bombardment of the Belgian coast continued. From their anchorage to the north-east of the Ratel Shoal – a matter of some 15 miles – the monitors were underway each day for about twenty hours out of the twenty-four. The barrage procession, usually consisting of two or three monitors creeping slowly towards their firing positions, accompanied by a small anti-submarine escort of perhaps two or three 30-knotters, became so predictable that those taking part actually questioned the rare enemy intervention. The grey graceful shapes of the destroyers steaming round the long line of drifters which puffed along behind was equally impressive as the paddle minesweepers in three pairs out ahead. The paddlers had arrived at Dover on 14 July 1915, under the command of Commander W. Rigg RN. While they were faster and better suited to work with the patrol ships off the Belgian coast, they were not at all suitable for heavy weather conditions. They were usually engaged in sweeping areas quickly and always swept the positions where the Dover-based submarines exercised for two days out of every four. But their special duty, where they became indispensable, was to sweep ahead of the bombardment force. Equally important, however, and also regarded as a special duty, was to sweep ahead of the steamers who carried important people to and from France – such as the politicians, heads of state and not least King George V.

The first loss of a paddle minesweeper was on 6 October 1915 when *Brighton Queen*, sweeping off Nieuport at night, struck a mine and sank almost immediately. Seven crew were lost and, from that day onwards, the paddles refrained from night sweeping. On 1 May 1916 the PMS *Kylemore* had two men killed with another seriously injured when a mine exploded sideways and swept the paddler's deck with shrapnel.

When lying at anchor at Dunkirk on 2 September 1917, the paddlers suffered severe damage during a two-hour air raid. *Albyn* was hit by a bomb which set her stern on fire. Lieutenant King and the 2nd Engineer Officer were killed. The PMS *Lingfield* received over 100 holes in her and lost two men killed. Dunkirk, only 12 miles distant from enemy lines, had more than fifty air raids in just a two month period, not to mention the long-range shelling incidents.

Soon after the first German mines were laid near Dover on 18 June 1915 *Albyn*, commanded by Lieutenant A. Daniels RNR, together with *Jupiter II*, commanded by Lieutenant G.P. Spooner RNR, came across these mines close to South Goodwin Sands and were disposed of by rifle fire.

As for the bombardment force, once the monitors were in their correct positions the shoot began, laying 12-in and 15-in shells on to specific targets but ever careful not to overshoot so as to avoid civilian casualties around Ostend and Zeebrugge. As the shooting season progressed, the monitors, for various reasons, began to lose speed and became rather sluggish in their forward movement. The *Marshal Soult* on one occasion in particular was not capable of a speed in excess of about 4 knots and *Prince Eugene* and *Prince Rupert* were once caught in a severe westerly gale against which neither vessel could make any headway at all. Their captains wisely anchored and, their holding gear being quite efficient, they rode out the storm with engines at half-ahead. Even so, the monitors were beaten sideways by the rending force of the gale and the peak of it became too enormous for the crews to do anything other than think of their immediate survival. Those on watch saw the landmarks of the world vanish completely. As for the destroyers who stood by them throughout and were tossed about like corks, their crews hung on for dear life.

The Vice-Admiral was constantly visiting his patrol lines and his heavy naval ordnance used in shore gun emplacements, of which he was particularly fond. He usually flew his flag in *Crusader*, which became known as the 'taxi-cab', but as the accommodation and messing facilities were hardly suitable for his rank, he slept on the *Marshal Soult* and remained there for his meals. The monitor became known in signals as 'the restaurant'. If Bacon made one of his visits to the Burlington Hotel, it was likely to strain even the most generous naval budgets. So, looking for somewhere to alleviate the boredom of office, he would wrestle with the outrageous dietary concoctions on board ship, washed down with a bottle of claret.

Working closely with Dover Command in 1916 were the French destroyers *Francis Garnier*, *Adventurier* and *Intrépide*. Their usefulness was crucial in daily patrol work but, like their British counterparts in the earlier vessels, their armament was not sufficiently modern to out-gun enemy destroyers, unless it was a close skirmish action. The enemy

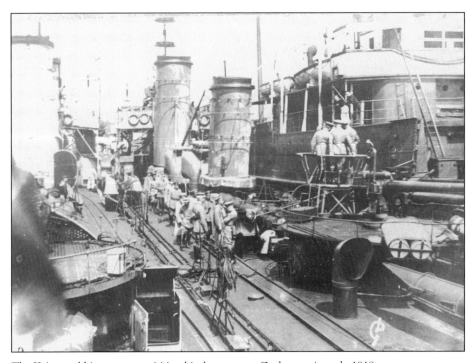

The Kaiser and his entourage visiting his destroyers at Zeebrugge in early 1918.

did not waste their vessels in useless attacks but kept them tied up in harbour until, as a striking force, they could attack either the Downs or Dunkirk. It was often the subject of debate in Admiralty circles that German destroyer attacks were rarely made upon shipping anchored in the Downs. A captured German officer explained their tactics to Bacon. He revealed that they so seldom risked their ships in close-range fighting because they feared unwarranted damage. The only repair facilities that were available for their torpedo craft were at Bruges and even there any extensive damage was almost impossible to correct. The later class of German destroyer carried three 4.1-in guns and six torpedo tubes. Compared with the British Tribal class they were superior and the Sixth Flotilla could not lay claim to damaging any of the enemy boats until they too were given updated craft.

The increased air activity in early 1916 led to the discovery of one of the enemy's most active aerodromes at Mariakerke, where the larger Gotha bombers were kept. The Vice-Admiral decided to 'get in the first blow' and so, on 5 May, nineteen aircraft took off from St Pol aerodrome each carrying 65-lb bombs. They were met by a fierce anti-aircraft fire that sent up a firework display of incendiary shells which burst among the attackers in a vivid jade green light. They called them 'flaming onions' and they were showered with magnesium sparklets as they doggedly flew through them with a

A DH4 day bomber seen at Guston Road aerodrome, before flying to St Pol, France, where it served with the RNAS squadrons.

wonderful sense of courage and determination. They had never before seen such a concentration of gunfire and their particular experience of it was locked in their minds for the rest of their lives.

There was a marked improvement in equipment that provided suitable machine-guns and wireless transmitters – the latter could now reach a distance of 100 miles. In June 1916 a reliable camera evolved which was suspended in a vibration-less mounting with a lens pointing vertically downwards through a hole cut in the under fuselage. The first test of the new camera system was made by Flight Lieutenant Mach and Sub-Lieutenant Simms during a bombardment of the Tirpitz battery on 9 June from about 14,000 feet.

For obvious reasons the long patrols flown over the vast expanse of sea at considerable distances from the coast was theoretically more suited to seaplanes than the landplanes. But there was one nagging problem with them. The Vice-Admiral was convinced they were 'becoming hopelessly handicapped for fighting a duel with the [German] aeroplane types that were now becoming common'. He was most concerned at the end of 1916 by the too-frequent reports landing on his desk saying 'Seaplane failed to return'. As a direct result, he commenced using landplanes in preference.

There was another nagging problem that Bacon wanted to master: the accuracy at extreme range of the German shore batteries firing upon his bombardment monitors. He discovered this was largely due to the enemy's use of a kite-balloon moored one mile south-east of Ostend at Steene. Bacon decided to attack it. Flight Lieutenant C.R.

Mackenzie of 10 Flight A Squadron of 4 Wing volunteered for the task. The French had invented a Le Prieur rocket device which was already being used successfully by the RFC wings. Mechanics fitted four rockets to the interplane struts of a Nieuport 17B (Baby) 8750, a particularly strong aeroplane capable of a dive at almost 200 mph. Mackenzie's first attempt ended in failure because he accidentally brushed against the switch that activated the rockets. He returned to have more of them fitted and his next attempt on 7 September was successful when he sent the kite-balloon down in flames. He was awarded the DSO soon afterwards.

Vice-Admiral Bacon was never sure whether his mine barrages were ever the success the Admiralty had intended. His latest barrage was primarily to act as a protection for the Dover Patrol vessels on their daily tasks. But its secondary purpose was to impede U-boats which, of necessity, were forced to cross the mouth of the Scheldt before reaching the end of the net barrier and setting course for their south-westerly run into the Dover Strait. Bacon thought the evidence was strong enough in support of the barrage's efficiency and it was often assumed that a U-boat had been destroyed when an explosion occurred.

After Commodore Michelsen's Flanders destroyers had made their raid in October, the Admiralty instructed Bacon to extend the net barrage at the easternmost boundary of the Dover Command's limit of operations to reach the Snou Bank in December. But of course, net and mine barrages were not only laid by Bacon but also his opponent. The UC-type submarines constructed a formidable mine barrier of over 400 high explosive mines off the Dutch coast from the Maas Light Vessel to Ymuiden. Just the year before an enormous amount of material was conveyed to Dover by train and ship – steel wire, jackstays and all manner of associated equipment – to make a more dangerous barrier. Bacon was furious when he received a signal from the Admiralty to transfer the whole lot to Gallipoli to provide a much needed boom defence.

Until 1916, the evidence was strongly in favour of having destroyed *U5* and *U11* in 1914 and *U8* and *U37* in 1915. When one or two bodies were found soon after an explosion, a search of their clothing would often reveal a pass allowing the bearer to visit Bruges. This sort of evidence was circumstantial enough to be accepted. But mines exploded for many other reasons and if every explosion reported meant the destruction of a German submarine, then the Dover Patrol would have sunk all the German U-boats several times over. On 17 June, for example, the drifter *Lord Charles Beresford* had reported six heavy underwater explosions during a two-hour period. As far as mines were concerned, the German device was considered really dangerous, while the British mines, whatever their merits when placed in position, possessed the unfortunate trait of breaking adrift too easily and were often found floating on the surface. By 1917, however, the British mine was just as deadly as its opposite number.

There was never a dull moment in Dover Command. The drifter *Ocean Crest* came upon a disabled seaplane near the Elbow light buoy on 19 June. She towed it as far as the Tongue lightship before it sank. *Reclaim* threw a line to a French schooner on 2 July which had entered the mine barrage area without knowing of the danger. Then the drifter *Rooke* was sunk on 3 August, having collided with SS *Mereddie* near the South Downs. Six crew members lost their lives in the tragedy. *Paramount* rescued the pilot and observer of a seaplane on 19 August, then towed it to the RNAS station at

Westgate. A week later *Buckler* fired on a Zeppelin, then *Lord Claud Hamilton* disgraced herself by going around in Pegwell Bay. When *Ocean Crest* was in collision with SS *Chatburn* on 10 September, the Vice-Admiral ordered oxyacetylene lamps to be lit while ships negotiated the net barrage gates in foggy conditions.

The early morning air reconnaissance sortie on 26 October had reported a considerable increase in railway movements, barge activity on the Ostend canal system and the presence of several enemy destroyers in the harbour complex. The Vice-Admiral was alerted. He became rather anxious that either a concentrated attack on part of the Belgian coast was likely, or perhaps his shipping in the Downs would be the target.

Because of the increased U-boat activity in the western approaches of the Channel, Bacon had been forced to strengthen his traffic patrols in daytime; therefore, his hard-working Tribals, out every day, were required to rest in harbour at night. The destroyer force at his disposal on the night of 26–7 October was only one division of eight boats borrowed from Harwich. His own force consisted of six Tribals, eight 30-knotters, four P-boats and two TBDs. Bacon split his force into two, covering the Downs, Dunkirk and the beaches to the east of La Panne. The Tribals were on a ten-minute steam-up order in harbour.

One of those rare skirmishes with the enemy occurred on 27 October at about 2300 hrs. A German destroyer flotilla made an attack in the Dover Strait, carefully negotiating the British mine barrage which had been laid to prevent such a thing happening. But of course, German reconnaissance seaplanes had spotted the mine barrage the day after it had been laid and made accurate charts of its length and breadth. The defenceless drifters attending the nets were suddenly and without any warning attacked. They were no match for the well-placed 4.1-in shells which just blew them apart as if they were made of matchsticks: those that were lost included *Roeburn*, *Spotless Prince*, *Ajax II*, *Gleaner of the Sea*, *Launch Out* and *Datum*.

The yacht *Ombra* and the trawler H.E. *Stroud*, together with the old C class 30-knot destroyer *Flirt*, heard the gunfire and arrived soon after the decimation of the six drifters. The German flotilla strength was twelve, which split into two separate divisions – six steamed for Cap Griz Nez, while the others set course for Dover. In the darkness *Flirt*'s lookouts mistook the dark shapes as those of British ships returning to Dover. Nevertheless, she altered course to see what all the fuss was about.

The German guns were heard in Dover. Vice-Admiral Bacon heard them too and immediately issued orders for the Tribals to sail, sent a signal to the Downs boats to weigh anchor and sent another to Commodore Dunkirk. Meanwhile *Flirt* had switched on searchlights to help locate men swimming around in the water. The First Lieutenant and a couple of deckhands went away in a lifeboat to pick up the men when two of the enemy destroyers reappeared to fire on *Flirt*. A well-aimed torpedo struck her amidships. She sank so quickly there was little hope for the crew to abandon ship. Except for the First Lieutenant and his deckhands, still pulling about in the turbulent waters, the rest perished. No flotsam or wreckage was ever found afterwards.

Commander Gibbs, the senior officer in charge of the three M class destroyers on loan from the Harwich Force, and patrolling the eastern approaches of the Channel, ordered full steam ahead when he heard the gunfire and explosions. Water seethed under the forefoot as each vessel responded to the helm. Thick black smoke belched

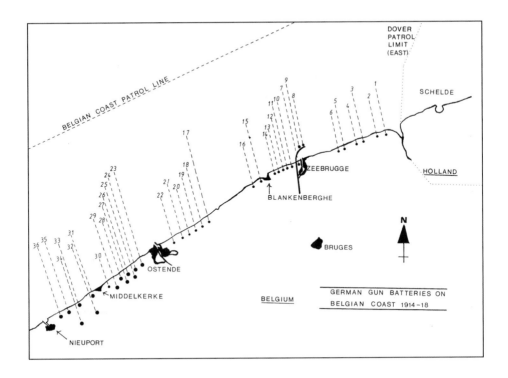

from the funnels, to snake back and down on to the surface of the water like a shroud. But it was too easy for the enemy to run in close for protection from their shore batteries. As if his life depended on it, Gibbs pursued them. In no time at all, the whole Belgian coastline became a blaze of gun flashes.

Having been cooped up in their Flanders bases for too long, partly due to the uncertainties of the British mine barrage but also German naval strategy, the destroyer commanders were out at last to make a killing. It was assumed they were expecting to cut off the British transport vessels running between Boulogne and Folkestone, carrying troops and equipment. They came across the steamer *Queen*, a troop transport that had left Boulogne without any escort because, fortunately, she was not carrying any troops at all. Vice-Admiral Bacon had abolished the night sailing of troops only recently. *Queen* was ordered to stop and her master obeyed, knowing he could not outrun the six or so destroyers poised to attack. Using a megaphone and speaking impeccable English, the nearest destroyer commander told the master to abandon his ship. When they had taken to their lifeboats and pulled away from their ship, she was torpedoed. She was reluctant to sink at once and for some time drifted eastwards on the fast-running tide, before plunging to the depths three hours later near the Goodwins. Only one man was lost while the rest of the crew were brought in to Dover by several small craft. Had Vice-Admiral Bacon not issued orders to stop carrying troops at night a disaster of some magnitude would have resulted.

But just before that episode, the undisturbed peacefulness in Dover harbour was suddenly broken by the shouts of 'Hands stand by wires and fenders!' The second division of the German destroyer flotilla had crept along the coast unseen by the drifter patrols. They began firing shells landwards, two of which exploded near the village of Hougham. The Tribals were raising steam at the time, having received orders to sail. Faint sounds were heard from several forecastles. The *Amazon* was the first to move. Lieutenant Coxon watched the proceedings from the Admiralty pier.

Amazon began to lurch as the screws beneath her slowly turned. She moved astern. Then after a few turns the engines stopped and there was silence again. The blacked-out hull swung slightly to port. Then a second and greater commotion from her propellers sent her forwards into the darkness. She slipped effortlessly past the now active shapes of the other destroyers, still secure at their moorings but soon to join her, and quietly entered the boom defence barrier. Once her full length had passed the eastern pier-heads she began to rise and fall to the swell of the tide outside the harbour.

Signals flashed between *Amazon* and the port war station. Within a few minutes three more destroyers were riding into the deep swell, following *Amazon*'s wake. The speed rapidly increased to 27 knots and they were fast on a course to intercept the enemy vessels. On seeing the British destroyers the Germans opened fire, then altered course. The chase began. Neither side did much damage, although *Amazon* was hit twice and suffered some casualties. In the gloom the vessels were mere shapes behind vortices of spray. Sounds were all fused together into one massive assault rather than a distinct noise, through which speech could only travel a distance of inches at the utmost pitch of the lungs.

As luck often plays a hand in sea actions of this kind, something was about to happen that was quite unforeseen. Amid the gunfire, *Nubian*'s bridge was strangely silent as she had become separated from the others. Suddenly the officer of the watch shouted out 'Alarm . . . bearing Green, Nine-O!' Commander M.R. Bernard ordered, 'Starboard on O-Eight-Seven!' Above the subdued noises of the ship, another sound was heard, a distant deep thrumming, a sort of long pulsation. *Nubian* altered course again intending to ram a German destroyer but that pulsation sound was a torpedo. While the alert gun crews listened intently to orders being given in quick succession, the missile struck home with an enormous explosion. Several men lost their lives instantly but *Nubian* refused to sink. She was taken in tow by the tug *William Gray*, during which the wind strength increased so suddenly that the tow parted, allowing the ailing vessel to drift ashore. She ended up going aground on the South Foreland rocks but not before the tug's skipper Thomas Smith had courageously rescued everyone left on board.

There was another casualty when *Mohawk* received holes in several places. Lieutenant-Commander H.S. Braddyll brought her into Dover by the skin of his teeth. *Viking*, which some months before had been damaged in a mine explosion, had been fitted with a larger calibre gun and, although she took part in the fracas, her new weapon proved disappointing. There were eleven bodies landed at the Admiralty pier from the damaged destroyers and nine were buried at the St James's cemetery with full military honours.

This particular German action caused a rumpus, not only at Dover, but a great deal of criticism also came from the House of Commons. The weakness of the Dover Patrol's

The F class *Nubian* went aground on the
South Foreland rocks, after the tow
parted in heavy weather.

fighting ships was not generally known to the public, mainly due to wartime censorship.
Admiral Bacon, however, was convinced that the German High Command was *au fait*
with their weakness. In any event Dover Command was strengthened by the transfer of
more modern ships from other commands. But after Lord Beresford had said in the
House of Commons, 'What is wrong at Dover?', the Vice-Admiral was hard-pressed to
stem the flow from his ardent critics. Almost immediately he adopted what became
known as the 'dark night patrol' system. During ten days or a fortnight of each month
when there was no moon, his destroyers were employed in two divisions to patrol the
Straits in case of further enemy raids. While this concentration of destroyers meant
better protection against surface vessels, it forfeited the vigilance against the submarine.
An even bigger outcry ensued because the German ships had been allowed to penetrate
the net barrage. It was, however, felt rather strongly by those who were operational in
destroyers that the obsolete ships in the command went some way to display the
hardship under which they worked. As Evans succinctly put it, 'Their rotten collection
of craft could not be compared with the splendid vessels in other commands'.

Take the eastern patrol division as an example, working near the tail of the
Ruytingen Shoal. It was only a short two-hour run to Ostend and the crews of these

ships were called upon to exercise the greatest degree of vigilance and readiness, often for ten nights at a stretch in awful winter conditions. By day they were required on anti-submarine patrols when they were not oiling, or carrying the snobbish officials across the Channel who refused to use the normal troop ships. It was considered fair comment, therefore, that the men who proudly served in the Grand Fleet, compared to those who served in Dover Command, had a gentleman's life.

But even when Dover Command became stronger it could not, by any stretch of the imagination, be everywhere at once and stop an enemy raid over a 25-mile front. Use of the Flanders bases, in spite of the net barrage, allowed German boats increased activity in the Strait. Until now they had remained elusive and unwilling to venture out into the Strait. Their strength, perhaps, was in offensive tactics and not defensive. Admiralty intelligence sources were convinced Germany knew of the Dover Patrol's weakness.

The Kaiser had sent his master spy Gustave Steinhauer to England in as early as 1908. He set up his spy network in London and enlisted the help of German Nationals, such as waiters, barbers and commercial travellers. During the years leading up to 1914, Steinhauer possessed over twenty agents, many of whom regularly visited Royal Naval dockyards and the surrounding areas. Suspicion was, at first, centred on a German called Stieler, who periodically visited every German waiter in Dover and Folkestone. He was believed to be a commercial traveller but carried no samples and the waiters all seemed very afraid of him. The Germans were fascinated by the Royal Naval gunnery drill and all the information collected passed through Gustave Ernst, a London barber, who sent it on to Berlin by post.

In 1909, MI5, the Military Intelligence Agency, under the tutelage of Colonel Vernon Kell, set about listing all the known German agents under suspicion of spying. The Official Secrets Act came into being in 1911, passed quickly through Parliament by the then Home Secretary Winston Churchill. Kell enlisted the help of every Chief Constable and arrests soon followed. One of the first was George Parrott, a Royal Navy gunnery instructor based at Sheerness, who was arrested on 14 July 1912. Karl Hentschel, a language teacher, was arrested on 22 October 1913; then Frederick Gould, who ran a public house called the Queen Charlotte in Rochester, was arrested on 22 February 1914. Gould's wife, Maud, a music teacher, was carrying naval documents when she was arrested on a train *en route* to Dover. The last five agents were arrested in 1917. Thirty-three agents were caught, fourteen shot, seventeen imprisoned and two discharged through insufficient evidence.

Lieutenant G.E. Johnson in the drifter *Paramount* rubbed his eyes in disbelief. He had seen a small boat under sail in a prohibitive area near the East Goodwins. It was late afternoon on 8 November. Johnson signalled the vessel to heave-to but the little lateen sail remained set. He then fired a well-aimed 6-pounder shell across its bow. The sail was hauled down at once and the little boat stopped. *Paramount* went alongside and Johnson discovered he had stopped a felucca named *Virgen de Socorro*. On board her were thirteen German officers and non-commissioned officers who had escaped from Spain.

The felucca, without either a motor or dinghy, had sailed from Vigo on 7 October

Lieutenant G.E. Johnson, skipper of *Paramount*, saw a small boat under sail in a prohibited area.

under the command of Carl Koch, a German colonial army officer, who intended to sail round the north of Scotland to Norway. They ran into a south-westerly gale in the Bay of Biscay, where their rudder was seriously damaged. They managed to rig a jury rudder but it failed to get them round Cape Wrath, so they allowed the vessel to run before the wind. Short of provisions, they sailed round the Scilly Isles, and set course for the English Channel. They ran past Falmouth, Bolt Head, Portland Bill then round the Isle of Wight, without ever being challenged once by the Royal Navy. It was the most incredible journey, in a small foreign vessel and carrying a rig that was totally out of character with any other ships encountered along the way.

Koch had moved along the shipping route in company with other vessels. Surprisingly, no one reported this strange, unfamiliar craft. They had passed through the Folkestone Gate without arousing suspicion, passed Dover and headed for the Downs. It was growing darker by the second and a sea mist shrouded the coastline. Unfamiliar with Admiralty regulations, Koch altered course out of ignorance and steered east of the Goodwins. It was his only mistake. Stopped by *Paramount*, the adventurous voyage ended.

Admiral Scheer's strategy to attack the watching forces on the Channel barrage, therefore assisting the U-boats to get through, was not successfully pressed home because his Zeebrugge destroyers were not fully trained. After the October skirmish, the British First Sea Lord had suggested that at least two flotillas would be needed on patrol with a third kept in reserve. This resulted in the flotilla leader *Lightfoot* with four destroyers being sent from Harwich to join up with *Carysford* and the eight destroyers already on station. *Lapwing* and *Phoenix* came to replace *Nubian* and *Flirt*.

The German flotilla at Zeebrugge, commanded by Commander Goehle, was ordered to make an attack upon the northern entrance to the Downs anchorage on the night of 23 November, with explicit instructions to destroy every vessel in sight and shell Ramsgate. Goehle's force of thirteen destroyers reached the North Hinder lightship just after 2015 hrs. Within thirty minutes they were approaching the North Foreland and could see Ramsgate's lights. Steaming slowly along the north end of the anchorage near Broadstairs Knoll the armed drifter *Acceptable*, one of twelve boats of the Ramsgate 2nd Division, spotted half a dozen destroyers. The drifter's skipper, Lieutenant W.T. Fitzgerald, unaware they were enemy boats, watched them cross his stern on a south-westerly course. He altered course to give them clearance and when they were less than a cable's length away noticed they all had high topgallant forecastles and were painted a lighter grey than British warships.

As the last destroyer passed Fitzgerald's stern it opened fire on *Acceptable* and *Buckler*. Fitzgerald sent up a red Verey light and returned fire with his 6 pounder. Although the drifters were out-gunned, their shots were so accurately placed that the enemy could not ignore them. The spluttering red flare curved into the night sky and alerted the Downs destroyers *Crusader*, *Saracen* and *Mermaid* who slipped their cables and got moving. When they arrived the enemy boats had disappeared.

Soon after this series of German destroyer raids, Vice-Admiral Bacon was pleased to accept one of the more modern destroyers transferred from Harwich. But the first of these had arrived ten months before Lord Beresford had impertinently enquired, 'What is wrong at Dover?' She was the unique flotilla leader *Swift*, built in 1907, with a displacement of almost 2,000 tons; she was also the first to have 4-in guns mounted as her main armament. Powered by steam turbines, she was capable of speeds in excess of 40 knots and was one of the fastest boats afloat. In the winter of 1916–17, her guns were replaced with a single 6-in gun – the heaviest calibre ever mounted on a British destroyer. Bacon was more than pleased to accept a couple more modern flotilla leaders of the Botha class. One of them was *Broke*, just two years old, with an estimated speed of about 32 knots, and also carrying four 4-in guns facing forward; another was the *Faulknor*, similarly armed, but it was not until May of the following year that the *Botha* arrived.

As for *Broke*, which had seen action at Jutland with the Grand Fleet six months before joining the Dover Patrol, she made a spectacular arrival. Her captain was Commander E.R.G.R. Evans, who had been second-in-command of Captain Scott's ill-fated Antarctic Expedition in 1912, and who was to become one of the most distinguished officers of the Royal Navy in this century. 'Evans of the *Broke*', a statement which every schoolboy would remember from history lessons, proudly berthed his ship alongside the eastern arm on 7 December 1916, with ten marines lined up on her deck. Marines on a destroyer had never been heard of before and caused as much comment as the vessel itself.

Lieutenant-Commander Evans said of *Broke*, 'She was a comfortable ship, rode the seaway beautifully, had a splendid bridge, but had the dirty habit of covering her decks

Admiral Bacon was pleased to accept, on loan, destroyers borrowed from the Harwich Force.
Myngs was photographed from the airship SS. Z18.

with cinders and fine dust.' Originally built for the Chilean Navy, she had excellent
accommodation for her captain but questionable quarters for everyone else. *Broke*, like
Faulknor and *Botha*, had been requisitioned before delivery under the 1914 Emergency
War Programme. Her principal fuel was coal but there was a method of squirting oil
into her furnaces which gave an extra turn of speed in excess of her standard 29 knots.

The winter withdrawal from the Dunkirk area of operations was always a rather sad
occasion, as the ship's companies could no longer hear the guns of the opposing armies
which, more than anything else, kept their warlike instincts alive. They were to miss too
the infinitely more interesting excitement of the bombardments and the rare skirmishes
with enemy craft. By contrast, they were now relegated to the long night patrols in some
of the worst winter weather that one could imagine. Huge sheets of icy spray would
break over bridge and decks to freeze the sailors until their spirits were numbed and their
only pleasure was the occasional hot mug of cocoa to keep body and soul together.

But beyond the confines of the English Channel there were many incidents of
passenger liners being sunk without warning when more U-boat commanders blatantly
disregarded their written orders to stop this practice. Back in October, while *en route* to
Halifax, the liner *Rappahannock* just disappeared mid-ocean without trace. Then the *City
of Birmingham* carrying 170 passengers, including 90 women and children, was
torpedoed without warning. By December, a total of sixty-three U-boats were now
operating around the British Isles.

Admiral Jellicoe was appointed First Sea Lord on 3 December, with specific
instructions to defeat the U-boat menace. Four days later Lloyd George succeeded
Asquith as Prime Minister, while Balfour was replaced as First Lord by Edward Carson.
Between them they studied the anti-U-boat position.

CHAPTER FIVE

'Nothing Remained to Hurt the Eye'

More than half of *Nubian* was hard up against the rocks at the South Foreland and was almost abandoned because of the sheer cliff face making salvage attempts extremely difficult. Dover's salvage officer Captain John Iron, the third in direct lineage of harbour masters, liked nothing better than a challenge, however, and he eventually received permission to blast a cutting through the cliff face to reach the destroyer. After many weeks of hard work he successfully refloated her and triumphantly towed her into Dover harbour.

While on passage from Dover to Dunkirk, another F class Tribal, the *Zulu*, had struck a mine on 8 November the previous year. The explosion occurred below her engine room, throwing parts of her turbines up on to the forecastle. There was a fierce sea running at the time and the excessive motion caused the after part of the destroyer to break away and sink. The remaining fore part remained afloat long enough to be towed by the French destroyer *Capitaine Mehl*, arriving at Calais some four hours later. Eventually both halves of *Nubian* and *Zulu* were married together resulting in a new destroyer named *Zubian* being commissioned.

At the beginning of 1917 the Germans seemed to realize that, although they were far from being beaten, they somehow could not advance their army with any confidence. Whether the people in Germany were beginning to mistrust von Hindenburg, Ludendorf and the Crown Prince is another matter but the fact remains they would not risk another naval battle after Jutland. Had they done so, the Admiralty was confident of success.

Pressures of the Allied blockade were being felt in Germany, augmented by the anti-German attitude of President Wilson of the United States government. Admiral von Holtzendorff issued some interesting figures which showed that an average rate of sinkings of near to 600,000 tons per month was possible and, what was more to the point, if this figure could be maintained for several months, Britain could be brought to her knees. On 9 January the Kaiser issued a statement: 'I order the unrestricted submarine campaign to begin on 1 February with the utmost energy.'

Throwing off their restrictions, the U-boat commanders unleashed their pent-up talents with sickening ferocity. Before the Kaiser's edict U-boats had sunk 282,000 tons of British shipping in January alone, with a further 464,000 tons in the following month. The losses were to rise alarmingly in April, reaching 834,549 tons, a total of 354 ships.

So far the Allies had struggled to eliminate the U-boat menace, in spite of the enormous strain imposed on the U-boat crews. German submariners were often at breaking point, having been subjected to the constant stress of a dangerous voyage where they experienced being hunted by allied warships; they had to exercise extreme vigilance to avoid minefields; they put up with lack of sleep, poor food, and having to drink the inevitable brackish water.

It was estimated there were now over eighty U-boats operating from the German and Flanders bases, using both the Scottish and English Channel routes, and causing some anxiety among the merchantmen carrying supplies. The convoy system was discussed at some length by the War Cabinet on 23 April but Admiral Jellicoe was not convinced it was feasible if the convoys were inadequately protected. Even so, convoys were already operating on a small scale in the Channel, where groups of merchant ships were escorted to French, Dutch and Scandinavian ports.

The large steamer SS *Sussex* struck a mine near the West Dyck sandbank on 1 January. Paddle minesweepers in the area went immediately to her assistance and discovered the vessel had fouled mine nets. The *Duchess of Montrose* and *Nepaulin* crossed over the nets safely as their draught was only drawing about 8 to 9 feet maximum. *Goodwood*, however, had the misfortune to strike another mine. *Redcar* altered course to assist and eventually she managed to tow the sinking *Goodwood* into Dunkirk. *Redcar*, meanwhile, had returned to the *Sussex* incident and, between all three paddlers, had towed her clear of the minefield.

Redcar was busy sweeping up mines with *Chelmsford* on 15 January when another large cargo vessel, SS *Port Nicholson*, struck a mine near the Gravelines buoy. Both paddlers approached her to pass towing lines. *Redcar* made slow progress to beach the crippled vessel on the Gravelines sandbank but the steamer turned over and sank within half a mile of the sands.

Just to the westward of Dungeness in a fierce gale at night, the destroyer *Gurkha* struck a mine on 8 February. In this incident the Dover Patrol lost one of its most respected officers when Lieutenant-Commander Woolcombe-Boyce went down with his ship. A good many men also lost their lives on that occasion. There are many unsung heroes when a ship is lost at sea, acts of bravery often went unnoticed in the heat of the moment, and all too often there were no survivors to tell of the infinite gallantry. Lieutenant-Commander Lewin, the gunnery officer of the 6th Flotilla, was on board *Gurkha*. It was due to his bravery that several of the crew were saved. He had seized a Kisbie life buoy and by his efforts kept men afloat until they were picked up by a trawler. Although Lewin had been swimming around in the cold rough sea, he insisted the men should be taken on board the trawler first. He was awarded both the Stanhope and the Humane Society's medals.

Daylight came slowly on 8 February, with a dullness that reduced visibility to two or three miles. There was no sign of land either as *UC46*, commanded by Oberleutnant F. Moecke, edged cautiously between the net barrages mid-Channel. The conning tower lookout scanned the immediate sea area for any sign of smoke that would indicate a British vessel. The submarine was in surface trim running back up Channel towards the Goodwin Sands area and home and, more importantly, charging the batteries. There was a stiff breeze that put the bow into a deep swell, which kept the submarine heaving

'*Liberty* rode over her prey. A few minutes elapsed before *UC46*'s bow rose from the water like some prehistoric sea creature.'

and dropping, with considerable turmoil in the beam sea. Moecke's anxious night was not yet over as he knew the dangers that confronted him. If he successfully passed the deadly Goodwins there were still the mine nets to avoid and even a rogue mine or two wallowing around in the tide. And then he might be spotted by a seaplane or flying boat on early morning patrol, or even a patrol vessel.

The breeze suddenly fell away completely and the tide changed, setting the submarine's bow dangerously close to the Sandettie Bank. Moecke was aware he was behind schedule so that running on the surface gave him a speed advantage. A shout from the lookout was accompanied by a scramble of feet on the iron ladder and the ominous thud of the closing conning tower hatch. Moecke, however, was too late in making his dive to avoid *Liberty* which seemed to come from nowhere. The destroyer's sharp bow sliced through the upper skin between the gun mounting and the conning tower when *UC46* was only partly submerged. She shuddered under the impact and rolled over on to her port beam. Water gushed into the submarine's inner skin with such force it knocked everyone off their feet. *Liberty* rode over her prey. A few minutes elapsed before *UC46*'s bow rose from the water like some prehistoric sea creature. She remained poised in that position for a few seconds, then majestically slid backwards out of sight. *Liberty*'s crew were jubilant but their excitement was tempered by thoughts of the drowning men. But this was war and there was no room for sentiment.

Several German destroyers appeared on 25 February to open fire with their 4.1-in guns, first upon the drifters near the North Downs, then upon the town of Ramsgate.

During this latter part of the winter the drifter crews tending their mine nets were often gratified by the suspicious damage to their nets. In strong tides and heavy weather conditions, it was beyond their capabilities to investigate further but they assumed a submarine had fouled them. It was a hazardous business. The drifter *Protect* was lost the following month while hauling in her nets. Quite unaware that a German mine was entangled in it, the explosion blew her apart and she sank in seconds. Only three deckhands survived.

Lower down the English Channel and beyond the scope of the Dover Patrol U-boats had already turned their attention upon the ships of mercy – the hospital ships, recognized and protected internationally by the Geneva Cross. A U-boat captain ignored the illuminated Red Cross of *Asturias* and torpedoed her while she was *en route* to Southampton in March. Another soon followed ten days later when *Gloucester Castle* was hit off the Isle of Wight, carrying over 400 stretcher cases.

The hours after midnight seemed to be the choice of the German destroyer commanders making their raids upon the English coast. When they arrived to fire upon the town of Broadstairs on 1 March, they encountered the three-year-old L class *Laverock* on patrol near the mine nets. They launched a torpedo at her but fortunately it failed to detonate.

During the dark night period of 17 March, several enemy destroyers actually crept up the Strait to the net barrage quite undetected. They settled down to wait for the British patrol ships to pass by. On seeing them the four-year-old *Paragon*, a K class destroyer, challenged with her aldis lamp. The prompt reply was a well-aimed torpedo which struck her in the foremost engine room bulkhead. She sank in about ten minutes. It was a well-executed piece of work and proved without doubt that the enemy were not yet finished with their use of surface craft.

Laforey, the same class of destroyer, arrived on the scene soon after hearing the explosion. She switched on her searchlights and began picking up survivors. It was almost an hour later when *Llewellyn* came on the scene. Before she sank *Paragon* had sent out a distress signal and when *Laforey* arrived she did the same. *Llewellyn* sent her signal and by now there was a plethora of wireless messages coming into Dover from all ships in the vicinity. Bacon immediately ordered all reserve boats to slip their moorings. The next signal from *Laforey* said that both *Paragon* and *Llewellyn* had been torpedoed and she was picking up survivors. There was then another signal which read, 'Sunk by submarine'.

The reserve boats were already under way, steaming for all they were worth past St Margaret's Bay, when the last signal was received. Bacon sent a 'recall' signal as it seemed likely now that a submarine was stalking his patrol boats. He replaced them with *P21* and *P11* to hunt the alleged submarine, then sent a signal to his patrol boats to fall back five miles at full speed. Yet another signal arrived to say that *Llewellyn* was not sunk and that both she and *Laforey* had only two survivors from *Paragon* on board. A tug was sent to assist *Llewellyn* which had actually been torpedoed.

At this stage in the proceedings Vice-Admiral Bacon was unsure of the situation, as each successive signal contradicted the former. Then, about to lose his patience, the telegraph reader began to chatter once again, dash-dot-dot and so on until the message read to his dismay, '*Paragon*'s survivors report seeing destroyers'. Bacon had to stop the

P11 with P21 were sent by Admiral Bacon to hunt for the U-boat near the Goodwin Sands on 17 March 1917. They were eventually recalled.

P-boats from going any further as they were quite unsuited to tackle enemy destroyers. *P11* was sent to relieve *Laertes*, who had begun escorting *Llewellyn*, while *P21* was recalled to Dover. *Myngs* and *Lark* were sent to reinforce the patrol line, both the captains half expecting to be recalled once again. *Llewellyn*, under her own steam, limped into harbour at about 0430 hrs. She had suffered the loss of five men killed in the explosion.

Meanwhile the four enemy destroyers originally sighted had approached the North Foreland, passed close to SS *Greypoint*, who was laying at anchor off Ramsgate with engine trouble, and torpedoed her. She sank just as the drifter *Redwald* was hit with several shells. The skipper was wounded along with three of his deckhands but they managed to beach their boat before further damage was done.

Both *Eglington* and *Redcar*'s skippers considered themselves very lucky to have survived when they hauled in a German mine with their sweep nets. *The Duchess of Montrose* was not so lucky, however, as she struck a mine on 18 March while sweeping off the Gravelines buoy. She sank in about one minute with the loss of twelve lives. *Nepaulin* was also mined near the Dyk Bank in the following month and took eighteen crew with her to the bottom. Paddle steamers were notoriously thin-hulled, not really

Because of her unreliable diesel engines the *Marshall Ney* monitor had her 15-in guns removed and replaced by 6-in.

built for wartime activities, and usually fell to pieces immediately they struck a mine. Commander A.D. Thomson recalled seeing the engineer officer and a steward with their heads showing through a porthole. They could not escape because the entrance to the wardroom was underwater. Thomson was picked up with about thirty others from the icy water some ten minutes later.

The monitor *Marshal Ney*, now refitted and bristling with 6-in guns, arrived off Ramsgate on 2 April. The Vice-Admiral had already organized the construction of 6-in shore batteries at Foreness and North Foreland. Now a floating fortress, the monitor was the third to be added to the two shore batteries, so that the whole of the northern sector – from the shoals off Margate to the Gull lightship – was covered by 6-in guns. Bacon insisted that these batteries should open fire on everything that was seen. His weekly memorandum stated, 'There will be no nonsense about challenging. Warn friendly vessels that if they do play around in the vicinity they will be sunk. And when they realize you are in earnest there will be no trouble.'

Visibility was poor and a dense sea mist hung over the waters on the morning of 19 April. The monitor's lookouts heard the aero engines long before the shape of a German seaplane appeared through murky clouds. They watched it circle round their vessel two or three times before the anti-aircraft guns opened fire. It veered off and disappeared from their view. But the sound of its engine persisted. The guns stopped firing and there was comparative silence, except for the lapping of the waves against the hull. Suddenly a lookout shouted, 'Torpedo!' The monitor was a sitting duck, its engines were stopped and she lay at anchor. The torpedo ran towards them, then, to everyone's surprise, it began to run erratically, travelling in a semi-circle until it made off towards Ramsgate Harbour. It ran through the mouth of the harbour to bury itself in thick mud beneath a dredger. The sound of the seaplane receding into the distance was lost in the excitement.

It was proof – if proof was wanted – that the Germans were showing greater initiative than ever before. The Flanders-based destroyer captains were beginning to believe they were invincible. Perhaps they were a little overconfident when, on 20 April, they made an efficient two-pronged attack upon Dover and Calais.

There was no moon and the sky was overcast but the night was fine. The flotilla leaders *Broke* and *Swift* were patrolling near the western end of the net barrage. Being a dark night with conditions so suitable for an enemy attack, both ships' captains were of the opinion it would be fairly easy for the enemy to fire a few rounds at a coastal town and then leave at full speed. The odds were in the enemy's favour to get clean away in the darkness. But in spite of these favourable conditions, what took place was to subsequently prove that the enemy force was no match for a couple of determined destroyer captains of the Royal Navy.

It was just after midnight when six enemy destroyers approached Dover at moderate speed. About three miles from the port they fired a star shell over the town. Their first salvo of 4-in shells was so badly aimed that they fell beyond the town at Whinless Down and at Chilverton Elms. The next salvo was not any better and exploded at the village of Church Hougham. In all, about thirty shells fell in the area without causing any serious damage.

Both *Broke* and *Swift* heard the commotion and saw the gun flashes, altered course immediately and headed towards Dover at full speed. Not seeing any enemy ships, they returned to their patrol positions so as to prevent an attack upon the prime targets of merchant shipping lying in the Downs. In line ahead, stem to stern, the six enemy ships actually passed close to the eastward of the Goodwin Sands without being seen. After steaming north-eastward, they then turned and retraced their original course, evidently expecting to be joined by the other division of destroyers that had shelled Calais.

The enemy destroyer's impeccable line-ahead formation was simultaneously observed by both *Broke* and *Swift* about seven miles east of Dover. The leading enemy vessel opened fire immediately to which *Swift* returned, firing her 6-in gun as she passed down the line at full speed.

Nothing could have suited the British captains better than the situation which presented itself. Although the comparison of numbers and armament left them disadvantaged, Commander Evans thought his right-ahead four 4-in guns were more than equal to the broadside of any single enemy destroyer. After the first exchange of rounds between *Swift* and the German column, the British ships converged on the enemy without any hesitation. Evans altered course slightly to get out of *Swift*'s wake and held his fire until the director sight on the bridge came ON for firing the port torpedo tube. He watched his First Lieutenant, Despard, making ready to launch a torpedo at the second ship in the line nearest them. Despard was deliberate about his

The flotilla leader *Swift,* built in 1907, was one of the fastest destroyers afloat and was said to have exceeded 40 knots.

aim. After giving the order to fire the port foremost torpedo tube, Evans held the ship 'steady' for a few seconds to allow the torpedo to clear the tube. He then conned *Broke* with the intention of ramming the nearest vessel against which they had just launched the torpedo. But before he could steady the ship, the controlling officer had already opened fire, at very short range, with the foremost guns firing independently. Despard then shouted, 'We've got her!' There was a muffled explosion, plumb amidships on the destroyer *G85.* Evans, realizing the futility of ramming a vessel he had already hit, put the helm hard over to port, and swung away to the starboard for a matter of seconds.

Broke's navigating officer Lieutenant Hickman quickly suggested a swing to starboard so as to ram the next vessel in the line. The helm was put over hard once again. The ship steadied. Everyone watched as *Broke* bore down upon her victim. It all happened so quickly. A cloud of smoke and sparks suddenly shot out of the victim's funnels as *Broke*'s bow tore into the vessel's port side with an almighty crash, abreast of the aft funnel. *Broke*'s strong bow had actually pierced the vessel's flank. In the flare of gun flashes the identification *G42* was clearly seen as her bow swung round towards her assailant. *Broke* continued to carry the crippled vessel bodily away on the impetus of the ram at about 27 knots, and almost turned *G42* on to her beam end. One of *G42*'s torpedo tubes had stuck into *Broke*'s side and was wrenched off its mountings. With her guns at maximum depression, *Broke* opened fire at point-blank range.

Shells crashed into the huddled mass of men who, terror-struck, were grouped about *G42*'s decks. So soon after the initial shock of the ram had been felt, the German sailors were being shredded where they stood. There was no question of the German sailors

Commander E.R.G.R. Evans, his eyes darkened by the terrific strain, walked round the decks of *Broke*, which were slippery with blood.

boarding *Broke* with the idea of inflicting damage. On the contrary, those who could were clambering up the sides of the destroyer to save their lives. But in the confusion of the action, *Broke*'s men took no chances.

After the SS *Lusitania* fiasco, when 1,195 innocent men, women and children were sent to a watery grave by a ruthless U-boat commander on 7 May 1915, Commander Evans had developed a loathing for the German race and all they stood for. He made sure his ship's company held similar views. His subtle indoctrination provided the patriotic impetus to fight to the death. On *Broke*, three loaded rifles with fixed bayonets were kept at each gun position, another at each torpedo tube and the after searchlight. Even cutlasses were provided round the upper deck, besides which loaded revolvers were supplied to Petty Officers and on the bridge.

When Lieutenant Despard had 'boarders' piped on the forecastle – one of the most dramatic signals a sailor could hear on active service – the weapons were literally snatched from their brackets. Unarmed, the desperately frightened men from the shattered bloodstained *G42* clambered up the sides of *Broke* to reach the forecastle and safety. Some of them met a bewildering death. Midshipman Donald A. Gyles RNR, who had been wounded when the German destroyer fired her first salvo, took charge and rallied his men from a gun crew who had suffered many casualties. Using his revolver he repelled German sailors swarming on board, while Leading Seaman Ingleson used a bayonet with devastating results. Gyles was awarded the DSC and Ingleson the DSM.

Meanwhile, the next German destroyer astern of the stricken *G42* passed ahead of *Broke*, while the one following passed astern of her. Evans shouted above the pandemonium to have a torpedo launched. But there was no answer. The controls had been shot away. At close range No. 1 tube managed to fire at *G85* but Leading Seaman Ivens was killed immediately and never saw the torpedo run true.

Amid the utter confusion, when all available guns were firing independently, while choking smoke from the funnels shrouded everything, the cries of wounded men and the shattering noise of exploding shells mingled with the whining of shrapnel, Evans thought, for a fleeting moment, that fifteen enemy vessels were involved in the action. To cap it all, passing down *Broke*'s starboard side, the enemy were firing at point-blank range. One shell hit a box of cordite on the forecastle. It shot up to the bridge, spilling burnt cordite everywhere. The flames lit up the ship and made it a perfect target. She was punished severely, while still pushing *G42* on her bow.

G42's stern was sinking fast until finally *Broke* steamed right over her. But not satisfied with that, Evans made to ram another vessel. The attempt failed, for just at that moment a shell had exploded in the engine room cutting the main steam pipes. *Broke* was now on fire amidships, as well as on the bridge, and steam was escaping with a horrible shriek from the cut pipes. She began to lose headway. The artificer engineer ran to the bridge and informed Evans that he could not maintain steam for more than half speed. Helm hard over *Broke* steered towards two sinking destroyers, passing through many German sailors in the water, 'their calcium lights on their life-saving jackets, twinkling like fairy-lights', Evans wrote. He ignored their cries for help, remembering, in sharp focus, the little *Flirt* incident.

Broke's first lieutenant saw, in the darkness, the phosphorescent wake of an approaching destroyer. The oncoming vessel flashed out the challenge but *Broke*, her electrical circuitry shot away, could not reply. The yeoman signaller used an aldis lamp to spell out B-R-O-K-E. The answer was even more gratefully received, S-W-I-F-T. Evans altered course to close with the sinking *G85*, whose survivors shouted 'surrender'. Her upper deck was a mass of flames and a large hole under the forecastle revealed more flames. Just as *Broke* was attempting to rescue the German sailors, a 4-in shell was suddenly fired from a turret gun. The shell passed straight through *Broke*'s bridge. *Broke* replied with three rapid rounds and the sub-lieutenant let go the port torpedo at no more than 200 yards range. Set to run at a depth of six feet, it struck the already sinking destroyer on the starboard side near her stern. *Broke*'s engines stopped through lack of water in her boilers. She was in danger of drifting towards the sinking vessel, which might have exploded at any moment. Then *Mentor* came to *Broke*'s assistance. She was being towed out of the way when *G85* finally sank.

Swift meanwhile had closed with the sinking *G42*. Some of her crew had saved themselves by taking to their boats. *Swift*'s damage was negligible, for she had been hit only once by a shell which had exploded beneath the forecastle, killing one of the crew while wounding four others. *Broke*, however, had received considerable damage. Her

'As dawn broke upon the scene the world seemed to lay clear to sight once again . . . the night, now turning into day, seemed spent like *Broke*'s crew.'

stern was bent and buckled, there were shell holes in every part of her and the funnels resembled sieves. The exploding shell in the boiler room had killed everyone in it. In the aftermath of the action *Broke* had suffered forty-eight casualties; twenty-one were killed while a further two died of their injuries later and twenty-seven were wounded.

As dawn broke upon the scene the world seemed to lay clear to sight once again. After passing through the fury of battle, the night, now turning into day, seemed spent, much like the crews, and marvellously still. Every one on *Broke* was covered in grime. Soot and cordite-stained hands clutched hastily prepared corned beef sandwiches and tin mugs of hot cocoa. Commander Evans, his eyes darkened by the terrific strain, walked round the decks slippery with blood and came across the doctor trying to identify the dead. When the dead sailors had been collected and reverently draped with canvas and bunting, the remainder of the ship's company began the unenviable task of scrubbing down the blood-splashed places, 'so that nothing remained to hurt the eye', Evans wrote.

Broke was eventually towed back to Dover by the tugs and berthed at the eastern arm. Evans admitted later that he could not help feeling a lump in his throat when other ship's companies gave a loud and prolonged cheer. The drifters blew their sirens until the din and hooting became quite unbearable. The destroyer's sailors never once considered they were heroes. Quite the reverse, for, in reality, their ship had been nine nights on patrol, had coaled twice during that period and on the afternoon of 20 April, they had taken on board eighty-seven tons of coal an hour.

Swift, *Mentor* and other boats sent to search for survivors brought back 140 German officers and men. They were assembled at the Admiralty pier before being marched under escort through the town where crowds had gathered along the route to jeer at the prisoners and cheer the British matelots. Two days later the German dead were laid to rest at the St James's cemetery, where a large contingent of men from the 6th Flotilla paid their respects. Vice-Admiral Bacon had sent a wreath upon which was written 'To a Brave Enemy'.

These words caused some adverse comment in higher circles, especially when the London newspapers printed 'To a Brave And Gallant Enemy'. When the Admiralty asked Bacon for an explanation, he was later able to produce the wreath which he sent to London by special courier. But there was no apology from the newspapers, let alone from the Admiralty. The trappings of office were rapidly diminishing for Admiral Bacon.

The British dead were buried on the following day. Children were hoisted up on their parents' shoulders to gaze upon the enormous wreaths of flowers which almost concealed the brightly coloured Union Jacks draping the coffins. Officers and men slow-marched behind a band that played solemn music, which seemed to echo and reverberate through the town. Towering above everything, proudly defiant with its Union Flag fluttering at half-mast, Dover's castle exclaimed to the dead, 'You did not die in vain'.

Strange to relate, the Germans were not deterred by the punishment they had received from *Broke* and *Swift*; seven days later they made another night sortie to fire upon Ramsgate. The recently installed shore batteries, now assisted by *Marshal Ney*, opened fire with such determination that their combined 6-in salvoes were more like a 15-in battleship broadside. Amid the huge columns of water sent up by the shells, the enemy vessels turned and fled. Steering clear of the North Foreland area, enemy destroyers decided to attack Dunkirk, where their strong force was immediately intercepted by four French destroyers then attached to Dover Command. The Harwich flotilla met another strong force of enemy vessels outside Zeebrugge on 10 May and drove them off before they could do any damage. The Harwich destroyer captains were disappointed, as they were hoping for a skirmish to settle old scores.

Vice-Admiral Bacon decided there was too much light in the North Foreland area, giving the enemy a distinct advantage. He revised the lights showing in the Downs area in particular and put his new proposals to the Admiralty. They approved them without question. It was to Bacon's lasting regret that civilians had been killed and injured during his term of office, in the area consisting of Margate, Broadstairs, Ramsgate and the North Foreland – an area which jutted out into the English Channel like the proverbial sore thumb, and so close to the enemy.

The Admiral's proposals were quickly implemented, which led to the Gull lightship and the wreck lights being extinguished; the Goodwin and Deal pier lights dimmed; the South Goodwin lightship was altered to show only in an up-Channel direction; the *Marshal Ney* was ordered to show only one red light at her masthead and the North Foreland lightship was to show a single white beam up the fairway. In a nutshell, everything was extinguished that had previously shone out to sea, making it very difficult for enemy destroyers to 'fix' a particular position on shore, whereas vessels using the Downs fairway could navigate with a degree of safety.

DAILY SKETCH, WEDNESDAY, APRIL 25, 1917.

HINDENBURG THROWS IN HIS RESERVES.

DAILY SKETCH.
THE PREMIER PICTURE PAPER.

No. 2,535.   Telephones: London—Holborn 6112. Manchester—City 6581.   LONDON, WEDNESDAY, APRIL 25, 1917.   [Registered as a Newspaper.]   ONE PENNY.

DIED DEFENDING OUR SHORES; Burial Of Gallant Sailors Who Defeated The Channel Raiders.

The funeral procession starting from the market square at Dover.

Some of the floral tributes from the shipmates of the dead heroes.   Carrying the bodies of their comrades to the grave.

Seven of the twenty-two Navy men who died fighting—and defeating—the German destroyers in the Channel fight on Friday last were buried in St. James's Cemetery, Dover, yesterday. Photographs of the funeral of the German sailors who fell in the same fight will be found on the Back Page.—(Daily Sketch Photographs.)

One of several newspaper tributes to the men killed in the destroyer action in April 1917.

German sailors killed in the April action of 1917 were buried in St James's cemetery, Dover.

The first Handley-Page O/100 bomber arrived at Coudekerque RNAS station on 4 March 1917, and bombed Bruges in June that year.

Even so, traffic through the Downs, which was regulated by the Downs Flotilla, did suffer some losses during strong tides, fogs and gales, which was unavoidable. Quite apart from the ships mined, only one merchantman was lost by collision and no less than nine were salvaged after having accidents. Two flotilla vessels were lost, the tug *Char* was reported as having sunk after a collision with all hands going down with her, and the armed yacht *Marcella* suffered a similar fate.

The arrival at Coudekerque aerodrome of the new Handley-Page O/100 twin-engined bomber on 7 March 1917 caused quite a stir among the RNAS personnel. The obvious advantages over the Short and Sopwith light bombers in respect of the bomb load being twice the capacity was a sensation in itself. Five had been delivered by the last week of April and anti-submarine patrols began but the twin-engined bomber was a larger target for both anti-aircraft gunners and enemy aircraft.

During a routine anti-submarine patrol on 25 April, No. 3115 attacked enemy destroyers off Nieuport. The O/100 was pounced on by a large enemy seaplane, during which action the pilot, Flight-Sub Lieutenant T.S.S. Hood, was drowned when the bomber was forced down on to the water. While enemy shore batteries opened fire on the victim two French FBA flying boats attempted a rescue. One of the FBAs was shot down while the other rescued gunner Kirby just before fast enemy motor boats shot out of Ostend to take the rest of them prisoners of war.

The French-built FBA flying boat was used to rescue aircraft crews forced down in the sea by either enemy action or engine failure.

German U-boats were still passing through the British mine nets. The *Loyal Star* reported a submarine at 1030 hrs on 13 May, close to the Goodwin Sands. Two hours later there was a huge explosion heard in the area, which sent up a column of water 50 feet into the air but no wreckage was found by searching drifters. Near the Elbow buoy next day the drifter *Try Again* quickly signalled the Admiralty Vessel SS *Waterville* to heave-to at once, as she was about to enter the mine nets. The signal was too late for the master to stop. The steamer struck a mine. Reversing engines the master only succeeded in winding up the nets with his propellers. Skipper Eves slowly edged through the gap made by the steamer, missing deadly mines by just a few inches, then secured a towing line. It took over five hours to tow the vessel anywhere near the Gull lightvessel, where Dover tugs were waiting to beach her near Sandown castle. Her bow section was filled with concrete and after refloating she was taken to the Thames. The irony of this salvage operation was that *Try Again* was not considered when the salvage award was made.

Called the 'Sisters of Sorrow' the UC-type minelayer submarines were not a popular craft on which to serve. There were many casualties and quite often the sudden disappearance of these vessels were never recorded other than being listed as 'overdue' or 'missing'. *UC26*'s sortie leaving Ostend on 9 May was not atypical of the coastal submarine. Her commander, Oberleutnant Graf von Schmettow, took her out through the shoals off Zeebrugge and set course for the open Channel. She was spotted off Calais

The American-built H8 and H12 flying boats, operational at their Felixstowe base, were often used by the Dover Patrol, at either Dover or Dunkirk.

at dawn by the duty destroyer *Milne*, which almost ran her down. Commander V.L.A. Campbell on the bridge gave full speed ahead, while action stations was piped. *Milne* bore down on her quarry at full engine revolutions. Too slow to react after being taken by surprise, von Schmettow had lost any advantage he had by submerging. *Milne*'s bow cut into the submarine's pressure hull. The blow was devastatingly fatal. *UC26* sank almost immediately and her fate was sealed when depth charges were rolled over the sterns of *Mentor* and *Miranda*, two destroyers who had answered *Milne*'s signal for assistance. There were only two survivors who managed to escape through the airlock system – von Schmettow was not one of them.

In spite of their losses submarine commanders toiled relentlessly. There were increased sightings either near the North Hinder lightvessel or the Sunk lightvessel. While not part of Dover Command, the Felixstowe-based Curtiss flying boats were, nevertheless, extremely useful in spotting U-boats and attacking them. Their extraordinary achievements with just a couple of bombs weighing 230 lbs are legendary. A pair of Curtiss H8 flying boats visited Dover and Dunkirk at various times but they were quite unsuited to the busy harbour traffic. One of them (8663), on patrol near the North Hinder lightvessel on 20 May 1917, spotted *UC36* lying on the surface. Since the introduction of flying boat patrols as far south as where the English Channel meets the

North Sea, the Flanders U-boat commanders were extremely apprehensive of being caught on the surface. The Curtiss H8 was being flown by Flight-Sub Lieutenant Morrish who immediately swooped down out of a bright sky to drop two 230-pounders right on target. Kapitänleutnant G. Buch was attempting to dive but he was in shallow water when the explosive smashed vital equipment. The submarine turned over then sank with just her periscope sticking out of the water. Morrish circled the area, ever hopeful he would see survivors shoot to the surface in the turmoil of bubbles and sand. Not one member of the crew was seen. The discipline of flying was, however, marred by a lack of extreme caution. Perhaps Morrish was over-confident, elated by his 'kill', and his judgment was impaired while making his final approach at Felixstowe. In the event, his fast run on to a heavy swell flipped the H8 over in a spectacular fashion, sustaining so much damage that 8663 was written off charge three days later. The crew were pulled out of the wreckage by a harbour launch, none the worse for their experience.

The Admiralty accepted that the May shipping losses were deceptively misleading and the June figures had exceeded 600,000 tons, despite a convoy system being introduced. As for the Dover net barrage of mines, considered impenetrable by the hard-working officers in the command, U-boats were still using the Channel route with impunity and most often remaining submerged for most of their journey to the western approaches.

Before the introduction of the Military Service Act (1916), which led to conscription, there had been many volunteers to serve in the Royal Navy as 'Hostilities Only'. These men were known as HOs and most were in the lower-deck rating. Training was provided by petty officers and leading seamen who had been transferred from other commands but few HOs were given any specialized instruction in gunnery, torpedo handling or wireless and signals. Those who were sent to vessels in an operational command, such as the Dover Patrol, were usually obliged to eat their meals on separate tables and were usually treated as lower-lower-deck, being given the most menial of tasks to perform. This lack of experience in the specialized duties was the cause of loss of life in certain, and quite unforeseen, circumstances.

Torpedo boat destroyer No. 4 was lying alongside the cross-wall in Ramsgate's harbour on Saturday 26 May 1917, and was being systematically washed down by HO matelots on the forenoon watch, while the regulars were below deck. An 18-in torpedo was being manhandled into a tube on the foredeck when it suddenly exploded. No one will ever know if the safety mechanism was deactivated while the torpedo was being washed down. There was a huge burst of flame which seemed to envelop the whole ship from stem to stern. The men close to the explosion were simply blown to smithereens, while three others standing on a gun platform close by were unscathed. They stood transfixed until the smoke had cleared, then calmly walked off the vessel on to the quay side. The deck plating had been torn and twisted as though made of tin; huge pieces of brass, iron, wood and torpedo fragments, together with bits of arms and legs and lumps of flesh, were hurled into the air. Fourteen men lost their lives in a split second.

The coastal motor boats, CMBs for short, and the motor launches (MLs), both products of the internal combustion engine, were eventually evolved to take up their share of work in the Dover Patrol complex. The first three CMBs were completed by

Built by Thornycroft the coastal motor boats were essentially motor boats of high speed, small size and light construction.

Thornycroft in April 1916 and by the end of that year a division of four boats were sent to Dunkirk to await the first suitable operation. CMBs were, essentially, motor torpedo boats of high speed, small size and light construction with, unfortunately, poor sea-going capabilities. The original design was built to a length of 40 feet but a later design increased the length to 55 feet. The first batch had a maximum speed of about 33 knots, they carried one 18-in Whitehead torpedo only, which was discharged via a trough aft and tail fin first, the craft being fast enough to steer clear of the torpedo once it was launched.

The 55-foot CMBs used at Dover and Dunkirk could either accommodate one 18-in torpedo and four depth charges or two torpedoes only. In addition to the two officers they also carried two motor mechanics and a wireless operator, the former largely recruited from Canada, Australia and New Zealand. The speed had also been increased to reach 40 knots but Thornycroft were having to rely on various aeroplane-type engines, such as Greens, Fiats and Sunbeams, to supplement their own marine-designed engines.

The CMB base at Dunkirk was quite successful in that they covered thousands of miles on various patrols and in quite dangerous mine-infested waters, which were protecting the approaches to Zeebrugge and Ostend. Commodore Lynes, senior officer at Dunkirk, was able to obtain vital information from Belgian civilians living in those particular areas. These firsthand reports suggested that the Germans were rather apprehensive of the CMBs, as they never knew when to expect them. The German patrol motor boats (PMBs), however, never ventured outside their ports at night or when weather conditions were the least bit rough.

Built at Eastchurch in 1916, this Short Bomber served with Dover Command's No. 4 Wing RNAS at Petite Synthe, France, and was later damaged by flak over Ostend.

It was generally accepted that the CMBs were really smooth-water boats for, when at high speed, they usually were bow up and stern down, jumping from one wave top to another and landing with a heavy thud on the water, providing a bone-shuddering experience for the crews. In particularly unfavourable sea-going conditions, their continual bouncing sometimes caused hull damage. But their greatest value, in a practical sense, lay in their high speed, manoeuvrability and small size. The Vice-Admiral was not slow to use them, although he was the first to recognize their limitations. In spite of these, however, he was quick to acknowledge their potential as a new weapon under his command. Opportunities to use them, in the event, were few and far between.

They became useful mainly at night, especially during the first and last quarters of the moon. As soon as the crews had practised their role, an attempt was made to attack German destroyers in the approaches to Zeebrugge on 7 March 1917. On that particular occasion they were assisted by the RNAS squadrons, who were to carry out a simultaneous bombing raid. The same ploy was used on several occasions, as Bacon recognized that enemy ships would tend to leave their moorings and head for the safety of the open sea.

Four CMBs were approaching just east of Ostend when the RNAS began their bombing raid. The CMBs moved in closer to the shore and before long enemy destroyers were seen by Lieutenant-Commander Welman against the lunar halo. He increased speed so as to make a better and faster run for an attack but the problem with all CMBs was that their loud engine noise gave his position away. The nearest destroyer altered course

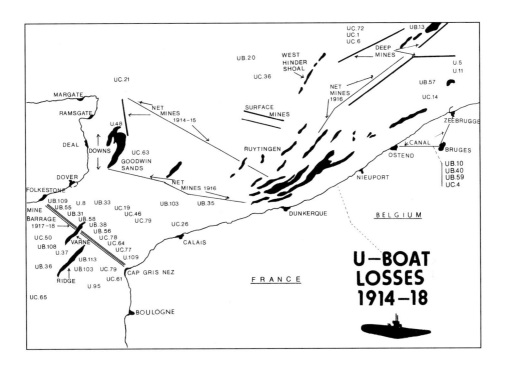

towards the noise and the CMBs were spotted. Welman launched his Whitehead torpedo
from about 400 yards range. It ran true and appeared to hit the destroyer as it was turning
to starboard. While the concussion of the explosion reverberated across the water,
Welman edged back towards a red glow showing in the darkness. The redness became
larger as he approached it but it slowly disappeared beneath the surface of the water,
accompanied by a loud shriek of steam. It was assumed that Germany had lost a destroyer
to Dover's CMBs but this singular success was never confirmed.

In reality the CMBs could only operate off the Belgian coast about one night in
twenty, and the targets were few. After what was considered their first success, the
young commanders, skilled in handling small craft and especially small yachts in civilian
life, were keen to see action and perhaps cover themselves in glory. They were in-line
astern and almost in sight of Ostend on the night of 2 May, accompanied by the
destroyer *Falcon*, when they discovered four large enemy destroyers bearing down on
them. They had, quite unexpectedly, become the hunted. They had left Dunkirk after
dark, while Lieutenant C.H. Lightoller RNR, in *Falcon*, had already dropped anchor off
the shoal banks long before the CMBs had arrived at Zuidcoote Pass. Lieutenant
W.N.T. Beckett RN was in charge of the operation in boat No. 4, with Acting-
Lieutenant F.C. Harrison RN in No. 5, Lieutenant A. Swann RNVR in No. 6 and
Lieutenant A. Dayrell Reed RNR in No. 9. They had been battered mercilessly by a
choppy sea since leaving their anchorage but had managed to find the German-laid light
buoy that marked a minefield just north of Zeebrugge.

They were at reduced speed to lessen the noise when the enemy destroyers were spotted off Weilingen Channel. Beckett closed to within about three cables length from the nearest destroyer before launching his torpedo. It missed and, as the 40-foot CMBs only carried one torpedo, he stood off to watch the rest of the action. The three remaining boats delivered their attack within three minutes, which resulted in the enemy destroyer *G88* being struck below the waterline. Beckett's boat developed an exhaust fault giving much discomfort in the cabin section because of the fumes.

All the officers and men were decorated, not least because of the night's work, but also for their fine seamanship in very poor weather conditions. Engine failures of one kind or another dogged all the boats during their return journey and it was a remarkable quirk of fate which enabled all four CMBs to dissolve into the black night without further incident. Lieutenants Harrison and Dayrell Reed both received the DSO, Lieutenants Beckett and A. Swann received the DSC, while the rest of the crews were awarded DSCs and DSMs.

The Vice-Admiral was unsure if he should risk the lives of these gallant men on such operations and decided to relegate the CMBs to minelaying, although he did allow one further operation in August. In the meantime, enemy destroyers were now reluctant to sail close to the English shores, as the new shore batteries and the formidable *Marshal Ney* had already proved their worth, while extinguishing the lights in the Downs approaches had caused navigational problems for them.

CHAPTER SIX

'A Tin Kettle Full
of Men'

After the German destroyer raids had ceased in May 1917 Royal Naval operations in the Dover Strait were not sensational in any way. Plans had been made to re-establish a line of mines between Copt Point, Folkestone and Cap Gris Nez on the French coast but materials were slow to arrive from naval depots. Another five months were to elapse before the Vice-Admiral could implement his new mine barrage.

From the beginning of 1917, until Bacon was superseded by Keyes, there was only one major offensive undertaken. This was on 5 June, when the monitors successfully bombarded the Ostend basin where the German submarines and destroyers were based. The Belgian barrage patrol was still being maintained throughout and the British ships went almost unmolested, due to the RNAS squadrons which the Admiralty was quick to recognize as a supportive arm to the Dover Patrol. Nothing ever happened on the Dunkirk side in the way of German operations from the air without the fiercest of opposition. During the barrage patrols enemy reconnaissance aircraft were always in the vicinity but soon left when the RNAS put in an appearance.

There were more than 100 merchantmen lying at anchor in the Downs on 17 June, awaiting escorts when a Zeppelin approached Ramsgate to bomb the area. The navy yard within the harbour complex received several bombs which blew up an ammunition store and severely damaged other buildings. But, surprisingly, the shipping was ignored.

Tartar, one of the original Tribal class destroyers, suffered mine damage while escorting the paddle minesweepers near the Gravelines buoy on 24 June. Three ships abreast, *Redcar*, *Kempton* and *Gatwick*, were busy sweeping for German mines when *Redcar*, having already exploded two mines, was approaching a third when she unfortunately bumped against another one. The whole of the forepart of the vessel from the bridge forward was cut off by the explosion and wiped out a 12-pounder gun crew instantly. On investigation her captain, Lieutenant Daniells, found the bottom bulkhead had actually carried away and his ship was in danger of sinking. *Kempton* and *Gatwick* slipped their sweeps and raced towards *Redcar* who was well down by the head. Daniells, meanwhile, had given orders to abandon ship but he and the chief engineer remained on board in case a tow was made. The crew scrambled over the sides into lifeboats and pulled towards *Kempton*. They had just swarmed up the side of the vessel, leaving their lifeboat to drift away on the swell, when *Kempton* also struck a mine. Amid the confusion a couple of quick-thinking seamen jumped into the water to retrieve their abandoned lifeboat and managed to bring it back alongside the crippled *Kempton*. By their action they saved many lives. Drifters in the immediate vicinity arrived to save many more, while *Gatwick*, the last of the three minesweepers, picked up the remainder. *Tartar* had remained afloat and was towed to safety soon afterwards but the Vice-Admiral read the report of the incident with certain misgivings; *Tartar*'s captain had steered the wrong side of a marker buoy. Lieutenant-Commander G.K. Twiss was killed in the explosion.

The Vice-Admiral was used to signing reports of mine damage, collisions, accidents of one sort and another and minor bumps which, on the whole, were not infrequent. Dover harbour was recognized by everyone as being one of the most difficult to negotiate where destroyers were entering the western boom defences in gale force winds and especially at spring tides. Trawlers and drifters were apt to pop up out of nowhere and at the most inconvenient times. Bacon rarely took much notice of an accident report unless it was grossly serious; this was not the result of carelessness but gave the captains the benefit of the doubt.

At a time when the Vice-Admiral was actually receiving one or two modern destroyers, he was most displeased to have one or more relegated to the dockyard for extensive repairs. But he made allowances for youth, long hours spent on dreary patrols, and put the rest down to lack of experience. He emphasized the dictum of 'close shaves' to the lucky and 'accidents' to the less fortunate. Of course the absence of certain lights, coupled with foggy conditions, especially at night, were all against the captains. Everyone was more than anxious to avoid moving destroyers in the Downs complex of shipping after dark but all too often this was quite unavoidable. Reasons for accidents were many and Bacon summarized his reports by saying, more than once, 'Some captains allow the coxswain to steer while the captain operated engine revolutions'.

A major scheme was envisaged in 1917 to land troops on the Belgian coast and was planned right down to the last detail. Monitors were to push between them, one on either side, long pontoons packed with marines and bluejackets and carrying the new-fangled tank. The Vice-Admiral had spent many long hours planning this *tour de force*, spent thousands of pounds constructing the quite elaborate pontoons, and had trained a storming force of hand-picked troops. It was a colossal enterprise in ingenious engineering techniques but the failure of the Ypres offensive forced the scheme to be abandoned. It was not only a considerable blow to the Admiralty but also to Bacon who had set his sights on the success of such an enterprise.

There can be no doubt, however, that the whole operation would have been quite hazardous if the Germans still held successfully the Ypres sector, while if the allied armies had defeated them it would not have been necessary at all. The most optimistic could hardly have expected success so long as the incomparable German heavy artillery batteries remained in their positions along the Belgian coast.

As for the Flanders submarine flotillas now totalling about thirty-eight craft, they were working as far westward as the Bay of Biscay. But their losses steadily increased. *UB36*, commanded by Oberleutnant von Keyserlinck, went 'missing' in the Dover Strait on 24 June, although she was not claimed as sunk by any of Dover Patrol's vessels. But when one considers the utter confusion on that day involving the paddle minelayers it leaves room for speculation, as the U-boat did not return to her base. Flying boats had already done for *UC1* near the entrance to the Thames Estuary on that same day, and a similar attack off the North Hinder lightship five days later had sent *UB20* to the bottom with her captain Oberleutnant H. Glimf and his crew of twenty-four. Admiralty intelligence found out that the German Army headquarters in Bruges were investigating the sudden disappearance of several of their officers. Glimpf, it was discovered, had invited several army officers and their girlfriends on board for an unofficial pleasure cruise. When *UB20* was spotted lying on the surface near some sand shoals by two Curtiss H.8 flying boats, 8662 and 8676, there was a terrible inevitability about what was to follow.

Flying boat pilots usually attacked U-boats with the sun behind them and rarely did they consider being shot at. They would swoop down upon their quarry before it could effect a dive. But a submarine diving deep enough to avoid an attack in an area notorious for its shallows was quite impossible. Glimpf knew that his boat would be visible against the sandy bottom. Even more calamitous was that *UB20* was undermanned; half the crew were in sick bay with influenza.

When Glimpf heard the roar of aero-engines he ordered every one off the decking. Using the voice-tube attached to the conning tower bulk-head he bellowed, 'Stand by to dive. Open all vents. Clutches out. All switches ON. Depth 20 metres. DIVE!'

The girls, having plucked up enough courage to even board the U-boat, sensed the exhilaration of an *unterseeboat* about to dive. *UB20* hit the sandy bottom bow first, even before Glimpf had vacated the conning tower. Over half of her 120-ft length was still exposed above water when the bombs burst upon her hull. One can imagine the harrowing experience for the girls, whose emotions of hysteria suddenly turned to despair as gushing sea water overwhelmed their screaming, innocent minds. Glimpf's body was the only one washed ashore three weeks later. The pilot of 8676 Flight-Lieutenant W.R. Mackenzie was awarded a Bar to his DSC, while Air Mechanic H.L. Curtiss and Wireless Telegraphist W.H. Grey received the DSM.

After the re-laying of deep mines off Zeebrugge on 27 July, *UC61*, commanded by Kapitänleutnant G. Gerth, successfully negotiated the new barrier and the Goodwin Snou barrier at night, intending to lay mines off Boulogne. Running in close to the shore to avoid the destroyer patrols she became stranded in fog off Cap Gris Nez. Gerth's frantic attempts to get clear of the sand shoals ended in failure, so he blew the bottom out of his boat before he and his crew were taken prisoner by a Belgian cavalry unit the next morning.

Much the same procedure was followed as in previous years when a new net mine barrage was laid off the Belgian coast on 25 July. The only difference was that the vast experience so far gained enabled the 12 miles of nets to be laid in just one and a half hours. Enemy ships of the TBD class came out to observe the operation and began firing on the drifters but the monitor *Terror*, with two flotilla leaders *Broke* and *Nimrod*, chased them off without firing a shot. Vice-Admiral Bacon, accompanied by the French Admiral Ronarch, were on board *Broke* to witness the laying operation. Bacon feared his destroyers were being drawn within range of the enemy shore batteries and might easily run into the net mines. He signalled them to retire.

But once the British ships had retired from the area German seaplanes put in an appearance. They bombed the nets and destroyed the battery cases which electrically

UC61, commanded by Kapitänleutnant G. Gerth, was stranded on the shoals near Cap Gris Nez
on 26 July 1917.

charged the whole mine system. Bacon was furious but as a direct result of this
interference produced an ingenious method of saving his batteries from further loss.
Hollow mine cases were used as a convenient battery compartment which were then
sunk to the bottom of the sea out of reach of the enemy.

The bombardment force of monitors presented features which differed only slightly
from those of previous operations. The 12-in monitors were still in the Thames Estuary
where they had been making preparations for the Vice-Admiral's ill-fated landing
operation. So the new bombardment force was now made up of *Erebus*, *Terror* and
Marshal Soult, together with a couple of smaller monitors and a destroyer escort spared
from other duties. More important was the main armament of these large monitors, for
they possessed 15-in main guns with a secondary armament of 4-in and 3-in anti-aircraft
pieces: they were formidable gun platforms.

Erebus fired a few rounds at Ostend dockyard on 21 August, having been instructed
to bombard it whenever the weather permitted. The chances of a successful shoot were
reported three times daily by a special code to the commodore at Dunkirk. If
favourable, motor launches were used to lay a smokescreen and the RNAS squadrons
received instructions to have their spotting aircraft ready. But sometimes the chance of a
shoot proved negative for a variety of reasons, not least of which was the serviceability

Built in America Dover's motor launches were originally fitted with 13 pounder guns, borrowed from the Horse Artillery, which were later given to merchantmen.

of the primitive wireless equipment used by the spotters. The hazardous use of the observation tripods, precariously perched in the shallows and so near to the enemy, had since been abandoned.

The Dover Patrol's motor launches, used so successfully in the 1917 bombardment operations, had originally arrived in November 1915 and were commanded by Commodore Hamilton Benn MP, RNVR. The effect of their arrival was to draw admiring glances from most if not all of the matelots who were fed up with their mundane duties. However the Vice-Admiral was unsure how to use them at first. They were, like the CMBs, a fine-weather craft with only thin wooden planking over a wooden frame and, being rather short in length and quite low at the bow, they were not really suitable for choppy sea conditions. But Bacon hit on the idea to use them for burning smokescreens. Experiments had already taken place at Dover using electrically fired phosphorous burners in rowing boats. In daylight the phosphorous smokescreen was perfectly adequate but at night the phosphorous emitted a flame which was visible through the smoke. Through trial and error, using all sorts of gadgetry and chemicals, such as chlorsulphoric acid sprayed on to the burners, a reasonable compromise was achieved.

Because the wind direction was mostly aft when they operated off the Belgian coast, the main burners were fitted at the bow of the MLs and this allowed the smoke to carry clear of the crew. After the first couple of operations it soon became obvious that to shield themselves while leaving the shoreline, a smaller version of the burner was required at the stern. Further experiments were made using a kite which had a small burner dangling beneath it and which was flown above the kite balloon ship *City of Oxford*. She was a well-equipped merchant vessel of considerable draught of water but too large for work along the coast, so she was replaced by a barge of shallow draught named *Arctic*. Ostensibly used to shield the monitors it was afterwards considered an unsuccessful ploy and was paid off.

During 1917 training was given to ML crews at Dover who had been sent from other naval establishments to have burners fitted to their own craft. One other useful gadget was the phosphorous smoke buoy, which burned for upwards of twenty minutes. When it was dropped to windward it would trail smoke along the surface of the water to hide vessels creeping up to the coast. There was always one division of MLs based at Dunkirk, ready to lay smokescreens whenever monitors moved out to their firing positions. On occasions they were also used with a light wire sweep, to locate mines in the more difficult shoal areas and where no other vessel could go. Although they were too light in construction to actually lift a mine, they soon knew when they had found one. In reasonably fine weather they were used for all kinds of errands but their noisy petrol engines, low freeboard and lack of any substantial armament was always a handicap. Even so, they performed a vital link in the chain of events that occurred almost daily in the Dover Patrol and, like their counterparts in the CMBs, they were mostly men used to handling small high-speed craft. Both the MLs and CMBs were used to pick up airmen who had alighted on the water and were invaluable in assisting rescues. Between them they had rescued over seventy people when *Anglia* and *Maloja* were sunk.

In the main the officers and men of the MLs and CMBs expressed a streak of bravado and were thirsting for action of one kind or another. Kicking their heels in harbour was not to their liking, in fact it was soul destroying, but when CMB No. 1 was attacked by enemy destroyers while searching for a crashed aircraft and was blown up, the Vice-Admiral called it a day. The erudite and energetic Bacon, good-humoured and immensely popular with all ranks, devoted the next two weeks in gentle persuasion, which culminated in stopping the young blades from venturing too far into enemy territory unescorted.

Their final action under Bacon's command, and conceived by him, was to attack enemy destroyers tied up on the inside of the Mole at Zeebrugge. The CMBs left Dunkirk harbour on the night of 22 August but there were unforeseen difficulties awaiting them. There is no doubt it was a most gallant and daring attempt. But the first and most telling problem was that the targets were not visible against the dark background of the Mole. The second problem concerned the Thornycroft-built CMBs themselves, because they could only launch their 18-in torpedo when they were running at full speed towards their target. The commanders were quite unable to clearly see any silhouette of the moored destroyers and were in no position to cruise round an enemy held harbour with noisy engines. In the event, they fired blind at what they supposed was their target, then raced out of the harbour at full speed. Aerial photographs taken the next day revealed unscathed destroyers still moored to the Mole.

ML 283, seen here in the Camber at Dover, rescued the crew of *Brilliant* off Ostend in May 1918.

The Vice-Admiral later said he regretted that particular action. The attempt had shown, perhaps belatedly, and as no other action had shown, that the inside of the Zeebrugge Mole was undefended. And so, within just a few days of that action, the Germans quickly strung a net line across from the Mole to the shore. Bacon remarked, 'It is a good maxim never to practise the enemy by useless operations; either hit hard or leave him alone, even if the gallant young officers in small craft do chafe and fume at inactivity.'

A whole section of the mine net exploded, blowing a large hole in Commander H. Oliphant's ship, the Broke class flotilla leader *Faulknor*. Until now, Dover Patrol commanders treated British mines with contempt but the new type of British mine introduced in 1917 was just as lethal as the German mine. Humour was never far away in such circumstances. One 6th Flotilla cynic declared, 'Commander Oliphant would not get into trouble with the authorities because they would be pleased to hear the mine nets were really dangerous'. *Faulknor* was eventually salvaged and lived to fight another day but everyone agreed the new mine was unpleasant to encounter closely.

One of the most fearless officers of the Dover Patrol in 1917 was undoubtedly Lieutenant-Commander Henry Forrester DSC, who commanded the M class minelaying destroyer *Meteor*. When the bombardment force withdrew at dusk after their action off the Belgian coast, they would usually anchor in the Dunkirk Roads, or just to the northward of the bank which protects them. A couple of hours before high water, *Meteor* would slip her moorings and take station abeam of the commanding flotilla leader and a little procession would form up to accompany her to the zero point from which she worked. The flotilla leader, with her destroyer escort following behind, would protect *Meteor* up to the zero point and if no enemy vessels were seen, the signal 'G' was flashed from Forrester's ship and she would proceed independently to lay mines.

The destroyer captains never ceased to admire Forrester's work, for he crossed and re-crossed the German minefields on almost every occasion. Acute apprehension crept over Captain Evans when, time after time, he watched *Meteor* disappear into the darkness. He recalled 'the cloud of black smoke, a phosphorescent wake and a tin kettle full of men, keen as mustard, while we waited in suspense, an hour or possibly two.' He knew *Meteor*'s position, her speed and could calculate to within five minutes the instant of her reappearance. Waiting for the lookout's shout of, 'Bow wave', he would then quickly flash the challenge signal. There was always a sense of relief when he received the correct acknowledgement. The dark shape of *Meteor* would take station abeam of the flotilla leader and together they would swirl away homeward to their anchorage at Dunkirk.

In the autumn of 1917 the seaplane fighter squadron was abolished and the pilots sent to St Pol. The bomber seaplanes, mostly Short Type 184s, were kept at Dunkirk, as they were now capable of carrying 600 lbs of bombs, suspended on three frames, three under each wing and three beneath the fuselage. When the single 500-pounder bomb was introduced several Shorts were fitted to carry just the one, the first of which was used on a raid on 9 November 1916.

The most common seaplane based at Dover was the Short Type 184, which eventually, through modification and local engineering skills, became known as the 'Dover Type Short'. This was due to a homemade radiator modification that this model proved to be highly successful. By mid-summer of 1917, several Sopwith Baby seaplanes had arrived for air-fighting techniques. To accommodate the increase in seaplanes of every description and including DH4s and DH9s fitted with air bags, the forerunner of

The Short (Admiralty Type) 184 seaplane served at both Dover and Dunkirk from 1915 to 1918.

the metal float, two additional hangars were built alongside the original. Until then it had been customary to launch seaplanes into the water by steam crane but two concrete slipways were built from the Marine Parade down to the water's edge.

When the American-designed Curtiss H8 flying boats arrived in Dover Command in August they were unable to use the hangars and were anchored offshore in the harbour. The Vice-Admiral, however, was not particularly impressed with their performance and remarked, 'there was no improvement over the Short seaplane'. Bacon had already discussed the inferior Short seaplane over the landplane with the Admiralty and, what was more to the point, intelligence sources revealed the Germans were also disappointed with their own seaplane performance. Studying reconnaissance photographs taken of the German seaplane base at Zeebrugge, it was observed the seaplanes were seldom used other than in making low-level patrols along the Belgian coast.

The success of the Handley Page 0/100 bomber was assured under the command of Squadron Commander Babington who arranged a first-class system of control, so that every night, weather permitting, every available bomber was used to attack enemy positions. In June 1917 over 5 tons of bombs were dropped on Bruges docks and in the following month the Short Type seaplanes were discontinued as a bombing force, returning to Dover for re-allocation.

The Vice-Admiral insisted that during an army advance, and usually at their request, he would supply aircraft from his command to assist them. The RFC had suffered heavy

The Sopwith Pup (Admiralty Type) Scout (N5199), seen here at Guston in 1916, was struck off charge in April 1917 after a crash.

losses on the Western Front in the late autumn and as the enemy were making even greater efforts to expand their air force, the balance of air power was in jeopardy. Consequently a complete squadron of RNAS Sopwith Pup fighters, commanded by Squadron Commander G.R. Bromet, was sent with Admiralty approval to Vert Galant aerodrome near Amiens. This was the first of the four original squadrons formed at Dunkirk who were to assist the RFC. From time to time there was an interchange of squadrons.

The Capel-based airships, crewed by men who showed great fortitude in a contraption of doubtful usefulness, were operating daily, searching for either submarines or mines laid during the night by the UC type. Favourable weather conditions were essential for operating airships of any design and any failure of either engines or gas bags often led to traumatic rescue attempts. One example which stands out above the rest occurred on 14 August 1917, when the SS.Z2 – one of the Zero-type airships developed at Capel by the local engineering officer – was on a routine patrol seaward of the Downs shipping anchorage. When the Z2 developed engine trouble she was forced to alight on the water. Winds and tides sent the buoyant gas bag scudding across the surface of the water like a child's toy balloon.

Drifters, tending their net mine barrage, tried unsuccessfully to capture the runaway by throwing lines across the partially deflated envelope. The destroyer *Mastiff* was on routine patrol in the area and joined in to quickly rescue the two-man crew, then set about retrieving the airship. Of extremely light construction airships were notoriously difficult to handle on the ground, let alone on water. When a stiff breeze got up, handling the misshapen gas bag became an absolute nightmare of enormous proportions. Part of the envelope inconveniently swung over the destroyer's hot funnels, whereupon the remaining hydrogen ignited like a Roman candle. The blazing envelope fell and spread the burning canvas over the ship's decking. *Mastiff*'s crew hurriedly cut away huge chunks of it and threw it over the side but, even so, two men were seriously burned in the process, one of them later died of his injuries.

Wing-Captain C.L. Lambe considered his HP 0/100 bomber squadrons to be the élite and was quick to signal a request for additional squadrons to bring his air arm up to scratch. He submitted lists which included not only bombers but also fighters, reconnaissance, training and even flying boat squadrons. The Vice-Admiral was astounded by the request and said it was nothing less than extravagant. Bacon relied heavily on his senior officers in the RNAS and, as they were responsible for their own supplies, maintenance and repairs, he sent a signal back with instructions to implement Lambe's request. Hidden in Lambe's request though was the suggestion to not only enlarge existing aerodromes but also to build more. The air operations under Dover Command were becoming a huge enterprise beyond the scope of the Vice-Admiral. Because of the intense workload pressed upon his detached squadrons supporting the RFC, he arranged for his weary pilots to take rest at Walmer aerodrome near Deal.

As for the American-designed flying boats, most of which operated out of Felixstowe, the overcrowded conditions at Dunkirk prevented more than one or two to operate from there. Those that did operate despite the awful congestion in the harbour managed to find and attack U-boats. On 22 September 1917, for example, Flight-Sub Lieutenant N.A. Magor, flying a Curtiss H8 (8695), spotted a submarine on the surface about

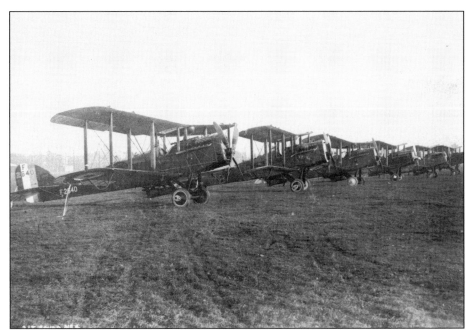

A line up of DH4s of No. 217 squadron, No. 4 Wing RNAS, at Petite Synthe in the autumn of 1917.

8 miles north-east of the East Hinder Bank. Magor dropped two 230-lb bombs from about 800 feet, one of which actually struck the conning tower. Recorded at the time as *UC72*, it was seen to keel over and sink with no survivors. It was later identified as being *UC32* commanded by Oberleutnant Ernst Voigt, as *UC72* was listed as being sunk two days before off Sunderland.

The re-laid mine barrage was feared by U-boat captains who were aware of its immense size both in length and depth. They had only the two options: try to run over the barrier and risk being seen, or accurately set the correct depth trim and go under it. Either option was a complete dilemma. Oberleutnant von Zerboni di Sposetti in *UC21* chose the latter on the night of 27 September and paid with his life and those of his crew. The following morning, 28 September, Oberleutnant G. Reichenbach had decided to take a chance while rounding the Thornton Ridge, and continued to run on the surface. It was a crisp September morning and the four-man crew of Curtiss H8 8676 were alerted by the tell-tale sign of a shimmering wake upon an otherwise calm sea. Flight Lieutenant B.D. Hobbs waved to his two air mechanics who knew what to do. Hobbs turned to the east so the rising sun would be behind him. When Reichenbach heard the Eagle engines it was too late. Hobbs dropped two 230-lb bombs on *UC6* before the conning tower hatch had closed behind the captain. The conning tower was suddenly enveloped in a sheet of flame. Hobbs circled the U-boat for more than half an hour, half expecting to see it rear out of the water and lie on the surface like a stunned fish. The sea was clear over the shoals and when the turmoil had subsided there was the dark shape of *UC6* clearly visible lying on the bottom. There was no sign of life or debris. Hobbs set course for home.

Captain Evans became senior destroyer officer in September, when Captain A. Peck left *Swift* to command a cruiser in another command. New blood was introduced to the Dover Patrol and one of the new arrivals was Commander G. Edwards, who took over *Botha* – another of the Chilean contract-built flotilla leaders. Both Evans and Edwards enjoyed their spacious cabins with the superb Chilean furniture and splendid amount of headroom, while from the ceilings were suspended silver-plated chandeliers. Evans recalled, 'they would have compared with those at Buckingham Palace'.

Broke steamed over to Dunkirk on 1 October to assist *Terror*'s captain who had asked for a light buoy to be lit south of Thornton Ridge. Passing through a gaggle of floating mines Evans signalled his escorts, *Mentor* and *Moorsom*, to stop and sink them while he proceeded to the buoy position. A lookout shouted 'Ship ahead!' Six enemy destroyers were waiting for him. Evans knew his broadside was hardly commensurate with the number of guns facing him. He decided to lead the enemy ships into the nearest minefield, convinced they would follow a single destroyer. His plan was to turn sharply about and make an attack using his four forward-facing 4-in guns. But the enemy were not so easily led. They remained in their area. Evans was furious when his trap failed. *Broke* heeled over as Evans made a sharp turn to port. *Mentor* and *Moorsom* had also turned, following their flotilla leader round in a smother of white foam, but in the gathering darkness the smoke from their funnels prevented the gunners from seeing their targets. Evans reached the edge of the minefield and opened fire. Two hits were recorded by the range taker but it was often difficult to spot hits in a destroyer scrap, as everyone was firing in the heat of the moment. The enemy destroyers disappeared behind their own smokescreen.

The monitor *Terror* had been brought up to fire upon Ostend and she successfully damaged floating docks, lock gates and two ships. In spite of the phenomenal accuracy of monitors in placing their shots where they liked, the heavy German, four-gun Tirpitz battery, to the west of Ostend, was equally accurate, and was able to reach a distance of 35,000 yards. Although the enemy artillerymen were considered first-class shots, they thought more of shooting at the slow-moving ships than attempting the more difficult task of catching the faster destroyers. From intelligence reports, it was soon clear that the Germans were under extreme pressure to use the Ostend dock facilities to repair submarines and destroyers after a bombardment. When the *Terror* suffered damage after being hit by a German torpedo, *Marshall Soult* was brought up to continue the shelling. She destroyed one vessel, damaged two others and then blew up a high explosive magazine.

Crucial to the success of these operations were the enormous efforts to train RNAS observers, who were required to face German anti-aircraft batteries while trying to accurately spot the fall of shot. They were encouraged not to use their wireless transmitters before spotting began and Vice-Admiral Bacon insisted they arrive over the target on time to signal 'Ready to observe'.

During the autumn bombardments Bacon used *Broke* almost like a taxi-cab. Evans, recently promoted captain after his April battle, remained with his ship, and was often impressed with the Vice-Admiral's deceptive wireless signals sent each morning to confuse the enemy listening posts. He was further impressed by the gunnery officers who attended the Vice-Admiral's breakfast table. The discussions on wind velocity, angular drift and the rotation of the earth, were, Evans observed, 'so perplexing as to give me a headache'. Evans had already established himself in the Dover Patrol as a courageous leader of men and had developed his own kind of bravado when handling ships. Beneath this exterior lay a personality which liked nothing better than to show off. After attending one particular breakfast session with the Vice-Admiral, he recalled, 'So as not to appear completely witless, I would put my destroyer alongside a pier at about 25 knots and then light a cigarette in a nonchalant manner, before going full speed astern. The gunnery officers almost stopped breathing, anticipating a dreadful collision.' His smugness, however, was amply rewarded by the looks of admiration.

There seemed little doubt that the Admiralty attached some importance to Dover's seaplane station. The Germans, on the other hand, seemed unimpressed with the conglomeration of both equipment and personnel. The Gotha air raids of 1917, an immense nuisance to the south-east of England and, perhaps, London in particular, tended to ignore Dover's seaplanes. But there was one incident which concerned a lone Gotha in October. It had negotiated the English Channel and dropped hundreds of incendiaries along the complete length of the seafront. More by sheer misfortune than any skill, it would appear, the seaplane hangars were set alight. Somehow the British were remarkably complacent about air defence measures, relying solely on anti-aircraft guns rather than using the splendid Sopwith fighters stationed at nearby Walmer aerodrome. The anti-aircraft gunners were not always aiming their guns at enemy aircraft either, as was disclosed in a parliamentary debate in the House of Commons on defence. It was disclosed that during a particular German air raid on Dover, RNAS seaplanes were shot at as they attempted to land in the harbour! The pilots were not amused and neither was the Vice-Admiral.

The air arm of Dover Command had reached its zenith in bombing power by the autumn of 1917. There were now two bombing squadrons of HP 0/100s based at Coudekerke, with a further day bombing squadron of DH4s at Petite Synthe, where the latter had replaced the Sopwiths in July. Bombing rates had leaped up to over 200 tons in October, an event which culminated in a special dinner at the Coudekerke officers' mess.

The flotilla leader *Botha* and her destroyer division were attacked by German aircraft on 27 October. The combined anti-aircraft fire from all ships soon broke up the enemy formation but not before matelots were injured on *Botha* and the French destroyer *Magon*. Then on the following day, a Sunday, an electrically powered motor boat was seen approaching the barrage patrol. *North Star*, an M class destroyer, hit the fast-moving boat with her pom-poms, and shortly afterwards it sank in a spectacular explosion. Another one was seen by the monitor *Erebus* about 9 miles off Ostend and heading towards her. It hit *Erebus* on one of her anti-torpedo bulges. Captain C.S. Wills suffered concussion and two ratings were killed, with a further fifteen being wounded by the blast. Unaware that the contraption carried explosives the monitor's crew had stood watching its progress without realizing the danger.

The German-built wireless-controlled motor boats, used off the Belgian coast in

It was disclosed during a House of Commons debate that Dover's anti-aircraft guns were shooting at Dover's seaplanes.

1917, were powered by twin petrol engines and were capable of very high speeds. From the stern they carried a drum of between thirty to fifty miles of insulated electric cable through which they were controlled by wireless signals from the shore operators. The shore operators received their instructions from a seaplane flying above the motor boat, which gave the required helm, either port, starboard or steady. In the fore part of the boat was packed a considerable charge of high explosive which was set to detonate on impact. This device was not a new invention. A similar boat had been used at HMS *Vernon*, the torpedo experimental establishment in 1885, although neither petrol engines capable of such high speed nor wireless equipment existed then.

Vice-Admiral Bacon first heard of the device when one of them ran into the pier at Nieuport, where sufficient pieces were recovered for a detailed inspection. His report to the Admiralty explained that 'the device was more suited to target practice than to endanger my ships, and further, they would ensure a constant vigilance by lookouts'. He thought the Germans would be concerned because, 'it gave ample warning of its approach by making a high feather travelling at such speed'.

It is perhaps interesting to note that the half-dozen or so submarines attached to Dover Command were based there for defence measures, to protect the Dover Strait against German cruiser attack, something that never happened. It deprived them of their

Dover's C class submarines were never allowed out on patrol unless certain restrictions were enforced to protect them.

only real objective. Their use in any other capacity was always overshadowed by their obvious shape to that of enemy submersibles. 'What the future value of these boats may be in naval warfare can only be conjecture', said the First Sea Lord in the announcement of the 1901 Naval Estimates, in which the first submarines were ordered for the Royal Navy. Bacon at that time was a captain and was appointed to oversee submarine development as an offensive weapon of war. There were many prejudices to overcome as hardly anyone in naval circles understood the submarine's potential. But even so, and in spite of these prejudices, there were, by 1914, seventy-four submersibles in Royal Navy service.

It is not therefore strange to relate that every periscope seen in the English Channel was immediately attacked. In consequence, the Dover-based submarine flotilla was never allowed out unless certain restrictions were enforced. When the Belgian coast patrols became firmly established in 1916, the Vice-Admiral used both British and French submarines to patrol the net lines at night. But because of difficulties in discharging their torpedoes while surfaced, the French craft discontinued their nightly vigil. There was also the inconvenience of escorting them to and from their respective positions at dusk and dawn. One of the most unpleasant tasks of Dover's submarines while they were fitted with occulting lights to resemble light buoys, was to lay closely moored to the high explosive mines. In that rather precarious position they were often in fear of drifting against a mine when the tide changed.

Two C class submarines left Dover to observe the Belgian coast on 4 January 1915. *C31* was never seen again, while *C34* was eventually sunk off the Shetland Isles in 1917.

Further difficulties were experienced with the C class submarines. The main problem being that they possessed bow tubes only, they were never in a position to launch torpedoes at enemy ships without first slipping their moorings to turn bow on to the target. On the few occasions when an enemy target was sighted, it had disappeared into the darkness before the British submarine could do anything about it. The months before aircraft were used for observation spotting during the bombardments, a couple of old A class submarines had been used as observation posts. They had been used submerged with only their conning tower visible above water level. As the aircraft spotting method was to prove satisfactory the submarines were withdrawn and the scheme abandoned. When *C15* signalled she was completely disabled off the Royal Sovereign lightship on 28 August, the aptly named drifter *Present Help* was sent to give assistance. A force five gale was blowing at the time and the little drifter took eight hours to tow her into Dover.

UC14 had been blown up in the minefield off Zeebrugge on 3 October. She had been disassembled at Pola after serving in the Adriatic and then sent by rail to Bruges, as it was beyond her capability to make the long journey by sea. Oberleutnant Fedderson, a reserve officer in the Flanders flotilla, went down with his boat as did the rest of the crew. During October the Vice-Admiral successfully obtained an E class submarine to hunt U-boats in an area often frequented by them and just eastwards of the old Goodwin Snue mine barrage. One of them, *E52*, commanded by Lieutenant-Commander P. Phillips, left its Dover anchorage at dusk on 31 October, escorted through the barrage by a destroyer before lying in wait with just its periscope showing above water. *UC63*, returning from her cruise and heading for home, was spotted early the next morning on the surface. Phillips fired a torpedo which ran straight and true and hit the minelayer below the waterline. The U-boat went down so fast only one crew member survived. He revealed that the captain, Oberleutnant von Keydebech, had sent a signal giving her last position before she sank. It was a simple matter for the German Naval Command at Bruges to signal all U-boats in the area to avoid that particular position. On hearing about the signal the Vice-Admiral said, 'After this the Germans were on the qui vive in this area'. Two days after *UC63*'s demise another was torpedoed near Beachy Head by the British submarine *C15*. Kapitänleutnant Klaus Lafrenz was captain of *UC65*, homeward bound, when he had to swerve smartly off course to avoid *C15*'s torpedo. Lafrenze was unaware that the British submarine had fired both bow tubes and the second missile, sent just a few seconds later than the first, found its target. There were five survivors and Lafrenze was among them.

Since the sinking of *UC63* U-boat commanders altered their route closer to the Goodwin sandbanks, known throughout the world as extremely dangerous and a graveyard for shipping. Strong evidence had filtered through the intelligence network to suggest that since January until November 1917, no fewer than 250 U-boats had successfully passed through the net and mine obstacles in the Dover Strait. The mine nets strung out in September 1916 across from the Goodwins to the outer Ruytingen had since sagged in many places due to extreme tidal movements and gale-force winds, giving the U-boat captains a positive advantage. The hard-working drifter crews patched them up as soon as they became obvious but the Vice-Admiral swept up the whole lot in anticipation of his new scheme using the latest H2 mine.

Having been torpedoed off the Belgian coast on 19 October 1917, *Terror* was proceeding to Portsmouth after temporary repairs had been made at Dover. On 23 October, before arriving off the Royal Sovereign lightship, she began to leak badly during a particularly fierce gale and heavy seas. At midnight near Beachy Head, she sent an urgent signal for assistance. The trawler *Elysian*, commanded by Skipper North, went alongside the ailing monitor and, despite the heavy seas and high wind, managed to rescue the entire crew, suffering considerable damage in the process. At dawn the next day the weather had improved and everyone was surprised to see *Terror* still afloat. Without any hesitation, Chief Skipper North sent the monitor's crew on board to secure a tow line and despite the colossal tonnage difference, towed the monitor to Portsmouth without further trouble. Chief Skipper North received the DSC for his skill, pluck and exceptional seamanship.

One of the latest ocean-going U-boats *U48*, captained by Kapitänleutnant Carl Edeling, left Wilhelmshaven on 21 November *en route* to the western approaches of the English Channel. She reached the eastern end of Dover Command's area two days later. She was first seen by an RNAS seaplane while running on the surface. Bombs were dropped all around her but Edeling dived to lay on the bottom until darkness would conceal his run through the Strait at night.

Photographed at Bruges, this German U-boat was a similar class to *U48*, which foundered off the
Goodwin Sands on 28 November 1917.

Edeling started up the engines just after midnight and began to move against a strong
westerly tide. At no more than a snail's pace, the U-boat slowly moved ahead but the
tide edged the submarine into the net barrage off the North Goodwins, where both
propellers became entangled in the wire mesh. At 0300 hrs *U48* was being held firmly
against a sandbank. The commander immediately jettisoned over 60 tons of fuel oil,
fresh water, ammunition and three of his torpedoes. But the vessel remained stuck fast.
An ebbing tide meant there was little water beneath the hull in which to manoeuvre.

As dawn broke, a watery sun gradually enveloped the horizon in a pink misty hue.
Minutes later the mist lifted. *U48* lay stranded and exposed, her steel decking glistening
in the morning light, her conning tower a sharp silhouette above the lapping wavelets.

To the south of her, two Ramsgate drifters *Paramount* and *Majesty*, accompanied by
the armed trawler *Meror*, were busy sweeping for mines along the war Channel route.
U48 stood out sharply against the background. She became the centre of attraction
almost immediately. The skippers made their identification through their binoculars. It
was too good to be true. The three vessels altered course to close with their 'find' and,
without any prompting, began to open fire with their 6-pounders. *U48*'s diesel engines
were running, giving power to her auxiliary equipment through the battery network,
while her gunners climbed out of the forward hatch to load their 4.1-in gun. The sound
of gunfire brought more drifters to the scene, *Present Help*, *Acceptable* and *Feasible*

steamed towards the action, but such a *tour de force* was more than the stranded submarine could take. Her gun crew had been killed before the other drifters had arrived. Shells whistled through the morning air with devastating results. Holes appeared in the conning tower and shells punctured the ballast tanks, while both periscopes were shot away into jagged-edged stumps. Another gun crew crawled along the decking – these courageous men, their lives held in fine balance, attempted the impossible. Their first and only shot struck the wooden side of *Present Help* but well above the waterline. *U48*'s captain was wounded in the head as he stood in his shattered conning tower. Below where he stood there were signs of a fire breaking out. He ordered explosive charges to blow up his crippled vessel and sent the rest of the crew over the sides into the seething water. Edeling and eighteen crew lost their lives. Answering a signal for assistance the destroyer *Gipsy* came up but the battle for *U48* was over. Smoke and flames enveloped the hulk when the charges exploded, ripping out her bottom. She settled on to the sandbank, all 900 tons of her. She would never again terrorize merchantmen in the western approaches.

The remains of *U48* reappear from time to time in the ever-shifting sands. She was first seen in 1921, again in 1939 and her most recent appearance was in June 1973. Carl Edeling's grandson recalled that *U48* last reappeared seventy years to the day after his grandfather had joined the German Navy.

An Admiralty award of £1,000 was paid to the three drifter skippers who each received the DSC, while there were five ratings awarded the DSM. Vice-Admiral Bacon wrote,

U48 had settled on the sandbank, never again to terrorize shipping in the English Channel.

'I wish to express my satisfaction at the gallant way in which the drifters [named] attacked this submarine armed with a 4-in gun. It is one more example of how the Ramsgate drifters and auxiliary service of the navy know how to meet and fight the enemy.'

Earlier in the year Vice-Admiral Bacon had organized the laying of mines at two depths to make a vertical screen, similar in construction to a ladder off the Belgian coast. The mines were fixed at intervals and staggered, one up and one down, in the line which, in effect, gave one mine every 20 feet. In February 1917, he began to prepare a similar minefield for the proposed Folkestone to Cap Gris Nez barrage, but the availability of mines was not expected until the end of the year. It was appreciated, both by Bacon and the Admiralty, that it was daily becoming more apparent that nets alone would not stop submarines and that the only sure way of stopping them was to lay another minefield. Bacon had estimated he would need two lines of mines at five separate depths, making a total of 4,000 mines.

After numerous discussions with Admiral Jellicoe and Vice-Admiral Sir Henry Oliver, details of the scheme were worked out and the section of the sea in which the minefield was to be laid was re-surveyed. The first move was to lay four parallel lines from the North East Varne to the traffic route off Cap Gris Nez. Laying the mines was started on 21 November and was almost completed by the end of December.

During the discussions the question of patrolling the minefield cropped up. Bacon had already considered the fixed light vessels along the line of nets supporting the mines. He favoured using searchlights on about four vessels anchored along the proposed route and, in addition, putting a searchlight on Folkestone's pier-head, with one other at Cap Gris Nez: between them they would illuminate the whole of the Channel. The Vice-Admiral's inventiveness was as perplexing as it was ingenious. The First Lord of the Admiralty immediately appointed a Dover Barrage Committee at the end of November whose experts visited Dover Command, saw the Vice-Admiral's plans and proposals and then returned to London.

Anxious to get things started, Bacon telegraphed the Admiralty for details on 12 December but was told 'the Barrage Committee had them in hand'. Throughout December he badgered them with more than one memorandum explaining in detail what he required to complete the minefield. He was not pleased with results so far and was even less pleased with, as he put it, 'the meddlings of an irresponsible committee'. His penultimate memorandum read:

I submit the present state of the minefield is not appreciated by their Lordships. In the letter under reply, in paragraph (1) it is stated that twenty-one [sic] submarines have passed through the Straits *since the deep minefield was laid*. I suggest it is intended to mean since the deep minefield was commenced. The minefield is not yet completed nor will it become a really effective danger to submarines for some weeks to come.

The Vice-Admiral Dover was not only furious with his Lordships but believed that it was better to leave the defence of the Straits to the Admiral who had local knowledge, experience and overall responsibility, than to allow dabbling by a committee who were far removed from it.

Admiral Sir Reginald Hugh Spencer Bacon KCB, KCVO, DSO, commanded Dover from April 1915 to December 1917.

When *UC44* was sunk on 4 August off Waterford, having run into a German minefield thought to have been swept up by the British, the sad episode had far-reaching implications leading to the removal of Vice-Admiral Sir Reginald Bacon from his post as C-in-C Dover. When salved, the submarine revealed confidential documents which showed, without doubt, the ineffectiveness of the Dover Barrage. The papers containing the operational orders concerning Dover's net defences clearly gave instructions how to avoid them. It was damning evidence and, sadly, Bacon was to pay the ultimate price of dismissal. He was not relieved of his post, however, until 29 December.

On 26 December it was announced that the Prime Minister, Lloyd George, had superseded Lord Jellicoe at the Admiralty by the appointment of Sir Rosslyn Wemyss, and a few days later Dover Command heard that Vice-Admiral Bacon had been superseded by Rear-Admiral Roger Keyes. The latter appointment, however, was not announced publicly, although news of it soon leaked out in the London-based newspapers, who revealed that in certain circles Vice-Admiral Bacon's term of office was not without criticism. But this criticism was quite unfounded for the facts speak for themselves and on record they invalidate the criticism. Bacon was to regard his shameful dismissal as 'brutal'.

During Bacon's two and a half years at Dover Command more operations were initiated and carried out than under any other naval command. The Admiral's secrecy throughout his tenure of office denied the British public full knowledge of the Dover Patrols efforts, their difficulties, disappointments and hopes, because he felt that any vital information would inevitably have been conveyed to the enemy. It was never appreciated that his 'least said' policy was the best policy. The Admiral would never reveal the slender nature of his forces which the Admiralty allotted to Dover Command. In his opinion 'the Germans would have been able to inflict irreparable chaos on the country if the veil of secrecy had been lifted just to allay public irritation.' The very existence of the Dover Patrol depended on his secrecy policy.

Bacon felt that the Barrage Committee would interfere with his own tactics, for he alone could see the difficulties of a system trying to arrange operations from London, especially the laying of the minefield from Folkestone to Cap Gris Nez. He alone knew the local conditions better than anyone else. When the First Lord, Sir Eric Geddes, appointed the Barrage Committee in November, Bacon was not asked to attend the meetings. Further humiliation was to come when the Admiralty declined to contradict statements made in the London newspapers, for they knew those statements were untrue. Just one example, of many, which appeared in the following year stated:

It was not until Sir Roger Keyes was appointed to Dover Command and a new atmosphere was created that remarkable departures in a new policy were inaugurated. This policy took two forms. The first was the establishment of a mine barrage from coast to coast across the Channel and, simultaneously with this, North Sea minefields stretching from Norwegian territorial waters almost to the Scottish foreshore, and another in the Kattegat, to intercept such German U-boats as base their activities upon the enemy's Baltic force.

The Admiralty knew well enough that the above statement was untrue. They were already aware that Lord Jellicoe had planned the North Sea minefields and had actually ordered the mines. They were also aware that the plans had been approved by Lord Jellicoe for the new minefield barrage in the English Channel and, more to the point, it was almost completed before Vice-Admiral Bacon's unfair dismissal. The Admiralty's insensitivity in allowing the country to believe that the new policies at Whitehall and the new Admiral in command at Dover were solely responsible for devising these schemes was regarded by many as reprehensible.

CHAPTER SEVEN

'Now I Suppose We Blow Up!'

Dover's first Admiral, the Honourable H. Hood, had been too fully engaged with bombarding the German advances along the Belgian coast to worry about laying minefields. But when Bacon took over the reins in 1915, though he lacked specific scientific qualifications, he became knowledgeable in the business of minelaying to either prevent enemy destroyers from using their new and recently acquired Flanders bases with impunity or, more importantly, to suppress the U-boat menace.

Captain Munro had already successfully sealed off Scapa Flow, Cromarty and the Firth of Forth. Although those areas were rarely challenged, he forwarded papers to the Admiralty detailing a scheme for closing the Dover Strait with anti-submarine nets of his own design. When Bacon was asked for his comments, he scathingly remarked, 'A glance at the scheme was sufficient to condemn it. Captain Munro's scheme would not last a single tide in the Channel. The Dover Patrol was up against hard facts and hard work and we have no men, vessels or time to waste.'

Rear Admiral Keyes was then Director of the Plans Division at the Admiralty and he considered, along with others in the planning division, that Munro's expertise in laying mines and anti-submarine obstructions was unrivalled. Keyes had already attended the Inter-Allied Conference where naval representations of all the Allied powers had met to consider measures to counter the U-boat campaign.

When Rear Admiral Keyes first reported to the First Sea Lord Sir John Jellicoe, he was handed a piece of paper containing a list of every conceivable offensive operation, from the capture of the Heligoland Bight and Borkum, to the blockading of Zeebrugge and of Ostend. Studying plans showing the German gun batteries at both these ports, Keyes did not think an operation to blockade them was at all feasible.

Discussion of an effective mine barrage in the Dover Strait continued unabated at the Plans Division and produced some of the most remarkable and hare-brained ideas ever suggested to the Admiralty. Some of them were, however, implemented with certain modifications and included nets – mined or otherwise; explosive jackstays to catch submarines on the surface; huge mines which lay on the sea bed and were fired by acoustic or magnetic impulse when a vessel passed over them; electric cables which detected an iron vessel above them. Then there was the suggestion to build concrete forts, floating or fixed, and equipped with searchlights, guns, hydrophones and lookout stations. In the event a Channel Barrage Committee was formed to investigate and report on every conceivable aspect for constructing a successful barrage between England and France.

Admiral Sir Roger J.B. Keyes KCB, KCVO, DSO, (later Lord Keyes of Zeebrugge and Dover). A portrait by de Laszlo.

While Rear Admiral Keyes realized that Captain Munro's net barrage was not necessarily the right solution, he was convinced that the passage through the Strait ought to be the most hazardous for enemy submarines. He was not pleased with Bacon's outburst as to the viability of Munro's suggestions but he was most impressed with Bacon's inventive ingenuity in providing 9.2-in and 6-in guns, manned by sailors and marines, just behind the Belgian front line. When he saw the 12-in gun, taken from one of the old pre-dreadnought battleships, mounted in a field and camouflaged to look like a house, he thought 'Bacon was at his best'. Given an elevation of about 45 degrees, the huge gun possessed sufficient range to place shells upon the German 15-in gun at Leugenboom. The colossal task of transporting the weapon to France by a monitor, then moving it into position by tractors, erecting it and manning it with specially trained marines was nothing short of a miracle.

When the Channel Barrage Committee visited Dover on 20 November 1917, to carry out their investigations on the spot, Vice-Admiral Bacon handed over eight closely typed sheets of foolscap, which explained in detail exactly how 'his' barrage and patrol system worked. After an excellent lunch on board *Swift*, the Keyes entourage embarked to examine the barrage at close quarters off Copt Point, Folkestone. But, unfortunately,

Swift ran over one of the new experimental 20-foot net sections, which was being tested for endurance under the extreme tidal conditions prevailing. The mines, like those fitted to the 60-foot vertical nets, were operated by an electrical battery system contained in special buoys and attached to jackstays, to which the nets were suspended. Standing on the bridge next to Bacon, Keyes remarked, 'Now I suppose we blow up!' Had this happened then perhaps history might have been considerably altered, for among *Swift*'s crew were Colonel A. Gibbs, Royal Engineers; Professors Bragg and McLennon, two very distinguished scientists; Captain Learmouth, the Assistant Hydrographer; Captain Lichfield Speer, the Director of Mines and Torpedoes; and Captain Fuller. Fortunately, the firing device proved faulty and failed to activate the mines. Instead, the net was torn to shreds by the destroyer's propellers. The indicator buoys on which the net system was suspended stood proud above the water and everyone guessed it would be easy for enemy destroyers to sink as many of them as they wished. That the enemy had refrained from doing so was only explained by the papers taken from the wreckage of *UC44*.

Among the documents found on *UC44* was this one which showed, beyond any doubt, that the barrage erected by Bacon was futile.

> It is best to pass this [i.e., the Dover net defence] on the surface; if forced to dive, go down to 40 metres. . . . As far as possible, pass through the area between Hoofden and Cherbourg without being observed and without stopping, on the other hand, the boats which in exceptional cases pass round Scotland are to let themselves be seen as freely as possible, in order to mislead the English.

On their return to London the Barrage Committee, having spent the best part of a whole day on the subject, wrote scathingly about Bacon's anti-submarine measures. Everyone quite expected Bacon to lose his temper as he read the adverse report but, to their astonishment, he agreed to almost everything that was in it, except he considered his Folkestone/Gris Nez barrage to be reasonably efficient. It was not appreciated at the time, however, that this much maligned barrage of heavy nets was actually responsible for denying the Dover Strait to German U-boats for more than a year.

During the month of October 1917, 289,000 tons of shipping had been sunk in the Atlantic and 62,500 tons sunk in the English Channel by enemy submarines, most of which had passed through the Dover defences. The Barrage Committee was frantically sorting through the various defence measures to deny this U-boat access route.

The Keyes report, submitted to the Admiralty, with a copy going to Vice-Admiral Bacon at Dover, was a scathing indictment of the latter's attempts to stop enemy submarines going through. The planners expected their next project to be approved by the Admiralty without question.

Their new plan was arguably the most daring, and involved the blocking of the Bruges canal system at Zeebrugge and the entrance to Ostend harbour. It was not a new idea, however, for in 1798 a combined naval and military operation had successfully destroyed the lock gates of the Bruges canal at Ostend. On that occasion the attacking force was unable to evacuate after the attack and, after a gallant action, was eventually captured. When Zeebrugge was vacated in October 1914, it had been suggested that the lock gates at Bruges should be destroyed. The military authorities thought this action foolhardy as they confidently predicted a reoccupation of the Belgian coast in the future. Today, no military strategist would uphold that view.

The first proposal to block these two ports was made by Admiral Bayley in November 1916, he anticipating to 'neutralize them as nests for destroyers and submarines'. He had suggested a combined naval and military operation to achieve this. Rear Admiral Keyes recalled, 'No action was taken on this proposal.' No action was taken either when Commodore Tywhitt at Harwich suggested the blocking of Zeebrugge using blockships, under cover of a bombardment force with smokescreens and poison gas! The Tywhitt paper was discussed at length by the Admiralty, at which meeting the Vice-Admiral Dover was present. Then Tywhitt submitted a further proposal on 8 January but after discussion it was abandoned. Vice-Admiral Bacon on the other hand suggested he could train CMB crews to go in and torpedo the lock gates. Keyes wrote, 'These papers were then locked in a safe at the Admiralty from which they did not emerge until February 1919.'

Commodore Tywhitt, undeterred by his rejection, submitted another paper on 7 May, which outlined:

(a) The capture of Zeebrugge Mole by assault and the occupation of Zeebrugge.
(b) Using Zeebrugge as a base for military action against Antwerp, with the ultimate intention of turning the German flank.

Discussion went on throughout the year until, on 3 December, an outline plan was completed. Intelligence reports suggested that twenty-eight destroyers and torpedo boats and thirty-eight submarines were based at Bruges, Zeebrugge and Ostend, and could pass between these ports using the inland canal system. There was no doubt that a scheme to block any movement of enemy vessels between these ports was a distinct advantage over any net barrage system.

Vice-Admiral Bacon studied the proposals to attack Zeebrugge and Ostend and, having read through them, he disagreed with most of it. In actual fact, he sat on the proposals for days, without making any comment, then laid his own plans in open defiance. Rear Admiral Keyes was furious with the delay and sent Captain Fuller down to Dover to find out what was happening. Fuller returned without the plans and reported that Bacon would visit the Admiralty with a copy of his own plans in just a few days. That there was a difference of opinion between Bacon and Keyes was now quite obvious.

Bacon's plan was really a regurgitated memorandum of his earlier great landing operation in which he favoured using monitors, not only to bombard the ports in question but also to land troops on to the Zeebrugge Mole, using a huge hinged gangway from the bow of a monitor. Keyes was all for blocking the ports with some old cruisers and only landing troops to attack the defences during the operation.

Rear Admiral Keyes reported the outcome of Fuller's visit to Sir John Jellicoe and asked for an immediate decision. Sir John, however, was not prepared to accept Keyes' indictment and was quick to point out that the Vice-Admiral Dover was better equipped to base his alternative plans on experience. The Vice-Admiral Dover, however, was summoned to the Admiralty on 18 December to attend a meeting in the

First Sea Lord's room, which was attended by Admirals Jellicoe, Wemyss, Oliver, Hope and Keyes. Bacon was asked questions, then given the opportunity to outline his own proposals to attack Zeebrugge and Ostend. He returned that same afternoon to Dover, with strict orders to patrol the new deep minefield at night and by day, and have it illuminated as directed by the Admiralty on 4 December.

Searchlights and flares were used for the first time over the deep minefield on 20 December and it seems rather ironic that *U59* had been forced to dive hurriedly and had blown up on a mine that very day. Keyes heard about it the following day and thought it was 'a great stroke of good fortune for the Plans division'. He wrote, '*U59* actually sealed Admiral Bacon's fate, for the First Sea Lord, Sir Eric Geddes, had been watching the battle about the Dover Strait with keen interest.'

Rear Admiral Keyes was incensed by the fact that Great Britain had never had to face a greater menace than the ruthless U-boat campaign of 1917–18. He felt passionately that the navy should overcome the submarine menace and 'the issue would be decided as of old, by the endurance and bravery of British seamen, not by passive physical defences, such as those which had been relied upon for the last two and a half years.'

On the morning of 28 December, Sir Rosslyn Wemyss sent for Rear Admiral Keyes. 'Well Roger,' he said, 'you have talked a hell of a lot about what ought to be done in the Dover area and now you must go and do it.' The shocked Keyes recalled, 'it seemed hardly decent that I should be sent to fill the vacancy, which my relentless efforts had caused – moreover it was a great surprise.' Vice-Admiral Bacon remembered that when he attended the Admiralty, almost on arrival he was told by the First Lord, Sir Eric Geddes, that he was superseded in his command so that any further action on his part was quite unnecessary. Rear Admiral Roger Keyes had been given the command of Dover. Keyes recalled Bacon returning to the room quite unperturbed and as friendly as ever, saying he thought the changeover had better take place at once. There was a ten year age difference between the two Admirals, Bacon was then fifty-five and Keyes forty-six, but the latter was a firebrand, full of energy and ready to tackle anything the Admiralty could throw at him. Keyes felt sorry for Bacon and secretly admired the way he had taken the knock. In retrospect, history had repeated itself as it often does, but this time with a vengeance. Hood had been superseded by Bacon just as ruthlessly and now Keyes had superseded Bacon, and the former wondered if a similar fate awaited him.

Dover Command's personnel, generally speaking, thought rather highly of Bacon and many had appreciated his small kindness in one way or another, especially one particular officer whose family had fallen on hard times. But they never lost sight of the fact that he had many strings to his fiddle. He was, they agreed, undoubtedly a man of brilliant professional attainments with a most original mind and perhaps the cleverest of many able officers of his time. When Admiral Fisher was First Lord, he had picked Bacon out as his principal lieutenant in the promotion of drastic reforms in naval education, strategy and ship construction. Bacon had won early promotion by sheer merit and his early work on submarines as well as his command of the Dover Patrol was of inestimable value to the service as a whole.

During his command at Dover he had seen 120,000 merchantmen pass through the Dover Strait. Nearer to the enemy held coast of Belgium than they were to Brighton in

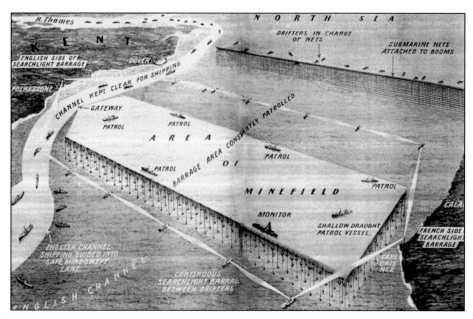

This artist's impression of the 1918 illuminated mine barrage appeared in newspapers and magazines around the world.

Sussex, the Dover Patrol succeeded in guarding that lifeline of food and materials so essential to the British in their hour of need. Throughout his tenure of office Bacon's work and conduct had the complete approval of his chiefs in Whitehall and he enjoyed the trust and enthusiastic admiration of his fellow officers.

Bacon's departure on New Year's Day was not without its poignant overtones. As he drove through the dock area at Dover, with his wife Cecily beside him, the ships in the harbour blew their sirens and whistles, while the sailors drawn up on the quay side broke ranks to cheer their Admiral. Bacon was so moved by this show of feeling towards him that he stopped to say a few words of farewell.

Acting in the rank of Vice-Admiral, Keyes officially took command of Dover on 1 January 1918. His headquarters, so recently vacated by Bacon, were three seaside lodging houses on Dover's Marine Parade. The one in the centre was the Admiral's official residence named Fleet House; those on either side were the offices containing the secretaries, telephone switchboard and telegraphic equipment connected to the port war signal station.

The new Admiral lost no time in visiting every unit under his command. The depot ship *Arrogant* lay at anchor in the Camber and had flown Bacon's flag. Laying next to her was *Hazard*, now the submarine tender, and on which Keyes hoisted his own flag to replace that of his predecessor which was hauled down at sunset. Keyes visited the dockyard and workshops, also the CMBs and MLs whose crews were billeted in wooden huts close to their craft. From there he was taken to the RNAS seaplane base on Marine Parade, then on to the Guston aerodrome, situated behind the castle. His final visit was to the Capel airship station above Folkestone.

Soon after his flag was fluttering at *Hazard*'s masthead Keyes sent for his principal officers. He recalled, 'and at once I sensed an atmosphere of hostility and resentment, which was, perhaps, not surprising after the summary supersession of their chief.' To allay any further resentment Keyes opened the Admiral's safe and produced facsimile copies of *UC44*'s captured documents. Confronted with the irrefutable evidence his officers were immediately on the defensive, pointing out that they had worked vigorously to maintain the net barrage complex while engaged on many other duties within the command. They had genuinely believed that German submarines were using another route rather than risk being sunk in the Dover Strait. Keyes allowed them time to digest the evidence then told them of his new proposals to abandon the old barrages and, in addition, emphasized the importance to concentrate all their efforts on the new illuminated minefield.

During the first weeks of January 1918, U-boats were being seen both by day and night but they were usually made to dive hurriedly by the presence of so many patrol boats. The old C class destroyer *Mermaid* reported seeing a periscope off Cap Gris Nez, steering west, on the evening of 19 January. *U95*, commanded by Kapitänleutnant A. Prinz, dived at once, but into the minefield. Ten minutes elapsed before there was an explosion. She was never seen again and was posted as 'missing'. The drifter *Beryl III* engaged another submarine steering due west just after 0800 hrs on 26 January. The drifter closed with its target, the latest ocean-going *U109*, commanded by Kapitänleutnant O. Rey, off Cap Gris Nez and the chase was on. It was noted the submarine had two large periscopes, one on either side of the conning tower, fore and aft. She was stationary in the water when *Beryl III*'s 12-pounder gun opened fire at almost point-blank range. *U109* – one of the latest U-boats built by the German shipyards – dived quickly but not before the drifter's shells had struck the conning tower. The crew of *Beryl III* assumed their quarry had escaped. Some time later several heavy explosions were heard in the vicinity, accompanied by a large oil slick that spread over the water. When divers went down later to investigate the wreck, *U109* was identified.

The coal-burning destroyer *Leven*, commanded by Lieutenant-Commander A.P. Melsom, was usually employed running a mail and ferry service between Dover and Dunkirk, without ever sighting the enemy at close quarters. Melsom was always optimistic and alert to the possibility that one day his luck might change and he had acquired additional depth charges for that very reason. It was about 2230 hrs on 26 January when a lookout spotted a periscope awash almost dead ahead. Melsom gave the order to the helmsman to ram but the old ship was rather sluggish to answer the helm and just wallowed into a large trough, which sent a huge sheet of spray over the forecastle. 'Reverse engines!' Melsom shouted. *Leven* drew backwards for up to 200 yards before the captain ordered all depth charges to be launched over the stern. *UB35*, commanded by Oberleutnant K. Stoter, had already dived beneath the surface. *Leven* rattled like a tin can when one after the other the depth charges exploded at intervals, culminating in a large air bubble surging up to the surface containing one officer and about six ratings. Although a boat was lowered to save them only one was boat-hooked to the side and he died soon afterwards. Melsom received the DSO but was more astounded by the performance of his crew and his old 30-knotter which had stood up to his bellows and changes of directions without faltering. He was quite proud of them.

The rising sun cast a feeble radiance over the sea as *Zubian* slid effortlessly through the calm waters with a strong offshore breeze on her port side. It was still very cold and the lookout was huddled behind a canvas canopy. The destroyer was about to pass Dungeness point about 3 miles out on the morning of 4 February, following the swept Channel route. It had been one of the coldest nights, bright and moonlit, which had produced 28 degrees of frost. Everything was frozen solid and there was two inches of snow covering the decking like a white blanket. Matelots were out wearing heavy sweaters and oilskins, sweeping the snow over the sides while others were banging ice off the gun mountings.

The lookout shouted, 'Submarine off starboard bow!' Lieutenant H.J. Hartnoll responded sharply. *Zubian* answered to her helm and the engine room telegraph swung to indicate 'Full Speed' revolutions. Shackle pins were knocked out of the depth charge holding frames while the starboard torpedo tube swung out from the deck. Hartnoll held his course until he reached a position where the submarine was last seen making its dive. Determined to destroy the U-boat Hartnoll let go his depth charges in a line following the course the submarine would have taken. At the same time he instructed the yeoman signalman to send for assistance. Within thirty minutes destroyers in the immediate vicinity arrived to spread out in a wide circle and drop their depth charges. It was not a long wait before a huge oil slick was seen. Hartnoll launched a buoy over the slick. The explosions had ceased.

Vice-Admiral Keyes, dressed in leather coat, helmet and goggles, climbed in the front cockpit of a Short seaplane and was soon conveyed aloft to join the hunt. Approaching Dungeness the engine spluttered and then stopped. Forced to alight on the choppy sea

The seaplane carrier *Riviera* (on the left) towers over the Short seaplane about to take off in Dover Harbour.

the pilot sent a signal back to Dover while the Vice-Admiral sat and fumed. They were picked up by a CMB two hours later. The reason for this quite extraordinary search was eventually found beneath the marker buoy, a total wreck. *UC50* and her crew, together with Kapitänleutnant R. Seuffer, had not stood a chance against a concentrated force of destroyers hell-bent in their destruction. Four days later *Goeland II*, a flare-carrying trawler, spotted a surface-running submarine about 4 miles out from the French coast. The trawler skipper gave chase and forced *UB38* into the minefield area where she dived to destruction. The submarine, crew and their captain Oberleutnant G. Bachmann were never seen again.

It was not unusual for Naval Intelligence to contact Vice-Admiral Dover by telephone when a particularly important situation was imminent. The Director of Naval Intelligence, Admiral W.R. Hall, made a call on 14 February to warn Keyes of an important ocean-going submarine about to pass through the Straits from west to east homeward bound. A signal was sent to all ships on minefield patrol to be on the alert but what transpired bore no relation to an ocean-going submarine.

The German Zeebrugge destroyer flotilla had shown some activity in January when it came into contact with the monitor *Erebus* and *M26* and duty destroyers on exercise near the Thornton Ridge on 23 January. The drifter *Clover Bank*, skippered by Lieutenant D.L. Webster RNR, was checking the net barrage when he came under fire from enemy boats. Intervention by the monitors saved any further action on that occasion and the enemy boats withdrew.

The Vice-Admiral had not altered the concentration of his patrols from that which his predecessor had arranged. The new minefield was still protected by one 12-in and one 15-in monitor, four 30-knotters, four P-boats, fourteen trawlers, sixty drifters, four MLs and two paddle minesweepers. The drifter divisions were protected by the flare-carrying trawlers, while the monitors were anchored near the Varne Shoal as support in case of enemy action.

While the Admiralty's intelligence service was fully aware that U-boats were using the north-bound route, the German High Command was preparing to attack the one thorn in their side, the Dover Strait mine barrage, at their earliest opportunity. Enemy destroyers had not made a serious effort to interfere with the mine barrage since about April 1917. When the *Clover Bank* incident occurred on 23 January, it was feared that immunity from further attacks was slim. Every destroyer in the Dover Patrol was being used at night except for those on a rest period, who were sent to the Downs where they remained at anchor but under strict orders to slip and be ready to protect shipping at short notice.

The concentration of vessels on 14 February was as follows: the light cruiser *Attentive*, the destroyers *Murray*, *Nugent* and *Crusader* at anchor in the Downs. The flotilla leaders *Swift* and *Marksman* were at the west barrage patrol area, *Termagant*, *Melpomene*, *Zubian* and *Amazon* at the east barrage area. The Folkestone deep minefield to southward was guarded by nine drifter divisions totalling about fifty-eight boats; they stretched on a line from Folkestone Gate buoy to roughly 3 miles north-west of Cap Gris Nez. The two paddle minesweepers *Lingfield* and *Newbury* were running on a line between the south-east gate and the Varne lightship, while four MLs cruised around near the shore. The destroyer *Racehorse* and P-boat No. 50 were stationary at certain marker buoys and the

Carrying only one 4-in gun and two torpedo tubes, the 600-ton P boat was introduced in 1915
for anti-submarine use.

French were covering the extreme end of the line off Cap Gris Nez. The whole gamut
of defence was being swept by the powerful searchlights on either side of the Strait.

Skipper Lieutenant W. Denson RNR of the drifter *Shipmates* reported seeing an
ocean-going submarine on the surface just before midnight. It was heading eastwards
but in the hazy conditions and in complete darkness he lost sight of it. About one hour
later the port war signal station reported that it had seen the red and white Verey light
sent up by Denson and could hear gunfire from the direction of the illuminated
minefield. The Vice-Admiral was informed and he immediately ordered the Downs
destroyers to steam to a rendezvous with the duty destroyer *Moorsom* south of the
Goodwins. Then the small monitor *M26* reported gunfire south of the Varne lightship,
and confirmed she was steaming in that direction to investigate. By 0130 hrs the
mysterious gunfire had ceased but the monitor reported a drifter had seen a green Verey
light shoot up from a trawler. The old 30-knotter *Syren* sent a signal to say she was
closing with the burning drifter *Cosmos*, and which sank at 0216 hrs.

The incoming signals became infrequent and Keyes was unclear as to the real
situation. Then the drifter *Chrysanthemum* reported seeing a submarine near the
Folkestone Gate, where red and white Verey lights were being fired off rapidly,
indicating a patrol vessel had actually spotted a U-boat. At first all the signals pointed to

more than one submarine attempting to pass through the minefield but when the flotilla leader *Termagant* signalled '*Amazon* reports three destroyers passed. Steering east at 0224 hrs. Position one mile SW of No. 11 buoy', Keyes knew at once that enemy craft were in his area. The plethora of confusing signals had influenced the whole night's events. Keyes was unable to understand why that particular signal had been transmitted to *Termagant* from *Amazon*, instead of being transmitted to the port war signal station. Perhaps the answer was in the forty-minute delay between sending and receiving a signal, as each message was coded and sent by Morse telegraph during darkness.

When dawn broke the truth of the ghastly night's vigil became apparent. The enemy destroyer raid had been quite successfully carried out. They had sunk the trawler *James Pond* and seven drifters – *Jeannie Murray*, *Clover Bank*, *W. Elliott*, *Cosmos*, *Silver Queen*, *Christina Craig* and *Veracity*. The paddle minesweeper *Newbury*, commanded by Lieutenant A.D. Thomson RNR, was severely damaged and another five drifters also damaged. The *Newbury* was towed back to Dover in a sinking condition with nine crew killed and seventeen wounded. Her bridge was smashed, the after mast shot away and her funnels perforated like sieves. The drifter *Violet May* limped into harbour with only two survivors, the rest of the crew had been killed.

In hindsight, if *Shipmates* had reported the attack on the drifters then perhaps the destroyers close by might have intervened more quickly. It really came down to lack of communication, for if the raid had been reported to Dover immediately then the Downs destroyers, on rest, could have been diverted to the action more precisely. Experience had already shown, however, that any action in darkness was a hit and miss affair, and chances of defeating the enemy force decisively under those conditions were very slight. Had the green Verey pistol lights been fired, announcing to everyone that enemy destroyers were in the area, then considerable forces were available to bring the raiders to action. There were too many ifs and buts.

The Vice-Admiral was dismayed by the casualty lists, eighty-nine officers and men had been killed while another thirty were wounded. He visited the damaged vessels next morning to talk with survivors. He listened to several cases of extreme bravery but, to his horror, learned at first hand that the auxiliary crews were disgusted with the navy's failure to engage the enemy. Keyes said, 'I was consumed with cold fury against those whose failure had let the patrol down so badly.'

There was no doubt, however, that an atmosphere of utter confusion existed because of the effect of searchlights, flares and smoke. One is tempted to suggest that this was the reason why Vice-Admiral Bacon had been reluctant to illuminate the Folkestone/Gris Nez minefield and had delayed its use until forced by the Admiralty to use it. Without adequate protection, the little drifters were sitting ducks, brilliantly lit from every conceivable angle, while their slightest moves were plotted by the enemy destroyers and submarines. Bacon, you will remember, with Admiralty approval, had reduced the lights showing seawards in the Downs and at North Foreland, so as not to give the enemy destroyers an advantage in making their attacks. Bacon's local experience had paid off in denying the enemy knowledge of the weaknesses of the Dover Patrol.

Vice-Admiral Keyes had experienced his first real setback, and realized that the Dover Command was not a force to wage an offensive war. He felt obliged to inform the

The drifter *Jeannie Murray* at anchor in Dover Harbour. She was lost with all hands on 15 February 1918.

Admiralty of this fact and, further, asked for the latest class of destroyer to help bolster his ageing craft. Bacon had been asking for new, fast and well-armed destroyers for years.

Vice-Admiral Keyes was furious that no signals had been received until after the enemy destroyers had made their attack and made good their escape. He appointed a Court of Inquiry, presided over by Admiral Dampier. That same evening, the patrol of the illuminated minefield was re-established. Keyes wrote, 'and that night the minefield was more brilliant, more aggressive, and more thickly patrolled than ever.'

Kapitän Heinecke, the commander of the Heligoland Bight destroyers, boasted a victory over the Dover Patrol in a wireless broadcast, claiming to have sunk a large guardship, twenty-five armed fishing vessels, a torpedo boat, a U-boat chaser and some small motor boats. Whether Heinecke was responsible for an attack on Dover by a submarine on the following midnight, we will probably never know. The submarine lay about 3 miles off the harbour, without being challenged, and fired twenty-two shells into the area. The flotilla leader *Swift* was the nearest vessel patrolling the minefield but when she arrived the raider had left after depositing mines near the eastern entrance. Although the gun flashes were so plainly seen, no effective attempt was made by Dover's defences. The reason for this lack of effort was put down to the instructions issued to battery commanders not to open fire without the authority of the Naval C-in-C as he considered 'they would not know a hostile vessel from a friendly'. Bacon's order had not been rescinded and no one had questioned why a 'friendly' vessel was shelling the town.

The convened Court of Inquiry could not fail to lay blame squarely on the shoulders of those who had commanded *Amazon* and *Termagant* and the *M26* monitor, although they mentioned the confusion between signals that had been in operation for over two years and those more recently introduced. On reading their report Vice-Admiral Keyes could not find any excuse for the delay in engaging the enemy vessels who had not replied to a challenge signal. There was, he concluded, sufficient evidence to frame a charge for a trial by courts martial upon the commanders. All three were relieved of their respective commands immediately.

It had always been an accepted practice in the Dover Patrol that ships passing in the night should show dimmed navigation lights and, during an action, the fighting lights approved for that particular night. 'Suspicious vessels were to be regarded as enemy; unnecessary challenges are to be avoided; if the challenge is made and not immediately answered, offensive action is to be taken without further delay.' The noteworthy example of *Swift* and *Broke* the year before had not permeated the minds of every commander in the 6th Flotilla, it seemed. The Admiralty had no alternative in the light of the evidence but to act as they did. The commander of the *M26* monitor, however, was not tried by courts martial.

Admiral Keyes, impressed by the courageous response of drifter and trawler crews who were, after all, fisher folk and quite untrained in the disciplined service of the Royal Navy, suggested to the Admiralty that they should receive prize money for driving submarines into a minefield. It was approved without question and sums of up to £1,000 were paid. The first was made for the destruction of *UB56*, sunk on 19 December 1917, the first U-boat destroyed in the new illuminated minefield.

An earlier suggestion to use towers manned by Royal Marines, mounted with searchlights and guns placed at intervals across the Strait, immediately above the illuminated minefield, was now considered with some urgency. But the costs of such a scheme were prohibitive and only the Prime Minister could sanction such an expense. Admiral Wemyss told Keyes he should explain the scheme to Lloyd George, emphasizing the importance to wield an absolute and effective anti-submarine measure. As luck would have it, the opportunity to explain everything came when the Prime Minister was visiting France on a troop transport. Such a golden opportunity could not be missed. Keyes arranged to meet Lloyd George on the boat and mentioned that, '£1,500,000 was but a drop in the ocean of war expenditure'. The Prime Minister gave his consent and construction of the towers began soon afterwards at Shoreham.

One or two U-boats were still attempting to negotiate the illuminated minefield. At about 0400 hrs on 10 March, a submarine was forced to dive when six drifters appeared in her path directly ahead. The inevitable explosion occurred. Identified later as *UB58*, commanded by Oberleutnant W. Lowe, the U-boat had blown her seams and sent up to the surface the usual tell-tale signs of flotsam and debris. There were no survivors. One other submarine was seen on the surface the following day. She was fired upon by the drifter *Tessie* but she escaped in the mist to fight another day. Vice-Admiral Keyes was anxious to eliminate every small coastal-type submarine attempting to pass through his area but all too often the UC and UB class were observed as far west as the Royal Sovereign Light Vessel, which was the limit of his patrol area.

Keyes sent a signal to the Admiralty, reporting the inability of his drifters and trawlers to match the speed of surfaced U-boats, due to the conglomeration of equipment they carried. He asked for more torpedo craft to assist his ageing ships. But the Admiralty regretted that they were unable to increase the force at Dover. Keyes argued that most of his destroyers were too old to cope with the conditions prevailing in the Dover Patrol. He explained that repairs, maintenance, refits and even navigational problems were probably greater than in any other locality in the United Kingdom and, further, no other flotilla was so continuously employed in high speed convoy work during the day and kept ready for any emergency at night. The line of argument was similar to that used by Bacon, who had used the same ploy to activate his superiors, and which resulted in *Swift*, *Broke*, *Faulknor* and others being transferred to the command. In the event, Keyes was loaned a division of the Harwich destroyers to assist him during difficult periods of deployment.

When a large slick of oil came up to the surface after a heavy underwater explosion on 19 March, there was no debris to indicate a 'kill', despite depth charging the area. The spread of oil was so large it was assumed a submarine had perished and so drifters received the £1,000 prize money. The victim might have been *UB108*, as she failed to return to her Flanders base.

Captains Douglas and Haselfoot were busy fixing marker buoys off the Belgian coast in preparation for Keyes' attack on Zeebrugge in April. The buoys were anchored at specific distances from the sand shoals. Because of the intense interference by the German shore batteries, a covering force of monitors, destroyers and smoke-carrying MLs escorted them. The whole operation to fix just eight buoys accurately lasted nearly one month, due in part to poor visibility and the accurate shelling from the enemy.

In broad daylight on 20 March, Commander R.L' E.M. Rede in *Botha*, with *Terror*, small monitors *M25* and *M26*, drifters and minesweepers, having been out all day in worsening visibility, decided to await darkness before completing the task. *Botha* was steaming towards the Dunkirk Roads when an enemy air raid occurred over the port itself. Communications with the signal station became quite impossible as anti-aircraft guns blazed away and exploding bombs caused chaotic reverberations. Even worse was the dense smokescreen put up by the military at Dunkirk which blew seawards, enveloping every vessel attempting to approach the harbour. Rede decided to anchor in the Dunkirk Roads overnight and, except those on watch, the remainder of the crews went to their beds.

Everyone was startled to hear the fire gong alarm at about 0345 hrs. In no time at all the cables were slipped and the engines were started. *Botha* moved slowly ahead through the smokescreen, illuminated occasionally by umpteen star shells. Everyone was completely mystified by the sound of gunfire. Torpedo men and gun crews were at action stations and the magazine personnel were already down aft. In line astern of the flotilla leader came *Morris* and three French destroyers, *Capitaine Mehl*, *Magon* and *Bouclier*.

Botha's speed increased as she steered north-eastwards to clear the shoals, then a lookout shouted 'Bow wave!' Away to port there appeared some blurred shapes. At once orders were given on range and bearing coordinates. The gunners and torpedo men responded. A recognition signal was fired into the sky, quickly followed by star shells which burst in a myriad of sparklets. The blurred shapes, two German torpedo destroyers, and no more than about 137 tons displacement, acknowledged with red fighting lights. Within seconds *Botha*'s fighting lights were also switched on then her forward guns opened fire independently. The French destroyers began firing simultaneously – main guns, pom-poms and even machine-guns – the noise was so intense it soon resembled a battleship broadside.

Bearing down on the enemy vessels at full speed *Botha*'s commander ordered 'Prepare to ram!' There was a slight jar as *Botha*'s bow sliced through the leading torpedo boat *A19* amidships, effectively cutting the vessel in half, the two portions passing down on either side of *Botha*. Commander Rede, intending to ram the next torpedo boat *A7*, put his helm hard over but he was too far in front and crossed *A7*'s bow. *Botha*'s two aft-mounted 4-in guns fired at point-blank range with devastating results. *Morris*, meanwhile, had closed behind *Botha* and also made an attempt to ram *A7* but missed by a hair's breadth in the excitement of the action. Both the destroyers disappeared in a heavy smokescreen put out by the enemy vessels.

After ramming *A19*, *Botha* had steered in an arc of about 180 degrees to suddenly reappear through the smoke without any lights showing at all. Her electrical circuits had been shot away completely. The torpedo officers of *Capitaine Mehl*, seeing a large destroyer bearing down on his ship, and without any lights showing, launched a torpedo without a moments hesitation. *Botha* shuddered under the impact as the missile exploded in her stokehold, stopping her engines at once. She lay in the water with her guns silent, completely surrounded with dense smoke and steam hissing from dozens of cut pipes.

As the horizon grew brighter every second the French destroyers were observed picking up survivors from the sinking two halves of *A19*. *Botha*'s captain was pleased to see *Morris* steaming towards him as his ship was lying helpless in the water with a huge hole in her port side. A tow was passed and, escorted by the French destroyers, the two ships made slow progress back to Dunkirk.

In the confusion of battle no one had noticed a lone CMB joining the fray. Lieutenant Willetts in CMB 20 pursued the retreating enemy vessels and actually caught up with five of them in line astern, steaming eastwards. Closing to within about 600 yards range of the last ship in the line, he launched a torpedo over the stern while running at maximum speed. Helm hard over, Willetts drew away from the tremendous gunfire which suddenly opened up on his little boat. His torpedo ran true and struck the fourth vessel in line. Willetts later received confirmation of his hit from a reconnaissance aircraft off Ostend that had reported seeing enemy destroyers circling another that was obviously damaged.

Hearing of the action Keyes suggested that as enemy destroyers were obviously sheltering in Ostend, arrangements should be made to bombard them without delay. That very afternoon *Terror*, escorted by destroyers and MLs and preceded by the usual minesweepers, were at their selected positions 26,500 yards off Ostend harbour at about 1500 hrs. The monitor opened fire with her 15-in gun and the German shore batteries replied almost at once.

Captain Douglas on board *Terror* later wrote, 'The damage we did was pretty extensive, as was shown by the aerial photographs taken afterwards; the naval basin etc., was badly knocked about and it must have pretty terrifying for the Hun there, as a 15-in high-explosive shell, weighing something in the neighbourhood of a ton, makes a bit of a mess.'

The extrovert dashing Vice-Admiral needed little excuse to leave his desk. He arrived at the bombardment area in the destroyer *Phoebe* and noticed, to his astonishment, that *Terror* was surrounded by huge water fountains, leaping up higher than her mast head. She was obviously being singled out by the German battery at Jakobvnessen. He ordered *Phoebe*'s captain to make smoke above that which was being laid by the MLs. Keyes was also concerned about the angle of descent of enemy shells, which he considered very steep. If a shell hit above *Terror*'s magazine then she would have blown up at once as her decking was no match for a 15-in shell. Perversely, the MLs' crews were busy collecting up stunned fish, while the roar of shells through the air and the violent explosions close by seemed irrelevant.

But *Terror*'s accurate shooting soon induced the Germans to cover the whole area in a dense smokescreen that prevented any precise spotting of shot. Keyes was rather anxious not to run the risk of placing shells in to the town of Ostend, which might kill or injure the civilians there. After firing about twenty-nine shells, weighing a little over 34 tons, Keyes gave the signal to withdraw.

The importance of the waterways leading from Zeebrugge and Ostend could not be ignored by the Admiralty any longer. The Germans had transformed the inland town of Bruges into a modern destroyer and submarine base, 300 miles nearer to Dover than their home ports in the Heligoland Bight. Blocking these vital exits and destroying the ammunition dumps and supply depots, the repair facilities and the concrete submarine pens would, in a nutshell, deprive the enemy of their most valuable asset on the very edge of the Dover Strait and the southern route to the North Sea.

The approaches to both these ports were now amply fortified by at least 200 heavy coastal guns of various calibres. Vice-Admiral Keyes was the first to acknowledge, after his predecessor's observations, that no blockship would ever arrive unmolested. However, one new factor had emerged, the new and vastly improved smokescreen system that showed minimal flare at night. The chances of blockships approaching unseen and under cover of darkness would now be feasible. Keyes was in favour of an attempt to use blockships to close both canal entrances. It was a bold but simple plan. Escorted by destroyers and covered by a flotilla of MLs carrying smokescreen equipment, the obsolete cruisers would be sunk inside the piers guarding the entrances to the Zeebrugge canal, while two old cruisers would be sunk at the entrance to Ostend at the same time.

When Keyes first walked into his office at Dover, one of his actions was to pin up on a wall a quotation. It read: 'It is thought combined with energy, preparation combined with aggressiveness, knowledge combined with application, that overcomes obstacles and makes achievements sure.' The ubiquitous Keyes was poised to play an even greater role in shaping our island's history. A firm believer in the staff system, he soon organized an efficient and congenial group of officers around him. But more important still, his recent involvement with the Plans Division gave him new impetus to draft plans to strike the necessary blow upon the enemy. Working with tireless energy, he started his two-month-long planning and preparation for the job ahead. Meanwhile, he had redoubled the night patrolling of the new minefield which, in the words of Winston Churchill, 'from end to end became as bright as Piccadilly'.

The Bruges/Zeebrugge canal system was known to the Vice-Admiral. The system was navigable by the destroyers and submarines and ran almost dead straight throughout its length of some 6½ miles. The canal was tidal as far as Zeebrugge lock with the result that submarines could not enter or leave the canal at low tide because of silt build-up. Both harbours at Zeebrugge and Ostend were protected by a large number of heavy and medium artillery, mounted on the shoreline. In addition, there were no less than forty of these guns in the immediate vicinity of Zeebrugge, all interconnected by an up-to-date signal and command system. The latter harbour was further defended on either side by entrenched infantry with machine-guns. To seaward was the famous Mole, the largest of its kind in the world, sweeping eastwards in a semicircle and protecting the entrance to the canal. The whole provided a deep-water quay from which ships could operate, protected from the westerly and northerly gales.

There were four separate sections of the Mole which carried footways, roadways and a double-track railway line. The Mole itself was a vast construction of granite paved blocks over one mile long and 80 yards wide. It was a formidable barrier in its pre-war guise but by 1918 the Germans had built barracks and stores on it and had emplaced six 3.5-in and 4-in guns on the Mole extension, which could fire through an arc of 360 degrees at any vessel approaching the canal entrance. As if that was not enough, there were also three 5.9-in guns mounted at the extreme end of the Mole proper. These nine artillery pieces were going to be the main targets of the marine attacking force after it had been landed on the Mole before the arrival of the blockships.

Intelligence reported there were over 1,000 Germans defending the Mole, with a back-up of about three or four destroyers, usually moored alongside it at night. The final hazard for the blockships, after entering the harbour and within point-blank range of the guns, was a long line of barges and buoys, supporting a line of anti-torpedo nets strung out between them. These had been introduced after Bacon's aborted attempt to torpedo enemy destroyers by CMBs the year before. The intended operation at Zeebrugge alone would need immense fortitude, courage and supreme skill.

But what of Ostend? Here, there was no protecting Mole. The harbour entrance was guarded only by coastal artillery and light guns at the two extreme pier-heads.

It was immediately apparent to the Vice-Admiral that in the face of such strong opposition, if there was any hope of the blockships reaching their objectives they must approach under cover of darkness, preferably on a moonless night, and at a critical time to allow their escorts to withdraw before daylight. The operation, therefore, could only be done during a period of four or five nights in every lunar month, and then the weather conditions had to be compatible. A navigational difficulty reared its ugly head in the shape of dangerous shoal waters, constantly shifting with the tides. They would need careful negotiating at night and without lights or buoys – other than those provided by the attacking force.

A dilemma of some magnitude was that the advance of a large number of vessels, steaming for 70 miles in open water and in daylight to start with, and at about 10 knots speed, might be spotted by either enemy aircraft, submarine or even surface craft. Precise navigation; speed to deliver the marines and bluejackets on to their targets; the withdrawal of the whole force, or what was left of it, could not take more than one hour, and were, therefore, overriding considerations.

The Vice-Admiral decided that the whole operation should be preceded by a heavy coastal bombardment from Nieuport, an air bombardment and a further bombardment by monitors from out at sea. The monitors, he suggested, should start their bombardment on a nightly basis for at least one week before the actual attack, thus duping the enemy into thinking there was nothing unusual happening.

The number of vessels used was estimated to be no less than about 140, which would not include the Harwich Force of twenty-three ships under the flag of Rear-Admiral Tywhitt; this fleet would provide a protective screen to the east of the operation. With meticulous precision Keyes revised the plans time and again until he was absolutely satisfied of success. On 24 February he took his final plan to London for the approval of the Admiralty Board: the scheme was approved. A week later he was instructed to implement the multifarious preparations, including the training of the landing parties, whose job it was to blow up installations and knock out the formidable gun defences.

During the preparations, it was generally accepted that if the blockships were ever to succeed in reaching their respective positions, much of the credit would go to the MLs providing the smokescreens. One of the officers assisting the planning was Wing Commander F.A. Brock RNAS who was an authority on all forms of pyrotechnics. Son of the founder of Brock's Fireworks, he was brought to Dover by Keyes to help improve the flare illuminations of the new minefield. It was through his inventive genius that the whole of the barrage was lit. One of the curiosities of the smokescreen mixture was the much acclaimed ingredient called saxin, a popular substitute for sugar. Brock had set up a small factory in the town of Dover to make his obnoxious smoke mixture.

The cruisers *Thetis*, *Intrepid*, *Iphigenia*, *Brilliant* and *Sirius* being converted to blockships at Chatham for the St George's Day operation.

The carefully surveyed route to the Belgian coast required a line of light buoys, spaced out about twenty miles apart. Brock's factory produced these lights and many other contraptions that were laid on the night of the operation, among them a number of specially designed smoke floats which were anchored in selected positions with an eye to wind direction. The task of the Fleet Guide Officer would be simplified by steering from buoy to buoy at a pre-arranged speed, checking all the while his time at each buoy and making the necessary adjustments to arrive at the last buoy at the exact time. The last buoy was roughly 16 miles north of Ostend and about the same distance from Zeebrugge in the north-west. It was at this point that the attacking force would split in two halves, the ships going to Ostend, turning south, while the main force continued to Zeebrugge.

Brock's inventiveness was, however, matched by the engineer officers, whose task was made all the more difficult by the strict time schedule for completion. Officers had already been chosen to command the vessels that were selected for specific duties. Three old cruisers built in the 1890s, *Thetis*, *Intrepid* and *Iphigenia*, were commanded respectively by Commander R.S. Sneyd RN, Lieutenant S.S. Bonham-Carter RN and Lieutenant I.B. Franks RN, each vessel destined to block the Zeebrugge canal system. Two similar ships, *Brilliant* and *Sirius*, commanded by Commander A.E. Godsal RN and

The Mersey ferry steamers *Daffodil* and *Iris*, each capable of carrying 1,500 men, were selected for the Zeebrugge operation.

Lieutenant-Commander H.N.M. Hardy RN were to block the fairway between the Ostend piers. The strengthening of these vessels was carried out at Chatham. Steering positions were duplicated, protected with bulletproof matting, and all controls were similarly duplicated, while engine rooms and other vulnerable areas were encased in cement. Furthermore, to increase the difficulty for the Germans in raising the blockships after they had been sunk, other parts were filled with concrete. Each cruiser was to retain light armament to engage the enemy shore batteries as the ship crept towards its final destination.

The old cruiser *Vindictive*, originally selected as the third blockship for Ostend, after much deliberation was chosen to carry the marines and bluejackets for their attack on Zeebrugge Mole. Her draft of 19 feet was not ideal for the purpose because she might encounter an uncharted minefield. However, Keyes decided to use two Mersey ferry steamers, *Daffodil* and *Iris*, each capable of accommodating about 1,500 men, and with their shallow draft could safely ignore any minefield.

To assist the raiding parties to reach the top of the Mole wall when *Vindictive* ran alongside it, a special upper deck was built with wide ramps leading up to it. The theory was that as soon as *Vindictive* had berthed alongside the Mole, gangways would be lowered on to it and the men would dash across to the quay. Like the blockships, it would be essential for *Vindictive* to engage the Mole batteries as she approached her berth. Three howitzers, pom-poms, machine-guns, trench mortars and two large, Brock-designed flame-throwers were mounted at strategic positions on the old cruiser.

Intensive training in grenade throwing, bayonet fighting and the more specialized work of demolition was undertaken by 200 bluejackets and 500 men of the 4th Marine Battalion. When the fitting out preparations were completed, the three assault ships, *Vindictive*, *Daffodil* and *Iris*, and the five cruisers converted to blockships, assembled in the Thames Estuary. The depot ship *Hindustan* also rode at anchor and was to act as a barracks for the six assault companies. They were unaware of their destination when they first embarked at Dover on 6 April. The 700 men assumed they were destined for France and were totally bemused when their steamer-come-troopship eventually berthed alongside *Hindustan*. Their commanding officer Lieutenant-Colonel B.N. Elliott of the Royal Marine Light Infantry was given absolute authority to inform them of their true destination. Strict secrecy was maintained and no one was allowed ashore.

Meanwhile the Flanders-based submarines were still dedicated to their tasks, the UC types sowing mines in the most unlikely places around the British Isles. Running the gauntlet of the Dover Straits was not so simple now that the deep illuminated minefield was increasing in size almost on a daily basis. It was a formidable and complex mine wall, as Oberleutnant F. Gregor in *UB33* found to his cost. Approaching the mine barrier on 11 April, Gregor saw a drifter division straight ahead and illuminated by flare-carrying trawlers. Gregor made his last dive. Some weeks later a salvage team recovered a steel chest from the wreckage containing confidential code and signal documents.

The day before the St George's Day operation – officially designated Operation ZO – *UB55*, commanded by Oberleutnant Wenninger, dived to avoid the drifters *Shipmates* and *Seaflower* in similar circumstances to those which had occurred eleven days before. The drifters bobbed about on the surface of the water when their depth charges exploded below them, setting the waters boiling like a cauldron. A huge air bubble broke the surface soon afterwards containing Wenninger and about twenty men. Only six survived the ordeal and Wenninger was among them. *UC79* was lost the same day but its wreckage was never found. Oberleutnant A. Krameyer went down with his men and the exact location where the submarine vanished remains a mystery.

CHAPTER EIGHT

'St George For England'

Vice-Admiral Keyes visited the anchorage in the Thames Estuary where all ships were ready and waiting for the signal to proceed. He spoke to the ships' crews and especially the men who would fight at the sharp end of the operation. As if to answer his critics, he had insisted that the risks involved in storming Zeebrugge were no greater than those sustained by soldiers in the trenches every day. It had been suggested that for this reason there had been no question of asking for volunteers. And yet, crews in the blockships, submarines, coastal motor boats and all other vessels associated with the operation were, one is led to believe, volunteers to a man. Despite the perversity, not one man offered to withdraw from the operation when given the opportunity.

Wind and tides were considered perfect on 11 April, after many days of tense expectancy. Late that afternoon the vessels slipped their moorings to assemble at their first rendezvous off the Goodwin Sands. At 1900 hrs they moved off at 10 knots towards the Belgian coast in three columns. With an overcast sky the night was dark, a light mist hung over the water then suddenly lifted to reveal the 140 vessels keeping perfect station. The very silence of their progress conveyed a tremendous sense of purpose and power. Every man on every ship was ready for action and held in check was the power to combat any opposition which might arise.

At the head of the starboard column was the W class destroyer *Warwick*, built the year before, and now flying the Vice-Admiral's enormous silk flag at her masthead. Hoisted within seconds of Keyes being piped on board, it looked extravagantly large for such a small boat. There was little doubt, however, of the whereabouts of the Vice-Admiral.

The wind was blowing in gentle gusts towards the Belgian coast when the armada silently crept towards its final rendezvous. The temporary light buoys were just ahead, where the thirty or so extra stokers allotted to each blockship would be transferred to a minelayer for their return to Dover. Prearranged signals were being rapidly sent by hand lamps between ships. Then the wind unexpectedly dropped. Soon afterwards it began to blow from the opposite direction. The success of the whole operation was now in jeopardy. Wing Commander Brock's smokescreens were vitally important to shield the approaching *tour de force*. Keyes was now faced with making a decision – either to continue with his well-laid plans or to call the whole thing off to fight another day.

It was no small matter to turn a large fleet of ships round on a reciprocal course, and at night, with no navigational lamps burning, to return the way they had come. Keyes made up his mind and signalled 'Course west'. Flashing aldis lamps immediately stabbed through the darkness. The briefest of messages were exchanged between vessels relating to the abrupt course change. Helmsmen spun wheels and ships began to roll round on to their new course. As dawn broke, the armada had reached its anchorage in the Swin.

This watercolour painting by Bernard Gribble shows the St George's Day armada of ships *en route* to Zeebrugge on 22 April 1918.

A second attempt was made the following morning but two hours later the wind rose alarmingly, producing conditions too rough for the smaller craft to endure. Once again, Keyes was forced to abandon his operation.

The difficult operation of turning the fleet round was only achieved by fine seamanship. And yet there were only three incidents, each of them concerning the fast coastal motor boats. Captain A.F.B. Carpenter VC, RN mentioned one CMB that, 'received a heavy blow in the bows from another craft'. The CMB's commander increased speed to about 27 knots which effectively raised the damaged bow clear of the water. He then decided to race around the whole fleet at high speed until daylight approached, then set course for Dover. Another CMB was too close to the Belgian coast for comfort when the signal was given to abandon and was fortunate to escape running ashore.

But no one was aware of the plight of CMB 33A, which had the misfortune to actually ground on an offshore sandbank. Even when Carpenter wrote his book in 1921, he seemed unaware of CMB 33A's plight, or elected not to mention it. The crew of the ill-fated craft were duly captured by German sailors the next morning. Admiral Ludwig von Schröder, commander of the Flanders Naval Force, which included the Marine Korps who manned the heavy coastal artillery, obtained a copy of Vice-Admiral Keyes's operational orders that was taken from the captured CMB.

A German official historian later wrote of the incident: 'the orders found in CMB 33A called for special attention. A heightened degree of combat readiness was ordered for the Flanders coastline but this measure was not transmitted to either the Mole

CMB 33A had the misfortune to ground on an offshore shoal on 11 April 1918, during the first attempt to block Zeebrugge.

Battery at Zeebrugge or the TBDs berthed alongside it.' Whoever was responsible for not informing everyone in the defence network at Zeebrugge caused an error of judgement that helped Keyes. But the young commander of CMB 33A had disregarded Keyes' instructions against carrying any documents on board.

The BEF in France were in a critical situation. In the last three weeks the army had suffered over 300,000 casualties. Sir Douglas Haig issued a statement which left no one in any doubt as to the gravity of the predicament facing the nation:

> With our backs to the wall, and believing in the justice of our cause, each one of us must fight on to the end. The safety of our homes and the freedom of mankind depend alike upon the conduct of each one of us at this critical moment.

Time was running out for Keyes, who was fearful of the Admiralty cancelling the operation altogether. Cooped up in *Hindustan*'s main decks the assaulting parties were showing signs of discomfort. A moonless night had always featured in the plans as an essential requirement for absolute success. The next moonless period would not begin until the second week in May. Keyes knew that the tide would be favourable on 22 April, although the moon, unfortunately, would be full. He decided, despite this major handicap, to press the Admiralty to agree to another attempt. Fortunately the First

Sea Lord, Sir Rosslyn Wemyss, was behind Keyes all the way and orders were given to make another attempt, weather permitting, on or after 22 April.

The meteorological summary was quite good for the day selected and there was every chance the operation could sail with confidence. At 1700 hrs on 22 April, the armada ships slipped their mooring cables for the third attempt. The Vice-Admiral had been reminded by his wife that morning that the next day was St George's Day. She begged him to use 'St George For England' as his battle cry and when the fleet approached the first rendezvous, the Vice-Admiral made this famous signal to his fleet. Captain Carpenter in *Vindictive* made the reply, 'May we give the dragon's tail a damned good twist.'

As before, the vessels were heading in three columns eastwards. Led by *Vindictive* in the centre column, with *Daffodil* and *Iris* in tow at her stern, she was followed by the five blockships and the minelayers, the latter to recover the surplus crews at the final marker buoy. Proudly flying Keyes' silk flag, *Warwick* led the starboard column, followed by the TBDs *Phoebe* and *North Star*, both towing coastal motor boats to save fuel. Astern of them was *Trident*, towing the submarine *C3* packed with explosives, and the destroyer *Mansfield*, towing the submarine *C1*, also packed tight with high explosives. The port column was made up of destroyers towing more CMBs, while between the three columns were the MLs, all manned by volunteers, many of whom were destined to take on some of the most hazardous duties ever experienced. The majority of the MLs were to operate the smokescreens, without which the whole operation would be in danger. A number of CMBs were to torpedo the enemy destroyers before they could slip their moorings, while others were detailed to rescue the crews of the blockships after they had been scuttled. Perhaps the most hazardous job went to the CMBs who would dash into Zeebrugge harbour to mark the canal entrance with calcium buoys. In case of an emergency, each small craft carried its own smokescreen equipment.

As the armada crept ever forward to its goal the moon shone in all its brilliance. Visibility was at least 10 miles. There was then a sudden suspicion of rain in the night air. The moon and stars became hidden. To starboard, a beam of light swung up from the rim of the sea, spilling a little of its radiance on the dark water. A lighthouse in less dramatic circumstances is always a symbol of peace and remembrances at home. But even as it waxes it wanes again. The ten-second cycle is all too short – its image barely offers hope. That it is there at all offers a crumb of comfort to the men who were closed up and ready for what the next hour or two may bring. In less demanding theatres of war this first degree of readiness would only be maintained for a limited period. But here, in the English Channel, this armada of warships heading towards the Belgian coast brought with it almost complete apprehension of the impending attack.

The comparatively confined waters lying between the two land masses, the proximity and strategic excellence of enemy bases holding fast destroyers, submarines and smaller craft meant that to avoid discovery and attack was almost impossible.

The decks became slippery with the condensation from the falling mists. The ships were butting into a short swell and they occasionally slapped a wave which sent a sheet of spray over their bow. Clouds veiled the moon, then it began to steadily drizzle and the visibility was suddenly reduced to less than a mile. The rain became intermittent but squally. Savage gusts then bore down on the ships and for a brief period blotted out what poor visibility there was. They continued their journey, more or less blind.

But the whole force had complete confidence in its Admiral, a confidence which showed itself dramatically when the ships arrived at the marker buoy, 16 miles from Zeebrugge. Here the surplus men were to be transferred to the minelayers for return to Dover. A dozen or more of the stokers could not be found when the launch came alongside *Iphegenia* to collect them. They had hidden themselves away so as not to miss the action to come. The launch was obliged to leave without them as time was critical. The launch that should have attended *Intrepid* broke down, and all thirty-four men remained on board. The task of rescuing these 'extra' men, after the blockships had been sunk in position, was going to be an additional problem.

Blockships for the Ostend part of the operation, with their destroyers and MLs, separated from the main force. They rolled round on their new course, while brief lamp signals blinked between ships. There was a change of watch. New voices were heard during the changeover but vigilance had not been allowed to relax for a second. They were on course for a rendezvous north of Ostend, where they would come under the command of Commodore Lynes, who was in charge of the Dunkirk flotilla.

Meanwhile the *Warwick* and four other destroyers pushed ahead of the main force, steadily approaching Zeebrugge. As they approached the coast the MLs, who had held their positions with remarkable skill in the wake of their larger companions, slipped their towing cables and forged ahead to lay the smokescreens. Some of them deposited smoke floats at strategic intervals so as to upset the enemy's gun batteries. CMBs, armed with a torpedo each, dashed for the harbour entrance to attack the enemy destroyers tied up on the inside of the Mole.

The rain began to cut down savagely. The small craft began to roll in a steady wallowing motion. They increased their speed to push into the swell. Although the wind had almost dropped there was enough of it to send the smokescreen in-shore. Visibility was reduced to about 200 yards. So far, everything was going to plan, and the critical timing of the voyage had been accurate. *Vindictive* was within ten minutes of reaching the Mole at midnight. Less than a mile away her crew heard the two monitors, *Terror* and *Erebus*, shelling the Flanders coast from far out to sea.

Through the all-enveloping smokescreens, the glaring enemy searchlights were observed, sweeping from side to side. Everyone hoped that the Germans were still unaware of the approaching armada. The rain fell in torrents but the wind had died away entirely. As the CMBs were racing towards the harbour entrance, the roar of their engines gave the game away. Night erupted into day, when dozens of star shells suddenly burst aloft. The coastal batteries at last opened fire on an unseen assailant. The British ships were still concealed by the choking smokescreen. The enemy shells screamed overhead to fall harmlessly into the water a mile or so beyond them.

Vindictive was punctual and was just 300 yards from the lighthouse when a slight breeze veered from the south. The billowing smoke, already restricted by the heavy rain and lying low on the water, rapidly cleared northwards, to reveal her high superstructure. She was bearing down on the Mole like some awful spectre. In the glare of the searchlights and star shells, she offered, at point-blank range, a ghostly target which must have shook the German gunners to their bones. Her only line of defence

These drawings by Charles de Lacey depict the assault by marines and bluejackets on Zeebrugge Mole on 23 April 1918.

was to open fire with every gun that could be brought to bear. Her speed was increased so as to pass through the danger zone and at one minute after midnight she came alongside the outer wall of the Mole, where only her superstructure was exposed.

But in those few terrifying minutes she had experienced dire misfortune. She had lost Colonel Elliot of the marines and his second-in-command Major Cordner, both of whom had stood on the bridge ready to lead the assault parties. Captain Halahan, in charge of the naval landing parties, with Commander Edwards beside him, was standing on the upper deck. Halahan was killed outright while Edwards had both legs shot away by a shell. Officers and men leaped from out of their cover positions when the firing began, only to fall in writhing heaps as they reached the deck.

Because of her increased speed, *Vindictive* had passed beyond her objective which meant that her raiding parties, trained to assault the gun batteries on the Mole, were out of reach. They were now in an area quite unfamiliar to them, disadvantaged even further by the barbed wire and fixed positioned machine-guns facing them. Drawing only 19 feet and at increased speed, *Vindictive* carried with her an enormous water surge. This high swell caused her to roll alarmingly, smashing many of her special gangways as she struck heavily against the parapet wall. Lieutenant H.G. Campbell of the *Daffodil* raised his engines to full power and was able to push *Vindictive* to hold her in position while she was secured to the wall.

The assault parties began to move but only two of the special gangways had survived out of a total of eighteen built. They were further handicapped by the heavy casualties already suffered; by the *Daffodil*'s contingent being unable to transfer to *Vindictive* while she was bow-on to the cruiser; and the unavoidable delay in getting any back-up from the *Iris*'s men. *Iris* had arrived just ahead of *Vindictive* and had berthed quite unscathed immediately ahead of her. But, because of the heavy swell that continued for more than half an hour, she pitched and rolled so violently that her scaling ladders could not be secured to the top of the parapet 20 feet above her deck.

Two single-handed attempts to secure a line to *Vindictive* resulted in the deaths of the courageous Lieutenant C.E.K. Hawkings and Lieutenant G.N. Bradford, both shot when they had reached the top of the wall. There was incredible gallantry shown by the men who actually succeeded in scrambling on to the Mole under a hail of merciless bullets. Having got on to the Mole, they were unable to reach their objectives to carry out demolitions, and were subjected to fierce machine-gun fire. They suffered severe casualties but, by their tenacious resistance, distracted the attention of the defenders from the arrival of the blockships.

One other important arrival was submarine *C3*, commanded by Lieutenant R.D. Sandford. She was on the surface, travelling towards the viaduct just after midnight, when she was suddenly enveloped in the glare of searchlights. The German shore batteries opened fire moments before the searchlights went out. Sandford increased his speed to 9 knots and, a few perilous minutes later, succeeded in forcing his small vessel between the cross girders of the iron pier. While his crew made good their escape in the motor dinghy, he calmly set the fuses of the tightly packed explosives.

Sandford and his crew had just five minutes in which to get as far away as possible from the inevitable explosion. The dinghy's propeller had been shot away, so they began to row to a safe distance in the short time available. But a strong tide was against

Damage to the Zeebrugge viaduct was the result of submarine *C3* being wedged between the girders and then blown up.

them. They had got about 100 yards or so before a searchlight on the viaduct illuminated them in its beam. Machine-guns opened fire and almost immediately Sandford and two of his men had been hit. Riddled with bullets, the dinghy began to fill with water. Sandford was then hit a second time. Then the viaduct blew up in a huge sheet of flame. The searchlight went out and the machine-guns stopped firing. They managed to keep the dinghy afloat long enough for the surviving men to be picked up by the boat detailed to rescue them.

The next phase of the operation was the actual reason for the whole enterprise – to block the canal entrance. It had been planned for the three blockships to make their final approach at least twenty minutes after *Vindictive* had been secured to the Mole. *Thetis*, under the command of Commander Sneyd, edged her way slowly through the choking smokescreen, preceded by an ML in the charge of Lieutenant-Commander Young, who was to mark the entrance of the canal with calcium buoys. Sneyd was to steam up the tidal canal, ram the lock gates, then sink his ship in the actual entrance. *Intrepid* and *Iphigenia* were to follow close behind and would be sunk, one behind the other, athwart the narrowest part of the canal.

Peering through the billowing smoke, Sneyd at last caught sight of the Mole when a star shell burst about 200 yards ahead. He altered course to round the lighthouse, then made full speed for the gap between the net barrage and the defence buoys. But, unbeknown to him, the ML was hit as it approached the harbour. Lieutenant-Commander Young and half his crew were either killed or wounded. Mortally wounded, the gallant Young supervised the sinking of his craft and made sure the survivors got away in the dinghy before he collapsed and died.

Until that moment *Thetis* had escaped close scrutiny but her enormous bulk, pushing a huge bow wave before her, attracted the attentions of the German batteries. The inevitable happened. She came under a fiercely accurate fusillade of shell. She replied with every available gun. *Thetis* had passed through the net barrage but fouled her propellers in doing so. She forged ahead for just a few more vital moments but just as the two pier-heads of the canal came into view, both her engines stopped. She became a sitting target at point-blank range. Motionless and illuminated by dozens of star shells, she was holed in several places below the waterline and began to heel over.

Commander Sneyd, realizing he could not get underway, signalled *Intrepid* to pass him. He then blew the charges in the bottom of his ship. Orders were given to abandon ship. Two of the cutters had been wrecked and a third was severely damaged. Still under a merciless fire, the crew used the damaged cutter and pulled away from the sinking *Thetis*. A few moments later they were picked up by the ML detailed to rescue them.

Intrepid now surged safely through the gap in the net barrage and entered the canal corridor without a shell hitting her. Her captain, Lieutenant S.S. Bonham-Carter, was now able to place his ship in the position which *Thetis* would have occupied. But Bonham-Carter stuck to his precise instructions – to sink his ship in the narrowest part of the tidal channel. One can criticize his decision but in the heat of the moment, and lacking any previous experience under fire, it was easier for him to obey orders than to think clearly of an alternative. Reaching his designated position he swung *Intrepid* athwart the stream, set the fuses to blow the bottom out of her, then abandoned ship.

Iphigenia meanwhile, just a few minutes behind *Intrepid*, was badly hit as she negotiated the canal entrance with extreme difficulty. Her captain, Lieutenant E. Billyard-Leake, managed first to miss the sinking *Thetis*, now enveloped in smoke, and changed course rapidly so as to miss the east pier-head. With *Intrepid* athwart the tidal stream, her captain could not proceed further down the waterway. He at once began to manoeuvre his ship backwards and forwards across the canal corridor aft of *Intrepid*. While this methodical tactic was going on his ship was being raked from stem to stern by machine-guns. Once satisfied his ship's position could not be improved, he set the fuses and ordered the crew to abandon her. The relief of the rescuing ML astern of *Iphigenia* was indescribable. 'It seemed,' the ML commander said afterwards, 'that the damned fellow was never going to stop juggling with his engines.'

The last rescue boat, ML 282, commanded by Lieutenant P.T. Dean, its carrying capacity about forty to fifty men, was heading for the harbour mouth with every inch of deck space packed tight with 100 men from *Intrepid* and *Iphigenia*. As she rounded the lighthouse, several of them were either killed or wounded by accurate machine-gun fire. Her chance of ever reaching Dover in one piece was diminishing by the second as she wallowed in a choppy swell at considerably less than quarter speed. Fortunately the Admiral's flagship *Warwick* was standing-in close to the Mole looking for stragglers, and Dean's little ML was spotted through the smoke and mayhem. In spite of being under a fierce attack *Warwick* managed to pick up all the survivors.

The marines and bluejackets, who had gallantly fought their action on the Mole under extreme difficulty, had now re-embarked on the battered *Vindictive*. With her two consorts she was soon steaming towards the rendezvous position, where the survivors of the operation were to assemble before heading back to Dover. Of these three vessels, *Vindictive*, *Iris* and *Daffodil*, only *Iris* had met with nothing but considerable misfortune. Commander Gibbs had tried in vain to secure his ship to the wall ahead of *Vindictive*, so as to allow his landing parties to get ashore. In the event, he was forced to go alongside the cruiser but, by then, the Mole diversion had reached a conclusion, as the blockships had already entered the harbour.

The contingent on *Iris* were eager to mix in with the battle raging all around them but were told they would not be required. Commander V. Gibbs was ordered to take *Iris* out to the rendezvous position, where both *Vindictive* and *Daffodil* would join her. She drew away from the Mole and had just cleared *Vindictive*'s protecting bulk when she was spotted by the German guns on the Mole extension. Fate took a hand in what followed. *Iris*'s smokescreen equipment failed her and, almost immediately, she was hit by an accurate salvo of shells which burst on her main deck where the landing parties crouched like sardines in a tin. Gibbs and several other officers were killed or wounded, along with the crouching men. She was saved from further punishment by an observant ML commander, who swiftly closed on her and put out a dense smokescreen round her. But this commendable action was too late. By then *Iris* had suffered a total of 77 killed and 105 wounded. Not one of them had fired a shot in anger.

Among those killed in the Mole action was Wing Commander F.A. Brock. He should not have been there at all. Vice-Admiral Keyes had relented when Brock asked for permission to join the operation, as he was anxious to discover how the German sound-ranging system worked.

After satisfying himself that all ships had evacuated Zeebrugge harbour, Keyes took *Warwick* in closer to the Mole for a last look round before leaving. Already the brilliant flashes of bursting star shells were becoming desultory. Then the searchlights went out. In the contrasting blackness of the night a solitary white flare fell slowly, burning brighter as it descended over the harbour, the scene of so much fierce fighting, then it too went out.

But the destroyers were still dashing about like greyhounds, their decks tilting alarmingly as they made abrupt turns, trying to avoid the Mole battery's guns which had not been silenced. It was a fine show of bravado but *North Star* was hit by two salvoes. She stopped in her tracks, exposed to even more shells which completed her destruction. The remaining destroyers moved further out to sea. The operation was now complete.

Keyes had already returned at full speed to Dover, anxious to make his report to the Admiralty, but the news had reached them long before *Warwick*'s arrival. Within a few hours Keyes was being proclaimed a hero. The War Cabinet, Admiralty and War Office each sent their praises of his achievements. Eventually, the decorations awarded for gallantry, bravery and courage came to 11 VCs, 21 DSOs, 29 DSCs, 16 CGMs and 143 DSMs. In the final analysis of the night's action, the total casualties killed, wounded or missing had amounted to 635 of all ranks. One marine officer and fourteen marines failed to re-embark and were taken prisoners of war.

Before and after. The *Vindictive* cruiser, built in 1897, was used to disembark troops on to the Zeebrugge Mole on 23 April 1918. The emotive drawing by Charles de Lacey shows her returning to Dover after the action.

'In the contrasting blackness of the night a solitary flare fell slowly, burning brighter as it descended over the harbour.' *Intrepid* and *Iphigenia* blocking the Zeebrugge canal.

The canal system at low water was unusable by the Germans but at high water small TBDs could pass through the locks the next day. On 25 April six TBDs went through but the destroyers under repair at Bruges were confined to their moorings. One or two small submarines negotiated the obstructions at high water. *UB16* was one of the first to do so but she was torpedoed by a British submarine, *E34*, off the Essex coast on 10 May. Later, when the suggestion to raise the blockships was rejected, the canal banks were widened.

The Admiralty had considered the operation a success, despite the awful sacrifice of the gallant landing parties and the loss of *North Star* and two motor launches. A German historian said, 'The English attack on Zeebrugge is a model of a meticulously planned, magnificently prepared and boldly executed attempt to eliminate a strongly defended enemy base by blocking it from the sea. The leadership was in the hands of a battle-proven, experienced and determined Admiral.' Vice-Admiral Keyes was later awarded a peerage, to take the title of Baron Keyes of Zeebrugge and Dover.

There can be no denying the fact that Keyes' monumental achievement at Zeebrugge cast a shadow over his predecessor Admiral Bacon, whose resourcefulness to adapt to any given situation had now paled into insignificance.

Total casualties in the St George's Day operation – killed, wounded or missing – had amounted to 635 of all ranks. Here, British prisoners are being marched away from Ostend.

Of all the nagging disappointments to arise from the action, the main one was the failure of the newly formed Royal Air Force, the amalgamation of the RFC and RNAS on 1 April, to bomb the German shipping interned at Bruges. The Handley Page bombers, formerly under the control of the Vice-Admiral Dover, had left the area after the reorganization of the two separate commands and the RAF commanders failed to appreciate the importance of knocking out the Bruges-based vessels.

In the event, one cannot overestimate the success of the St George's Day action. There was a sense that history had been made that day, which would always be remembered in the annals of naval engagements. But there was a more immediate effect of greater importance that was quite unforeseen. It was like a gleam of light in the darkness of war. Hope swelled in the breasts of the utterly dejected army in France. The long drawn-out trench warfare was so hideously repetitive. It lacked sparkle and achievement. The St George's day success also gave some credence to the overwrought civilians at home, that something had happened to which everyone could relate.

The Ostend part of the operation, however, seemed to go awry from the onset. For one thing there was no diversionary attack like that performed at Zeebrugge. Approaching the Belgian coast on a southerly course the two blockships *Brilliant* and

Men of *Vindictive* back at Dover. There was a sense that history had been made on St George's Day, which would always be remembered in the annals of naval actions.

Sirius, under Commander A.E. Godsal and Lieutenant-Commander H.N.M. Hardy respectively, reached their planned positions off the Stroom Bank buoy on time. Escorted by the destroyers under Commodore Lynes, the MLs and CMBs were to lay the smokescreens, mark the entrance to the harbour with calcium buoys and would eventually be responsible for rescuing the crews of the sunken blockships.

Everything was going to plan until the wind dropped suddenly and then a light breeze began to blow from the shore. The black sooty substance erupting from the fast-moving motor boats spread like a low-lying cloud upon the water. It then drifted slowly out to sea. The destroyers rushed to make more smoke, running back and forth until they were enveloped in the choking filthy cloud, reeking of oil and chemicals.

But the marker buoy was not in its proper position. Commander Godsal was quite unaware it had been moved overnight by the Germans to a new position rather more than a mile to the east. It was discovered much later that the Germans had swept up a British mine in the area of the buoy and had immediately adopted a new route for their vessels well to the eastwards. Godsal steered for the harbour entrance, despite the absence of the marker buoy. A few minutes later they spotted the buoy. Godsal altered course towards it, then, at least one mile to port, he altered course again.

The thickening smokescreens dampened by the rain, no other markers were visible to

'. . . there were no other markers visible to indicate an error. A few minutes later both *Brilliant* and *Sirius* ran aground.'

indicate a navigational error. A few minutes later both blockships, now just one mile to the east of the Ostend piers, ran aground. Realizing the futility of ever getting the vessels off, and coming under increasingly accurate shell fire from the German shore batteries, Godsal had no alternative but to blow the bottoms out of them where they lay. The attendant motor launches closed the sinking ships and rescued the crews without suffering casualties.

The Ostend operation had come to a sad end and all other vessels returned to Dover without further delay. But the abandonment was not to last. Officers whose enthusiasm had been sorely dampened were reluctant to admit to failure, and their obvious enthusiasm to try again convinced not only Vice-Admiral Keyes but also the Admiralty. Weather conditions permitting, it was decided to make another attempt.

The old *Vindictive* was still seaworthy, despite the battering she had received at Zeebrugge, and with a possible date of 9 May for the new attempt, there were ten days available for preparation. The Apollo class cruiser *Sappho* was obtained as the second blockship; *Vindictive* was to be commanded by Godsal and *Sappho* by Hardy. Commodore Lynes was retained to command the whole operation.

Intelligence reports suggested that a strong force of nine German destroyers had recently arrived at Zeebrugge. This force would have been a thorn in the side of Lynes' left flank, as he did not possess sufficient strength to protect it against enemy destroyers. The Vice-Admiral decided to perform this task in *Warwick*, supported by another three specially selected destroyers. He was also anxious to confront the enemy and hoped German destroyers would give him an opportunity to engage them.

All preparations completed for the new attempt, Keyes received a telegram on 8 May from the king of the Belgians, asking for a meeting next day at La Panne. Keyes left for Dunkirk in *Warwick*, quite unaware that he was to receive the Star of a Grand Officer of the Order of Leopold. After lunch, Keyes, while walking along the sands with King Albert and Queen Elizabeth, could not help noticing a slight breeze blowing from the seaward. He could not afford to miss this opportunity and sent a signal for all ships to stand by. Another signal was sent while he returned to Dover in *Warwick* at full speed. As *Warwick* made her approach *Vindictive* and *Sappho* were already pushing into the swell outside the harbour. Keyes signalled them to stop, went alongside each vessel in turn, boarded them, and wished them God speed.

But the Ostend operation was doomed to failure. *Sappho* developed an engine fault that reduced her speed by half. She could never expect to reach Ostend in the time remaining. Godsal received her signal with some trepidation. *Vindictive* continued her journey. This final leg was a proposition which Godsal viewed with the least enthusiasm, especially as a dense fog increased the difficulty of finding the harbour entrance.

When *Vindictive* at last began her final approach, the channel between the piers was being fiercely defended by the German shore batteries. Having already passed through the barrage of shells successfully, Godsal was on the point of swinging his ship across the channel when a heavy calibre shell exploded beside him. He was never seen again. *Vindictive* ran aground before Lieutenant V.A.C. Crutchley, who assumed command, could do anything further. Unable to recover his position, Crutchley had no alternative but to blow the ship's fuses where she lay. In doing so, it left a considerable seaway between her stern and the west pier.

Intense machine-gun fire presented the most hazardous conditions ever imagined, as the crew clambered over the railings to the waiting MLs *254* and *276*. Bullets smashed into everything and in a short space of time, the rescue boat *254* was near to sinking. The ML crews had suffered a number of casualties. Conditions were deplorable and both her officers had been hit. Lieutenant G. Ross had been killed, while Lieutenant G.H. Drummond was wounded. Crutchley, who was to win the Victoria Cross for his consummate bravery, succeeded in getting the craft away stern first. Meanwhile Admiral Keyes in *Warwick* had remained close-in to the coast, ever hopeful to engage an enemy destroyer. It was his persistence which enabled him to see Crutchley's distress signal from the sinking *254*. It was the ML's salvation. *Warwick* closed with *254* quickly. On board were wounded and dying men and those who had the strength were furiously bailing out. When the last man had been taken off the launch drifted away.

Warwick and her three consorts set course for Dover. But she was not out of the conflict yet. While still within range of enemy guns she had the misfortune to run into a rogue mine which damaged her stern. Her escorts closed in rapidly. One of them lashed a cable alongside to keep her afloat, while the other took her in tow. The third destroyer kept watch to the eastwards. Steadily approaching Dover at midday she was met by just about every vessel that could manage to raise steam and slip their moorings. It was an indescribable scene when she limped into the harbour surrounded by ships of every description.

SIX ZEEBRUGGE HEROES RECEIVE THE V.C.

ZEEBRUGGE D.S.C.

Sgt.-Maj. Thatcher, R.M.L.I., received the D.S.C. for his work in carrying heavy scaling ladders from his ship to the Mole.

At His Majesty's Investiture yesterday scenes of great enthusiasm marked the presentation of the V.C. to six heroes of the Zeebrugge and Ostend operation. They were: 1. Sergeant N. A. Finch, V.C., R.M.A. (on left), leaving the Palace with his relatives. 2. Lieut. P. T. Dean, V.C., R.N.V.R. 3. Lieut. R. D. Sandford, V.C., R.N. 4. Major Edward Bamford, V.C., D.S.O., R.M.L.I. 5. Commander Alfred B. Carpenter, V.C., who was in charge of the Vindictive. 6. Able Seaman A. E. MacKenzie, who limped to the dais on crutches, with his mother.

Heroes of the Zeebrugge and Ostend operation attending the investiture at Buckingham Palace.

The Flanders submarine flotilla was losing one U-boat every week. The average life of any class of boat, UB or UC, was down to about six patrols. If they had reached their base safely after passing through a formidable array of measures designed to stop them – aircraft, airships, destroyers or minefields – they were then subjected to nightly air raids. What should have been a haven of rest, Bruges, was under constant attack. The large concrete, bombproof U-boat pens, with roofs six feet thick, withstood the battering of

V.C. IN THE OLD KENT ROAD.

The Mayor of Southwark escorting Able Seaman Albert MacKenzie, R.N. (on crutches), to his home off the Old Kent Road on his return from Buckingham Palace, where he received the V.C. for his share in the Zeebrugge exploit. He landed on the Mole, advanced down it with a machine gun, and did great execution.

Captain A. F. B. Carpenter, R.N. (right), selected to receive the V.C. for his services in command of the Vindictive on 22nd-23rd April. Commander E. O. B. S. Osborne, R.N. (left), was responsible for the fitting out of the Vindictive with howitzers, etc. Awarded D.S.O. ("Daily Graphic" photo.)

Lieut. R. D. Sandford, R.N., in command of submarine C 3, awarded the V.C. for the hazardous enterprise of blowing up his vessel between the piles of the viaduct.

Lieut. S. S. Bonham-Carter, awarded D.S.O. for his success in sinking the Intrepid in the Bruges Canal. (Russell, Southsea.)

Lt. Roland Bourke, R.N.V.R., receives the D.S.O. for his rescue work with a motor launch under heavy fire. (Lafayette.)

There were six VCs who attended the Buckingham Palace investiture.

The concrete-built U-boat pens at Bruges withstood the intensive bombing raids made upon them by the RNAS of Dover Command.

the latest 500-lb bombs, but other less well-protected buildings associated with submarines, such as workshops and barracks, were plastered beyond recognition.

Oberleutnant H. Kukat took *UC78* out of Ostend harbour during the night of 1 May, turning west to avoid the first obstacles of mines around the Scheldt. Using this route he avoided the long detour through Dutch waters before altering course. He decided to run on the surface, not only to make a faster speed, but because he knew he could not dive below the first mine net encountered because of shallow water. Festooned with mines, some nets were laid very deep outside the shoals but Kukat's charts showed where the nets had been holed by the Flanders-based minesweepers. The only option open to him was to pass over the barrages on approach and hope that luck was on his side. If he succeeded Kukat's next encounter was another net strung out from the Goodwin Sands to Snou Bank. Again he would try to pass over it rather than go under it, either way it was a hazardous job.

Kukat had so far succeeded but even so he was not yet in the clear. Ordinarily sea mists and fogs assisted U-boat commanders in their ordeal but to run through the Straits on the surface in 1918 was a very brave act indeed. Kapitän Bartenbach, commanding the Flanders submarine flotillas, acknowledged the signals of both *UC78* and *UB31* as they passed the pier-head observation post. He was aware of the tremendous courage of his U-boat captains, acutely aware also, that few survived their terrible ordeal. No fewer than 75 of his submarines had so far been lost, taking with them 140 officers and 1,000 men. That they had destroyed 2,550 allied ships, either by

SS. Z29 hovered over the U-boats like a predator, the crew excited by the prospect of a grandstand view of impending action.

mine, torpedo or gunfire, a third of all shipping sunk, somehow seemed to him totally irrelevant.

Oberleutnant W. Braun in *UB31* decided to stay on the surface like his compatriot Kukat. Both U-boats were not more than three miles distant from each other when the anti-submarine airship SS.Z29 spotted them at 0800 hrs. The inevitable Verey light spluttered into the morning sky as the airship swung her nose towards the two unsuspecting submarines. The drifters *Mary*, *BTB* and *Our Friend* quickly left their positions on the eastern side of the Folkestone minefield, quickly followed by *Lord Leitrim*, *Loyal Friend* and *Ocean Roamer*. Both U-boats had dived below the waves as the drifters moved in for the kill. The days when the sea was sufficiently pure and transparent to reveal a submerged U-boat were few. But on this occasion the sun's rays were parallel and the U-boats' upper decks and bulbous hulls were thrown in shadow across the bottom of the sea. SS.Z29 hovered over the shadows – a silver-coloured predator – all the while circling like an albatross, the four-man crew excited by the prospect of a grandstand view of the action to come. The drifters moved in for the kill. Neither U-boat could avoid the concentration of explosives which tumbled over the sides of the drifters. They both perished without a fight. When the drifters moved away there were two red flags fluttering in the morning breeze secured to buoys that marked the spot where Kukat and Braun met their fate.

CHAPTER NINE

'It Was Like a Rowing Gala'

The new Royal Air Force bore no comparison to the humble force dispatched to France in August 1914. The aircraft industry alone had grown enormously by 1918 but since the amalgamation much of the strategic planning of air operations within Keyes' command was taken from him. Had the planning not changed hands, his squadrons would have been engaged in strategic bombing of German industry, as well as providing the photographic reconnaissance they so ably performed every day.

It is worth mentioning that when the Admiralty totted up their October returns for 1918, they were astounded to learn that the two sister stations, Dunkirk and Dover, had between them more aircraft than was available for the whole defence of the United Kingdom. A rapid tactical change resulted in seaplanes of various types being sent to less fortunate stations.

At last the RAF began bombing the enemy vessels still moored in the Bruges canal system. Keyes was delighted with this belated attempt but was quick to point out that similar bombing should have taken place immediately after St George's Day action. In the event, the bombing provoked instant retaliation. On 6–7 June enemy aircraft successfully attacked Dunkirk. Three officers and nine men were killed and several wounded at the former RNAS station, where four hangars were burned to the ground and others wrecked. Five aircraft were destroyed and forty-eight damaged. There was, however, one major stroke of luck. Fortunately the Handley Page bombers were actually attacking Bruges when their airfield was being bombed and were obliged to make a landing upon the sand dunes near Calais.

Retaliatory air attacks increased upon the RAF shore bases in and around Dunkirk, resulting in some ferocious air fighting where losses were inflicted on both sides. The monitor *Erebus*, at anchor in the harbour, was hit on several occasions and her anti-torpedo bulges were damaged. Considering the enormous bomb tonnage dropped over the whole area it was surprising that she was the only ship to suffer damage.

There were more mine explosions in the Folkestone minefield. On 31 May a huge explosion occurred that sent up an oil slick to the surface. It was not until two months had passed that a diver went down to investigate and found Oberleutnant W. Kolbe's *UB119* with her stern blown off. Then just before dawn on 20 June Oberleutnant F. Schwartz, commanding *UC64*, was forced to dive by approaching drifters and blew herself up in the process. In July all the special lightships were in their correct positions over the Folkestone minefield but even so the U-boats still used this deadly route. On

10 July Oberleutnant J. Ries, commanding *UC77*, tried to run through in the evening but he was inexperienced and left a trail of air bubbles behind him on the surface of the water while submerged. It was a simple task for the trawlers to depth charge him to destruction. The tally board, hanging up in Kapitän Bartenbach's office in Bruges, denoting the U-boats at home and those out on patrol, was showing an increase in 'missing' craft. Kapitänleutnant W. Amberger of *UB108* disappeared in mysterious circumstances. A big question mark was shown against his name on the last day of July.

A new ship *Gorgon*, originally built for the Norwegian Navy as a coastal defence monitor, edged slowly towards her mooring buoy at Dover at the end of July. Her two 9.4-in guns had been relined at Chatham so as to accept the British 9.2-in shell and she was also given an increased elevation of 42 degrees to enable her to reach 35,000 yards range. Her baptism of fire occurred on 26 July, when she calibrated her guns upon the German howitzer battery at Leugenboom.

To ensure enemy destroyers using Zeebrugge would remain hemmed in and unable to leave without hindrance, the Vice-Admiral decided to use the new magnetic mine. The flotilla leader *Abdiel*, together with five other minelaying destroyers, laid a string of these latest mines in the approaches to Zeebrugge on the night of 7 August. On the following day there were several loud explosions detected on the directional hydrophone system. Intelligence reports suggested the torpedo boat *A58* was a casualty and also *UB57* commanded by Oberleutnant J. Losz, which was lost on 14 August.

Field Marshal von Hindenburg, Chief of Staff, and General Ludendorff told their new Chief of Naval Staff, Admiral Scheer, that only German U-boats could win the war. At a meeting of the Crown Council at Spar, Ludendorff recommended immediate peace. The Kaiser warned that Austria–Hungary could only continue the war until December.

Since February 1918 almost all the larger U-boats had been ordered to use the northern route, resulting in a loss of six days' cruising time. The German High Command had already recalled a part of the submarine flotillas back to German bases during the summer months because of the tightening defence measures in the Dover Strait. One of the innovations was the electrical loop-line system, spaced at intervals between Beachy Head and North Foreland, which showed a meter reading when a vessel passed over it. This particular system assisted the hydrophone units also spaced along the Kent and Sussex coasts.

The Folkestone observation post reported a fast-running engine at 0310 hrs on 29 August, following by a blip on the meter of the loop-line. The order was given to fire the electrically operated mines, resulting in a huge explosion and which sent two officers and six men shooting up to the surface in a large air bubble. Kapitänleutnant Ramien was among the survivors of *UB109*, who revealed to the trawler skipper who picked them up that he had passed beneath the illuminated minefield successfully but was unaware of Professor Bragg's electrical loop system of detection. The new defence system was a marked success, even before the introduction of the armed towers, still under construction.

With the August offensive now in full swing and Sir Douglas Haig planning to reach the Belgian coast, all thoughts of a German invasion of England had long since been dismissed as impractical. Vice-Admiral Keyes had already shut down Dover's submarine depot and was now employing service women (WRNS) in almost every department, thus releasing sailors for other duties.

The monitor *General Wolfe* re-appeared at Dover with her new 18-in gun and in time to take part in the new offensive to assist Haig's push along the Belgian coast. She was accompanied by the monitor *Glatton*, a sister ship to *Gorgon*, and also built for the Norwegian Navy.

The all out offensive by Haig's forces began on the Somme and it was of such gigantic proportions that it took the German generals by surprise. It was in stark contrast to all previous large-scale operations on the Western Front and was to swiftly turn the tide of bloody warfare and horror into a changing scene of hope. As the British, French, Belgian and American divisions progressed with their counter-offensive, so the Admiralty was involved in the recapture of the Flanders coast.

With this in mind, towards the end of August the monitors assembled in Dover harbour to await their instructions to bombard. They took up mooring positions decided by their tonnage and draught. At about 1830 hrs on 16 September, a southerly breeze with just that hint of an autumn coolness tugged at two dozen naval ensigns at their stern posts. The immaculate monitors – grey and sombre, their guns capped with canvas hoods – hardly moved in the slight swell, the cables were drawn taut between bow and buoy, the line of ships was impeccable. They seemed aloof from the hectic comings and goings of countless lighters and barges which had brought fuel oil, water, provisions and ammunition throughout the day. Naval ratings on watch gazed longingly at the town bathed in the evening sunlight. Most wished it had been their turn to visit the public houses in Snargate Street. Along its entire length the Dover promenade was dotted with townsfolk and, here and there, the dark-blue uniforms of off-duty ratings could be seen with their girlfriends. This calm, almost tranquil scene of a typically English summer's eve was soon to erupt into the last disaster to befall the town during the war.

On 16 September there had been little movement on board the monitors since the second dog watch was piped. Bilge water cascaded from vents and pipes and the shrill blast of the ship's bulges, calling officers to wardroom, had long since penetrated the decks, galleys and cabins. In fact, the officers were already dressing for their evening meal on *General Crauford*, *General Wolfe*, *Lord Clive*, *Prince Eugene*, *Prince Rupert* and *Sir John Moore*. *Marshal Soult* with her 15-in guns was dwarfed by *Erebus* and *Terror*.

Near to the eastern arm of the harbour, some 500 yards from the beach, were the two new monitors built originally for Norway, carrying their nameplates *Bjoergvin* and *Nidaros* bolted to their respective superstructures. Armed with their re-lined 9.2-in and four 6-in guns in turrets and with an estimated speed of 15 knots, comparable with *Erebus* and *Terror*, they were now known as *Gorgon* and *Glatton* and were expected to prove very useful for the next offshore offensive.

First commissioned at Newcastle on 31 August 1918 at a cost of £513,000, *Glatton* was captained by Commander N.W. Diggle RN. She completed her sea trials in just under two days and left for Dover on 9 September, arriving two days later to join the rest of the bombardment force. She had tied up to No. 2 buoy close to the steamer *Gransha*, a small ammunition ship laden with shell and cordite charges ready for the big offensive. Several other vessels close to her also carried shell and cordite, not to mention the odd one or two that had no magazines at all and were obliged to carry their explosives on deck. By and large, there was enough high explosive around in one shape

HMS *Glatton* was anchored close to the Camber area in Dover's harbour, when one of her magazines exploded.

or another to blast the town and dockyard from the face of the earth, let alone try to blast the Germans from their entrenchments on the Flanders coast.

The Vice-Admiral, now Sir Roger Keyes, was dining in his bungalow near South Foreland when he received an urgent telephone call that a disaster had occurred in the harbour. Keyes had actually heard the enormous bang and rumble, which had reverberated between the hills on either side of the town. People on the seafront promenade were not only startled but some were knocked off their feet by the blast. The force of it shook the very pavements they were standing on and windows nearby were shattered. They saw a huge yellow flame leap into the evening sky from one of the ships lying at anchor, followed by a tremendous gush of grey-white smoke. HMS *Glatton* had erupted amidships.

It happened at a moment when seamen were relaxed in the comparative safety of a home anchorage: they were suddenly thrown to the decking and against the bulkheads. All thoughts of relaxation were lost in the rush of pounding feet on iron decks amid smoke and flames. Those below deck scrambled towards the nearest companion-way. Many of the already shocked matelots were beaten back by the fierce heat taking control of the narrow passages, eating up the oxygen as it seared through open hatches. Almost at once the decks of every ship in harbour became thronged with sailors. Then, as if acting under one supreme order, every ship began to launch their cutters and small lifeboats. It was an incredible sight. One onlooker recalled, 'It was like looking at a rowing gala night . . . small boats were pulling towards the *Glatton* and within a few minutes, there were dozens, including pinnaces, surrounding the stricken ship and taking off survivors.'

Gransha slipped her mooring and moved slowly away to safety. The tug *Lady Brassey*, with two small tenders round her like ducklings, moved in close in an attempt to extinguish the flames by pumping water. But the fuel oil had also caught alight by then. The situation was becoming critical. The after magazine was unable to be flooded and there was every possibility of an even greater explosion. It was then that every ship in close proximity was sent a signal to move away. Shackle pins were knocked out and the great monitors retreated towards the Prince of Wales pier. It was an extraordinary sight. One by one they slowly moved astern until there seemed little space left for water, for not only the monitors were seeking a new anchorage but other ships as well, including about two dozen destroyers, drifters, trawlers and minesweepers. The harbour soon became unbalanced to the eye. At one end of the harbour there was a conglomeration of funnels, masts and huge guns while at the other end, the stricken *Glatton*, now with a slight list to port, was alone, her starboard anti-torpedo bulge glistening in the evening sunlight like a disorientated whale.

Through the dense smoke there appeared small boats carrying the injured, many of them terribly scorched and some with mangled arms and legs. Both horse-drawn and motor-driven ambulances stood at the quayside to relay them to sick bay. No one knew for certain if a further explosion would occur. Only one of *Glatton*'s magazines had blown up, that amidships; the forward magazine was successfully flooded but not the aft. The valve which allowed water in to sink the ship could not be reached. There was imminent danger and yet the rescuing of survivors continued until the Vice-Admiral arrived. It was soon plain to Keyes that neither the flames could be quenched nor the ship sunk by conventional methods. He decided to sink her by torpedo. Garrison troops with fixed bayonets were ordered to clear the seafront.

It was now 1900 hrs and the explosion and resulting fire had cut off the aft part of the ship completely, killing or seriously wounding considerable numbers of the ship's company. However, in defiance of the obvious dangers, Lieutenant Belben, Sub-Lieutenant Evans, Petty Officer Stoker and Able Seaman Nunn, quite unaware that the destroyer *Cossack* was slowly positioning to fire her first torpedo, continued their rescue attempts on their own initiative. Without any kind of breathing apparatus, and despite the danger, they entered the superstructure, climbing down the companion-ways to the deck below. Time and again they were driven back by the intense heat and flames but they stubbornly refused to give up. They were successful in rescuing twenty-three men, eight of whom were seriously injured. All four men were subsequently awarded the Albert Medal for bravery.

As the last craft left the side of *Glatton*, screams and shouts for help from the lower decks were still audible above the noise of escaping steam and the roaring flames fanned by a persistent breeze. A signal was sent to *Cossack*. She fired her port tube. The torpedo failed to explode because it had not travelled far enough to deactivate the safety device. *Cossack*'s second torpedo drove through the starboard side amidships. A fierce shaft of flame belched from *Glatton*'s funnel but the 200 pounds of explosive was not enough to sink her.

Glatton heeled over on to her port side and settled to the bottom. *Cossack* and *Myngs* slowly moved astern in the disturbed waters.

In the fading twilight millions of yellow and red sparks flew into the sky, disappearing into a cloud of black oily smoke that hung above the harbour, then drifted over the town like a canopy of doom. Keyes watched the disappointing results of his decision to end *Glatton* as a fighting ship for ever. He signalled the destroyer *Myngs* to fire two torpedoes. *Glatton* keeled over on to her port side and settled to the bottom. *Cossack* and *Myngs*, their task done, slowly moved astern, while huge air bubbles disturbed the water around *Glatton*'s last resting place.

There had been a loss of nearly fifty lives and a further fifty-seven men were unaccounted for: they presumably had been trapped below decks when the torpedoes struck. More than three-quarters of the ship's company had either been killed or injured but afterwards it was realized that sinking the monitor had saved many lives. For many months *Glatton* was visible only at low tide, lying on her side, a sad reminder of the misfortunes of war.

Time was running out for the Kaiser's submarines. Kapitänleutnant P. Hundius, commander of *UB103*, left his Flanders base on the night of 15 September with thirty-four crew, six torpedoes and enough ammunition to serve his 4.1-in gun if it was needed to either defend his boat or to sink a ship. But Hundius and his U-boat were never given the opportunity to do either. *UB103* was to enter the record books as the last German submarine to be sunk in the Dover Strait during the First World War. Hundius had settled his boat on the bottom between net barrages during the night, waiting to surface and smell the clean autumn air next morning.

The sky was yet to change from night into day when the bows of *UB103* broke the surface to shake off the green water. The captain climbed up to the conning tower and breathed in the chill air. By coming up from the bottom Hundius had adopted a wholly convincing devil-may-care attitude. Unless he was about to die through circumstances other than war, he would not be thought well of for putting his crew in danger. It was almost suicide to run on the surface of the Straits in 1918. Suicide missions were not the brief of U-boat captains; after all, it is against nature, an insult to one's culture and would be viewed by his seniors as an ambitious, ostentatious act. Even so, given the result, it would have taken extraordinary bravery to attempt such a run on the surface. Whether Hundius was at all worried about his place in history, as he was about to go down in defeat, is difficult to imagine. He may have been too cynical and disillusioned and may have discovered that U-boat captains were merely playthings of the Kaiser. In any event, it was his first mistake.

SS.Z1 had wobbled into the early morning air from its green swathe above Folkestone on 16 September and set course out over the Channel, climbing all the while to reach 5,000 feet. Pilot and observer looked down on the water just as the sun broke through low cloud over Belgium. Hundius was recharging his batteries in more than one sense – his mind and the mechanical batteries of his submarine. He took one more gulp of fresh air and one last look at the breathtaking spectacle of the pink hue of dawn, then ordered 'Dive!'

But pilot and observer of SS.Z1 had already seen the dark shape running on the surface. The observer fired a Verey cartridge into the morning air while the pilot turned the nose of his airship towards its prey. Two barrage patrol drifters answered the call for help. It was another chance to reap the harvest of a £1,000 prize. The SS.Z1's pilot had already calculated speed, drift and tide to estimate the time it would take to reach his quarry. The airship crew watched the U-boat submerge beneath the waves. Hundius had seen the Verey light shoot up into the sky and was aware that drifters had been warned of his approach. From the air the submerged craft could clearly be seen and gave an indication of its course.

In line abreast, the two drifters saw a second cartridge splutter into the sky. UB103's slow progress at no more than 6 knots prevented Hundius from making a run for it. He then made a second mistake, for he was quite aware that he had been spotted. He ordered the periscope to be raised and saw the two drifters looming up ahead. The periscope wash gave his position away more clearly than anything else. It was a mistake which cost him his life and those of his crew. The airship crew watched the depth charges explode at intervals. The sea boiled but UB103 was not seen again.

Kapitän Bartenbach in Bruges was to strike off another of his U-boats on that same day. Oberleutnant U. Pilzeder in UB113 had disappeared without trace. The submarine's loss might have been due to an accident. UB113 probably sits on the bottom of the Dover Strait, still intact and in perfect working order, her crew poisoned by toxic battery fumes.

Field Marshal Haig's massive offensive due on 28 September meant there were three British, Belgian and French army divisions poised to attack German positions simultaneously at Ypres. Leading up to this assault Dover Command was to dupe the Germans into thinking a landing on the Flanders coast was imminent. Two divisions of monitors, together with the Royal Marine Artillery siege guns, were to open fire upon

The periscope wash gave *UB103*'s position away more clearly than anything else. The crew of SS. Z1 watched the depth charges explode.

the enemy shore batteries. The monitors were reinforced by a third division and between them would endeavour to destroy enemy communications, roads, railways and generally harass movements between Nieuport and Ostend. Keyes had decided to land a brigade of bluejackets and marines, a plan almost identical to that which Bacon had envisaged the year before his dismissal. Keyes agreed to embark troops in three monitors and to run them in under cover of smokescreens at high water. The idea was to prevent Ostend harbour being blocked or destroyed by retreating Germans.

The Vice-Admiral, his flag at the mast of *Prince Eugene*, left Dover for Dunkirk on the afternoon tide on 17 September. That evening the bombardment began in gale-force winds which fiercely blew from the north-west, accompanied by rain. The weather seriously curtailed the armies but both the British and Belgians managed to break through enemy lines. The French division, however, failed to consolidate their objective. History reveals that the French troops, who had fought so well on their own soil, were not prepared to die in Flanders. As a result, the whole offensive came to a standstill, which enabled the Germans to reorganize their defence and completely block Ostend harbour with a minefield.

The *Onward* cross-Channel packet boat, used as a troopship, lay beside Folkestone's pier waiting to embark troops on 18 September when she was suddenly consumed by a fire in the salon. Seacocks were quickly opened but she gradually settled lower in the water to eventually keel over on her port side. She was to remain in that position for

The monitor *Lord Clive* in Dunkirk harbour, showing some extra gadgetry attached to her anti-submarine bulges, port and starboard.

about a month while her funnels and masts were cut away and removed. She was later brought upright using five steam locomotives pulling cables running through enormous baulk timber tripods. Explosive experts discovered that a thermite incendiary device had been hidden in a pile of lifebelts.

The monitors continued to bombard the enemy shore positions and, in addition, Keyes used his CMBs to destroy the enemy's minefield laid to the approaches to Ostend. Lieutenant Welman tried vainly to blow up as many as was humanly possible in the most appalling sea conditions. He raced about the waters at high speed dropping depth charges over the stern of his craft. One of his boats was lost during the night's escapade, so the operation was called off. The bodies of the crew, three officers and two ratings, were washed ashore at La Panne a few days later.

Another offensive was begun on 14 October. The Vice-Admiral had already sent for one of the huge 800-foot-long pontoons, built originally for Admiral Bacon's 'great landing' scheme which was later abandoned. With an escort of small craft, Keyes was hoping to mislead the enemy into thinking that a landing was about to take place. He had hoisted his flag on *Termagant* and the pontoon had already been exposed to the enemy's view. His next bombardment commenced at 1730 hrs but there was no reply from the German gun batteries. No one quite knew if the Germans were still in their positions. The Vice-Admiral then received a signal to make a reconnaissance along the Belgian coast that afternoon. At 1400 hrs the monitor *Gorgon*, screened by three 30-knotters, and

Experts thought it was sabotage that sank the troopship *Onward* in Folkestone Harbour on 18 September 1918.

Funnels and mast cut away, *Onward* slowly moves to the perpendicular, helped by cables and tripods attached to five steam locomotives.

the flotilla leader *Termagant* took a course through the West Deep shoals at about 14 knots, followed by *Prince Eugene* and *Sir John Moore*, surrounded by smoke-laying MLs. *Gorgon* opened fire while still underway but the enemy withheld their fire until the monitor was closer to Westende. Both the Tirpitz and Raversyde batteries then opened fire. Amid huge columns of water thrown up by the high explosive shells, *Gorgon* turned sharply out of the way. Her escorting destroyers dashed about to cover her withdrawal with a black dense smokescreen. Three days later, the Vice-Admiral made another reconnoitre, this time making a series of slow, probing movements, stopping awhile, then edging ever closer to the coast. But nothing happened. He then advanced even closer until *Termagant* was almost at the entrance to Ostend harbour. Here he was stopped by some Belgian fishermen in a small dinghy, who warned him of the dangerous minefield ahead. Keyes was rowed into the harbour and considered that his ship was the first British vessel to 'take' the port.

Vice-Admiral Keyes, who had often visited King Albert and Queen Elizabeth of the Belgians at their small villa near La Panne, accompanied their majesties to Ostend that very evening, at their request. Zeebrugge was occupied by the Allies on 19 October. It was only when the advances of the Allied armies along the Flanders coast threatened to overrun the vast complex of repair docks, torpedo dumps and barracks, that the Germans reluctantly ordered the evacuation. All available submarines and TBDs escaped north to their German bases except for those caught in dry dock under repair. These were scuttled by the crews.

But it was not all plain sailing for the Dover Patrol. While the *Termagant* was making another tentative reconnaissance to the eastward and escorted by the French destroyer *Lestin*, the paddle minesweeper *Plumpton* struck a mine. The explosion ripped away the bridge killing her commander, Lieutenant G.A. Drummond DSC, RNR, Sub-Lieutenant Collet and seven ratings. The aft mess deck and the port-side stokehold were just a mass of tangled debris. *Plumpton* was eventually towed by the Dance class *Quadrille* paddle minesweeper by her stern and beached east of Ostend pier.

Commander Buckland, Port Minesweeping Officer Dover, accompanied by Captain Hamilton Benn, in charge of the ML Flotilla, began a sweep with the tunnel minesweepers which had arrived at Dover in December 1917. Their light sweeping gear was no match for the heavily moored German mines. They were assisted in locating the minefields by MLs and seaplanes. Mines were discovered everywhere, even inside the Zeebrugge Mole area. Over ninety-three mines were destroyed along the Flanders coast, twenty-one of them inside Zeebrugge harbour.

On 20 October the small *M21* monitor struck a mine and sank, and on the following day *ML 561*, attempting to sink a mine by gunfire, suffered the same fate. The mines were particularly difficult to beat as the mooring system used by the Germans was exceptionally strong. The Vice-Admiral stopped all operations to clear them and asked the Admiralty to send out a team of experts. In the event they were cleared by chain sweeping the sea bottom.

The Kaiser's empire was falling apart at the seams, his invincible army had retreated on all fronts. The new chancellor, Prince Max of Baden, had already sought honourable terms from the Allies. President Wilson of the USA was quick to respond to the

UC4 was blown up at Bruges on
1 October 1918, together with several
others after serviceable U-boats were
evacuated.

Armistice suggestions by sending a cable outlining the first requirements that all
occupied territory must be released and further, that 'all inhuman acts must cease'.
When the Kaiser heard of this, he approached Prince Max to continue the U-boat
campaign.

Admiral Scheer agreed, believing that Germany's submarine warfare was the most
valuable contribution made by any of the military forces. The politicians were
completely disillusioned by the fanatical Kaiser and his close advisers. They were
anxious to placate the American President and even refused point-blank to agree with
any proposed unrestricted U-boat campaign. Admiral Scheer sent a signal to all U-boat
commanders informing them that attacks on passenger ships would cease on
21 October. This important transmitted wireless message resulted in U-boat
commanders setting course for the home bases.

But Scheer never gave up hope. His High Seas Fleet was still operative and President
Wilson's conditions had not mentioned attacks on warships. The Chief of Naval Staff,
Admiral von Hipper, together with Admiral Scheer, laid plans which would involve
surface craft and the submarines in a one-off two-pronged operation to attack the Allied
forces now occupying the Flanders bases, and to strike at Allied shipping in the Thames

The Kaiser, his empire falling apart at the seams, visits Admiral von Schroder's headquarters at Bruges, April 1918.

Estuary. Scheer got as far as allocating U-boats in stand-off positions in the North Sea with the intention of intercepting Admiral Beatty's Grand Fleet when Beatty decided to leave his Scottish anchorages.

Had this particular plan been augmented then perhaps the ensuing battle would have been the greatest ever fought. But Scheer had rejected as nonsense the mutinous agitators that had suddenly arisen like a phoenix from the ashes in every naval base. Aided by seditious leaflets circulated to every ship the German sailors openly discussed their problems and their grievances, especially showing their discontent at being held back in harbours for nigh on two years. Scheer's plan was to spark off the mutinous sailors who, when ordered to raise steam for the ambitious operation, smashed the anchor capstans of two battleships, thus preventing them from going to sea.

On the day *Glatton* had blown up amidships in Dover harbour, President Wilson had rejected the Austrian request for peace talks. Another peace offer to the Belgians, referring to a no claims for restitution, was also rejected by the Belgians three days later. The Allies had continued their advance during which the BEF had taken 30,000 prisoners. Speaking to 400 of his submarine commanders on 25 September, the Kaiser lectured them against treasonable activities. But only two weeks before one of his U-boats had torpedoed the Union Castle liner *Galway Castle* in the English Channel with a loss of 154 lives.

The illuminated minefield off Folkestone's Copt Point was considered the most successful of all the offensive measures, largely due to the increase of patrol vessels attending it. The Vice-Admiral and his officers had succeeded in tightening the defence network and, by so doing, had forced the Germans to rearrange their entire submarine operations. There was no doubt in Admiralty circles that Vice-Admiral Sir Roger Keyes had ruthlessly persecuted the U-boat commanders with such energy and persistence that they were forced into less favourable tactics.

Fear of this Bolshevick-inspired revolt in the German High Seas Fleet gripped the rest of the armed forces and they finally surrendered. The Naval terms of the Armistice agreement laid down that the German fleet was to be handed over to the Allies for internment pending the signing of the peace treaty. U-boats which had, in 1917, brought Great Britain to the brink of defeat, were the only threat remaining to the Royal Navy. Paragraph 22 of the Armistice agreement stated, in no uncertain terms:

Germany is to surrender at the ports specified by the Allies and the United States, that all submarines at present in existence (including all submarine cruisers and minelayers) with armament and equipment complete. Those that cannot put to sea shall be deprived of their armament and equipment and shall remain under the control of the Allies and the United States. Submarines ready to put to sea shall be prepared to leave German ports immediately on receipt of wireless orders to sail to the port of surrender, the remainder to follow as soon as possible. The conditions of this article shall be completed within fourteen days of the signing of the Armistice.

Under Royal Navy escort, the first surrendered U-boats, with white ensigns fluttering at their masts, arrived at Harwich. By the following month, 122 submarines had crossed the North Sea to dock at Harwich but not all of those destined to make that final trip actually made it. While in tow of Royal Navy vessels, at least seven foundered before reaching their specified destination. They had sprung leaks and sank, so it was said, but it was not difficult to assume the real reason for their demise. Such an ignominious end for an intensely proud service was too much to bear for some U-boat commanders.

And so there it was – defeat after four long years, the war was at last over. At the eleventh hour, on the eleventh day, of the eleventh month, the Armistice was signed. Celebrating peace was done in so many different ways. In the Flanders ports where the peoples had been under German occupation, and who had sustained the awful threat of Allied bombardments from the Dover Command's monitors and aircraft, civilians spilled out into the streets and cheered and cheered until they were exhausted. Likewise in Dover the seafront promenade was thronged with people and all vessels in the harbour blew their steam sirens until the cacophony of sound became unbearable.

A week later the king's message was read out to the ship's companies.

Ever since that fateful 4 August 1914, I have remained steadfast in my confidence that the Royal Navy would once more prove the sure shield of the British Empire in the hour of trial. Never in its history has the Royal Navy done greater things for us, nor better sustained its old glories.

King George V
21 November 1918

UB21 is seen here in Ramsgate Harbour on 16 December 1918. Kapitänleutnant Ernst Hashagen had sunk 130,000 tons of allied shipping.

Within just a few weeks of the Armistice, however, several of the Dover Command's destroyers were sent north to bolster the Grand Fleet in case the German High Seas fleet was intending to make one last appearance. Their task over, men of the Auxiliary Patrol who had manned the trawlers, drifters and other small craft were now seeking their release from wartime duties. These were the gallant fishermen who had faced death daily, laying mines, sweeping up mines, patrolling the mine nets and conducting with constant vigilance the spotting of enemy U-boats. They wanted to go home: they were not in the least interested in sweeping up mines now that the war was over. Surely the Royal Navy could manage those duties. Hearing the grievances Keyes had no alternative but to speak with the men he so admired. It was a point of honour, he told them, to see that no British Tommy returning from France should run the risk of being blown up by a mine. Keyes won the day and the men elected to continue clearing the minefields.

And so, in December 1918, Commander Colin S. Inglis DSO, RN, was appointed to command a flotilla of sixteen drifters engaged on minesweeping off the Flanders coast. The skippers had retained their own crews and began bottom-sweeping over 3,000 square miles of sea with special chains. The whole operation lasted for over six months, the flotilla being paid off in September 1919. During their attempts to secure a safe passage for the ships in the Dover Strait, a Mine Clearance Service was formed in February 1919 and seamen were enlisted to perform these hazardous duties. The men received special rates of pay and conditions of service and also wore the Mine Clearance Badge on their uniforms, specially approved by the king.

Several of Dover's destroyers were sent to bolster the Grand Fleet, after the Armistice, while trawlers and drifters were mustered to sweep the Dover Strait for mines.

Ten minesweepers were based at Dunkirk. They were of the Tunnel class, fitted with twin propellers in hollow dishes beneath the hull, and were originally built for river service in Mesopotamia. Because of their light construction they could only work in calm waters but, even so, they also attempted the impossible, searching for thousands of high explosive steel canisters which had lain undisturbed in the constant eddying of currents on the seabed.

Perhaps the most peculiar minesweepers were the Flemish dray horses employed in sweeping the Bruges canal. There is evidence to suggest they were rigged fore and aft in true naval fashion, carrying an ensign staff at the tail, a jack staff at the head and a mast amidships.

The number of German mines destroyed by the Dover Patrol vessels between July 1915 and November 1918 was 1,507 – this does not include the British mine. And so, from the latter half of 1915, 132 were found, 313 in 1916, 755 in 1917 and approximately 307 in 1918. The French minesweepers employed on the opposite side of the Dover Strait accounted for 427 overall.

Total movements of merchantmen – hospital ships, transports, troopships and numerous miscellaneous vessels, crossing the Dover Strait between 5 August 1914 and 11 November 1918 – came to 147,674. In addition, the gross tonnage of materials transported was 1,250,000 tons, which included 650,000 tons of ammunition of every calibre, while an approximate number of troops transported both ways was a staggering 16 million.

Epilogue

One of the last duties performed by Vice-Admiral Sir Roger Keyes was to accompany King George V to France when, with the Prince of Wales and Prince Albert (later George VI), His Majesty crossed the Strait to pay an extended visit to his armies in the field. Accompanied by King Albert of the Belgians, they also visited the scene of fighting at Zeebrugge. It was during the return journey that George V again honoured the Vice-Admiral by awarding him the KCVO, an award that Keyes afterwards remarked, 'I reluctantly accepted'.

In November 1918 an Executive Committee was formed for the erection by public subscription of memorial obelisks to honour the Dover Patrol. These were eventually sited at Leathercote Point, St Margarets, Cap Blanc Nez, on the French coast, and a facsimile monument was put up in New York harbour. Over £45,000 was collected by subscription and one of the first donations received was a cheque for the sum of £1,000 from King Albert and Queen Elizabeth of the Belgians. The Dover Patrol Memorial at Leathercote Point was unveiled by HRH the Prince of Wales on 27 July 1921. A Book of Remembrance, containing the names of nearly 2,000 members of the Dover Patrol who lost their lives, is held in St Margaret's church.

When the donation was received from the king of the Belgians, it was accompanied by a letter addressed to Vice-Admiral Sir Roger Keyes and was written in the king's own hand.

Brussels, 16 March 1919

Dear Admiral

The Queen and I would be glad to be among the subscribers to the Memorial of the Dover Patrol, and to see our names associated with the manifestations of gratitude and respect towards the splendid sailors whose skill and heroism largely prevented the enemy from making efficient use of his naval base on the Flemish Coast.

Having been more than four years in close contact with the Dover Patrol, we have been able to realize the immense services rendered to the defence of the Allies left flank by the continuous action of your ships and artillery.

We send you the enclosed subscription for the Dover Patrol Memorial, expressing to you personally our feelings of greatest admiration and most sincere esteem.

I remain, dear Admiral,
Your very affectionate
Albert

The Dover Patrol monument, designed
by Sir Aston Webb RA, was erected at
Leathercote Point, St Margaret's, near
Dover.

Admiral of the Fleet Lord Keyes of Zeebrugge and Dover, the last Admiral to
command the Dover Patrol, died in his sleep in the early morning of 26 December
1945, after a long illness.

'We have lost,' said Sir Winston Churchill, in a radio broadcast to the nation that
night, 'one of the great sailors of the Royal Navy, who embodied its traditions and
renewed its glories. It was by men like him, in whom the fire and force of valiance
burned, that our island was guarded during perilous centuries. The fame of Zeebrugge
will hold its place among our finest naval actions. In this war, too [Second World War],
Roger Keyes, as Chief of Combined Operations, laid the first keels of landing craft of
many types without which the Liberation of Europe from across the channel could not
have been possible. The Admiral's countrymen and friends throughout the British
Empire salute his services and cherish his memory. Our hearts go out to his widow –
always his comrade and champion.'

With every honour a grateful nation could show, Roger Keyes was brought in state
through the silent streets of London to his funeral service in Westminster Abbey, where
all the world had sent their representatives to pay homage. At the end of the ceremony
he was taken to the St James's cemetery, Dover. There, in the reddish glow of a

winter's sunset, they laid him to rest beside his fallen Zeebrugge comrades in arms. The words of the Stevenson's 'Requiem', sung in the abbey a few hours earlier, seemed more poignant at that moment.

> Home is the sailor, home from the sea,
> And the hunter home from the hill.

Admiral Sir Reginald Hugh Spencer Bacon KVO, KCVO, DSO died at his home, Braishfield Lodge, near Romsey, on 9 June 1947. It is also perhaps fitting to associate the words of Stevenson's 'Requiem' to Admiral Bacon, who, throughout his tenure of office as commander of the Dover Patrol, applied himself with characteristic zeal to organize a command sadly lacking in modern materials. The measure of his success is borne out by the support he gave to the men under his command and the unquestionable support he gave to the sea flank of the armies in France. His knowledge of navigation in difficult waters off the Belgian coast, and operating in the face of formidable German heavy artillery, demands admiration.

In the eighty years that have elapsed since 1918, there has been another world war and several lesser skirmishes that have gripped the British people in a craven regard that they, and the Royal Navy, can proclaim beyond doubt to defend their country's interests. The white ensign is, and always has been, a symbol of chivalry, bravery and humanity both in peace and war. Throughout the many campaigns involving the Royal Navy, there are none, in my opinion, which evoke a sense of pride more than the Dover Patrol during the First World War.

Glossary

AA	Anti-aircraft
APS	Auxiliary Patrol Service
BEF	British Expeditionary Force
Bluejacket	Sailor (slang)
C-in-C	Commander-in-Chief
CGM	Conspicuous Gallantry Medal
CMB	Coastal Motor Boat
CO	Commanding Officer
DSC	Distinguished Service Cross
DSM	Distinguished Service Medal
DSO	Distinguished Service Order
GHQ	General Headquarters
HAA	Heavy Anti-aircraft Artillery
HE	High Explosive
HQ	Headquarters
Matelot	Sailor (slang)
ML	Motor Launch
MGB	Motor Gun Boat
MTB	Motor Torpedo Boat
RA	Royal Artillery
RAMC	Royal Army Medical Corps
RM	Royal Marine
RMLI	Royal Marine Light Infantry
RN	Royal Navy
RNR	Royal Navy Reserve
RNVR	Royal Navy Volunteer Reserve
TBD	Torpedo Boat Destroyer
WRNS	Women's Royal Navy Service
WT	Wireless Telegraphy
VC	Victoria Cross

Appendices

APPENDIX NOTES TO GUIDE THE READER

The most fraught aspect of listing every vessel that served with Dover Command during 1914–18 is to have a hard time selecting those which actually served for more than one month. The author decided to include the ships which were, at various times, detached from the Harwich Force but, when it was necessary to list the 4th Submarine Flotilla, many submarines served with other flotillas on the south and east coasts and abroad. The lists will, however, despite many anomalous entries in official documents, provide the reader with a clear overview of the many types of vessels which served in the command. Listing hundreds of vessels is one thing but to list every aircraft, seaplane and flying boat serving in the RNAS under the command of the Admirals of Dover Command would be a tedious exercise beyond the remit of this work.

GERMAN GUN BATTERIES DEFENDING ZEEBRUGGE

No.	Name	Number & Gun Size
1	Bremen	Four 4-in
2	Lekkerbek	Four 4-in
3	Hamburg	Six 4-in
4	Kaiser Wilhelm	Four 12-in
5	Freya	Three 6-in
6	Augusta	Four 8-in
7	Goeben	Three 6-in
8	The Mole	Four 4-in
9	The Mole	Two 6-in
10	Württemberg	Four 4-in
11	Grossen	Four 11-in (howitzers)
12	Belgische	Four 5-in
13	Donkerklok	Four 11-in

No.	Name	Number & Gun Size
14	Kaiserin	Four 6-in
15	Hafen	Four 4-in
16	Hertha	Four 8-in
17	De Haan	Four 11-in

GERMAN GUN BATTERIES DEFENDING OSTEND

No.	Name	Number & Gun Size
18	Deutschland	Four 15-in
19	Turkijen	Four 11-in
20	Irene	Three 6-in
21	Hindenburg	Four 11-in
22	Frederich	Four 4-in
23	Eylau	Four 4-in
24	Palace	Two 6-in
25	Tirpitz	Four 11-in
26	Cecilie	Four 6-in
27	Oldenburg	Four 6-in
28	Baesler	Four 6-in
29	Antwerpen	Five 4-in
30	Achen I	Four 6-in
31	Achen II	One 6-in
32	Lengenboon I	One 15-in
33	Lengenboon II	Two 6-in
34	Lengenboon III	Two 6-in
35	Lengenboon IV	Two 8-in (howitzers)
36	Lengenboon V	Four 6-in

Cruisers

Aboukir (Lost 22.9.14)
Active
Adventure
Attentive
Canterbury
Carysfort
Conquest
Cressy (Lost 22.9.14)
Foresight
Hogue (Lost 22.9.14)
Irresistible
Redoubtable
Revenge
Sentinel
Venerable
Sapphire

Monitors	Built	Armament	Remarks
Humber	1914	3 6-in 2 4.7-in	Ex-Brazilian
Mersey	1914	3 6-in 2 4.7-in	Ex-Brazilian
Severn	1914	3 6-in 2 4.7-in	Ex-Brazilian
General Craufurd	1915	2 12-in 4 6-in 2 3-in	
General Wolfe	1915	2 12-in 4 6-in 2 3-in	1 18-in added in 1918
Lord Clive	1915	2 12-in 4 6-in 2 3-in	Later re-armed with 3 15-in then a single 18-in
Prince Eugene	1915	2 12-in 4 6-in 2 3-in	Single 18-in added in 1918
Prince Rupert	1915	2 12-in 4 6-in 2 3-in	
Sir John Moore	1915	2 12-in 4 6-in 2 3-in	
Marshal Ney	1915	2 15-in 8 4-in 2 3-in	Re-armed with 6-in in 1917 and used as Downs guardship
Marshal Soult	1915	2 15-in 8 4-in 2 3-in	
Erebus	1916	2 15-in 8 4-in 2 3-in	
Terror	1916	2 15-in 8 4-in 2 3-in	
Glatton	1918	2 9.2-in 6 6-in 2 3-in	Sunk in Dover Harbour in 1918. Ex-Norwegian Navy.
Gorgon	1918	2 9.2-in 6 6-in 2 3-in	Ex-Norwegian Navy.

Small Monitor

M 21   (Lost 20.10.18)
M 23
M 24
M 25
M 26
M 27

Sloop/Gunboat

Bustard
Drudge
Excellent
Niger   (Lost 11.11.14)
Rinaldo
Seagull
Spanker
Vestal
Wildfire

P-Boats

P 11
P 12   (Lost 4.11.18)
P 17
P 19
P 21
P 23
P 24
P 34
P 47
P 48
P 49
P 50
P 52
P 57
P 58
P 64

DESTROYERS ATTACHED TO DOVER PATROL

30-Knot Turtle Back

Boxer   (Lost 8.2.18)
Crane

Falcon
Fawn
Flirt   (Lost 27.10.16)
Gypsy
Greyhound
Kangaroo
Leven
Mermaid
Myrmidon   (Lost 26.3.17)
Panther
Racehorse
Syren
Violet

River Class

Foyle   (Mined 15.3.17)
Hope
Lapwing
Martin
Phoenix
Ure
Teviot
Velox   (Mined 25.10.15)

Tribal Class

Afridi
Amazon
Cossack
Crusader
Ghurka   (Lost 8.2.17)
Maori   (Lost 7.5.15)
Mohawk
Nubian ★   (Torpedoed 26.10.16)
Saracen
Tartar   (Mined 24.6.17)
Viking   (Mined 29.12.15)
Zulu ★   (Mined 8.11.16)
Zubian ★

★*Nubian* and *Zulu* were joined together and commissioned as *Zubian* (2.7.17).

L Class

Laertes
Laforey   (Lost 25.3.17)
Lance

Landrail
Lark
Laurel
Laverock   (Torpedoed 1917)
Lawford
Legion
Liberty
Linnet
Llewellyn   (Torpedoed 1917)
Lochinvar
Lucifer
Lydiard

Acasta Class

Ambuscade
Paragon   (Lost 18.3.17)
Porpoise
Unity
Victor

Marksman Class

Kempenfelt
Nimrod

Talisman Class

Termagant
Trident

M Class

Manly
Mansfield
Mastiff
Matchless
Medea
Melpomene
Mentor
Meteor
Milne
Minos
Miranda
Moorsom
Morris
Murray
Myngs

North Star   (Lost 23.4.18)
Nugent
Phoebe
Sceptre
Scout
Stork
Teazer
Tempest
Tetrach
Truculant
Ulleswater

Flotilla Leaders

Abdiel
Botha   (Torpedoed 21.3.18)
Broke
Douglas
Faulknor
Lightfoot
Lizard
Marksman
Swift
Warwick   (Mined 8.5.18)
Whirlwind

French Destroyers Attached to Dover Command

Adventurier
Bouclier
Capitaine Mehl
Enseigne Roux
Entende
Francis Garnier
Intrépide
Lestin
Magon
Obusier
Oriflamme
Roux

Hospital Ships

Anglia   (Lost 17.11.15)
Brighton
Cambria
Dieppe

Jan Breydell
Newhaven
St Andrew
St David
St Denis
St Patrick
Stad Antwerpen

Trinity House Ships

Alert
Argus
Vestral

Transport Ships

Arundel
Golden Eagle
Invicta
Onward
Pieter de Coninck
Princess Clementine
Princess Elizabeth
Princess Henriette
Princess Victoria
Queen   (Lost 27.10.16)
Sussex
Victoria
Ville de Liege

Depot Ships

Arrogant
Hazard
Hindustan

Mersey Ferries

Daffodil
Iris

Tugs

Conqueror
Firm   (Paddle Tug)
Herculaneum
Lady Brassey

Lady Crudall
William Gray

Balloon Vessels

Arctic
City of Oxford
Menelaus

Steam Lighters

Bickford
Curran
Goole X
Gransha
Lewin

Blockships

Brilliant
Intrepid
Iphigenia
Livonia
Montrose
Sappho
Sirius
Spanish Prince
Thetis
Vindictive

Boom Vessels

BV.17
BV.18
BV.41
BV.42

Survey Vessels

Daisy
Esther

Airships (Capel Le Ferne)

SS.1	SS.29	SSZ.1
SST.1	C.21	SSP.1
SS.2	SS.32	SSZ.2

SST.8   C.23   SSP.3   Hero
SS.4   SS.37   SSZ.3   Highlander
             C.23A   Hull Trader
SS.5   SSZ.4   Jacamar   (Lost 28.1.17)
SS.8   SSZ.5   James Pond   (Lost 15.2.18)
SS.9   SSZ.18   John Sherborn (Lost 6.3.15)
SS.10   SSZ.26   King's Grey
SS.10A   SSZ.29   Kate Lewis
SS.11   SSZ.36   Laroone
SS.12   SSZ.46   Leander   (Lost 6.8.15)
SS.13   SSZ.69   Lena Melling   (Lost 23.4.16)
SS.14   SSZ.74   Lord George
SS.14A   Lydian   (Lost 18.9.15)
SS.26   Macfarlane
SS.28   Magnolia
                                      Meror
                                      Notre Dame de Lourdes

Trawlers

                                      Osta
                                      Ostrich II
Agate   (Lost 14.3.18)   Otello II   (Lost 31.10.15)
Angelus   (Lost 28.2.16)   Pitfour
Balfour   (Lost 13.5.18)   Princess Beatrice (Lost 5.10.14)
Ben Ardna   (Lost 8.8.15)   Raglan Castle
Bona Law   (Lost 27.10.15)   Returno
Carlilon   (Lost 24.12.15)   Russell II
Carlton   (Lost 21.2.16)   Sabreur
Carmania II   Savitri
City of Dundee (Lost 14.9.15)   Saxon Prince   (Lost 28.3.16)
Colleague   St. Germain
Columbia   (Lost 1.5.15)   St. Maurice
Cleon   (Lost 1.2.18)   Strathcoe
Corona   (Lost 23.3.16)   Strathgairn
Dagon   (Lost 8.12.16)   The Norman
De La Pole   (Lost 4.2.16)   Viernoe
Dinas   Weigelia   (Lost 28.2.16)
Drumlochly   (Lost 29.1.18)
E.E.S.
Electra II   ## Drifters
Elysian
Eros   Acceptable
Erna   Achievable
Equinox   Ajax II   (Lost 27.10.16)
Etoile Polaire (Lost 3.12.15)   Alaburn
Falmouth III   (Lost 17.11.15)   Arcady
Flicker   (Lost 4.3.16)   Arndilly Castle
Fraser   (Lost 17.6.17)   Au Fait   (Lost 25.4.16)
Glen Boyne   (Lost 4.1.19)   BTB
Goeland II   Begonia
H.E. Stroud   Beryl II

Buckler		Lord Claud Hamilton	
Campanula		Lord Cromer	
Calceolaria	(Lost 27.10.18)	Lord Howard	
Chrysanthemum		Lord Leitrim	
City of Edinburgh		Loyal Friend	
City of Liverpool	(Lost 31.7.18)	Loyal Star	
City of Glasgow		Ma Freen	
Clover Bank A.379	(Lost 24.4.16)	Majesty	
Clove Bank A.731	(Lost 15.2.18)	Mary Cowie	
Cosmos	(Lost 15.2.18)	Mary	
Christina Mayes		Mishe Nahma	
Christina Craig	(Lost 15.2.18)	Nevertheless	
Coleus	(Lost 4.10.18)	Ocean Crest	
Courage		Ocean Hope	
Covent Garden		Ocean Pilot	
Datum	(Lost 27.10.16)	Ocean Reward	
Devon County		Ocean Roamer	
Dewey	(Lost 12.8.17)	Our Friend	
East Briton		Paradox	
EBC		Paramount	
East Holme		Persistive	(Lost 9.2.16)
Eskburn	(Lost 30.11.16)	Pleasant	
Ethnee	(Lost 15.1.18)	Present Help	
Feasible		Protect	(Lost 16.3.17)
Fearless		Reaper	
Fraserburgh		Redwald	
Frons Olivae	(Lost 12.10.15)	Reward	
George V	(Lost 3.6.17)	Roeburn	(Lost 27.10.16)
Girl Annie		Rooke	(Lost 3.8.16)
Girl Eva	(Lost 2.10.16)	RRS	
Girl Norah		Scania	(Lost 2.8.18)
Gleaner of the Sea	(Lost 27.10.16)	Shipmates	
Glen Afton		Sibulus	
Golden Grain		Silver Line	
Gracie	(Lost 10.2.17)	Silver Queen	(Lost 15.2.18)
Great Heart	(Lost 24.9.15)	South Tyne	
Herring Searcher		Spotless Prince	(Lost 27.10.16)
Hyacinth		Tessie	
IFS		Treasure	
James Fletcher		Try Again	
Jeannie Murray	(Lost 15.2.18)	Veracity	(Lost 15.2.18)
Joe Chamberlain		Violet May	
John Lincoln		Waveney II	(Lost 27.10.16)
John Robert		W. Elliott	(Lost 15.2.18)
Kessingland		White Rose	(Lost 26.7.16)
Launch Out	(Lost 27.10.16)	Young Crow	
Lord Charles Beresford		Young Kenneth	

Drifters Engaged on Mine Clearance Duties Off Flanders Coast Between December 1918 and September 1919

Anticyclone
Black Night
Firmament
Hailstorm
Heat Wave
Imbat
Pack Ice
Red Sky
Runnel
Scend
Scour
Shadow
Sheet Lightning
Storm Centre
Sunlight
Swirl

Yachts

Aries	(Lost 31.10.15)
Diane	
Grainaigh	
Liberty	
Marcella	(Lost 24.3.16)
Ombra	
Paulina	
Queen Alexandra	
Sanda	(Lost 25.9.15)

Downs Boarding Flotilla

Carcass	
Cerberus	
Ceto	
Ceylon	
Char	(Lost 16.1.15)
Codfish	
Steel Castle	

Minelayers

Andromache
Biarritz

Latonia
Naiad
Opollo
Orvieto
Princess Margaret

Seaplane Carriers

Hermes	(Lost 31.10.14)
Riviera	
Vindex	

Oilers

Eupion

Coastal Motor Boats (CMB)

No.		
	1	(Lost 19.6.17)
	2	
	4	
	5	
	7	
	8	(Lost 27.9.17)
	10	(Lost 7.5.18)
	11	(Lost 2.11.17)
	12	
	15	
	16A	
	17A	
	18A	(Lost 12.4.18)
	19	
	20	
	21B	
	22B	
	24A	
	25BD	
	26B	
	27A	
	28A	
	29	
	30B	
	32A	
	33A	(Lost 12.4.18)
	34A	
	35A	
	39B	(Lost 28.4.18)
	71A	(Lost 15.10.18)

Motor Launch (ML)

11	
16	
17	
22	
23	
30	
60	
79	
105	
110	(Lost 23.4.18)
121	(Lost 22.12.18)
128	
223	
239	
241	
249	
252	
254	(Lost 10.5.18)
258	
262	
272	
274	
276	
278	(Lost 15.1.18)
279	
280	
282	
283	
308	
314	
345	
356	(Lost 11.4.18)
394	
416	
420	
422	
424	(Lost 23.4.18)
429	
448	
512	
513	
525	
526	
533	
538	
549	
551	
552	
555	
556	
558	
560	
561	(Lost 21.10.18)
562	

Paddle Minesweepers (PMS)

Albyn	
Balmoral	
Brighton Queen	(Lost 6.10.15)
Cotillion	
Coverley	
Chelmsford	
Duchess of Montrose	(Lost 18.3.17)
Eglington	
Gatwick	
Gavotte	
Goodwood	
Horn Pipe	
Jupiter II	
Kempton	(Lost 24.6.17)
Lingfield	
Marmion II	
Mazurka	
Minuete	
Nepaulin	(Lost 20.4.17)
Newbury	
Pirouette	
Plumpton	(Lost 19.10.18)
Quadrille	
Ravenswood	
Redcar	(Lost 24.6.17)
Sarabande	
Tarantella	

SUBMARINES OF 4TH SUBMARINE FLOTILLA

A Class

A11
A12

C Class

1, 2, 3 (blown up at Zeebrugge), 6, 7, 8, 9, 10, 12, 13, 14, 15, 16, 17, 18, 19, 20, 21, 22, 23, 24, 25, 26, 27, 28, 29, 30, 31 (Lost 4.1.15), 32, 34, 35.

D Class

1, 2, 3 (Lost 15.3.18), 4, 5, 6, 7, 8.

F Class

1

German U-boat losses within Dover Patrol area

U5   Mined off Zeebrugge, December 1914. Kapitänleutnant J. Lemmer killed.

U8   Sunk by destroyers, March 1915. Kapitänleutnant A. Stoss killed.

U11   Mined off Zeebrugge, December 1914. Kapitänleutnant F. von Suchodoletz killed.

U37   Missing in Dover Strait, April 1915. Kapitänleutnant E. Wilcke killed.

U48   Destroyed on Goodwin Sands, November 1917. Kapitänleutnant C. Edeling killed.

U109   Sunk by drifter *Beryl III*, January 1918. Kapitänleutnant O. Rey killed.

UB10   Scuttled at Bruges, October 1918.

UB13   Mined off Walcheran, April 1918. Oberleutnant A. Metz killed.

UB20   Sunk by flying boat, July 1917. Oberleutnant H. Glimpf killed.

UB31   Sunk by drifters, May 1918. Oberleutnant W. Braun killed.

UB33   Mined in Dover Strait, April 1918. Oberleutnant F. Gregor killed.

UB35   Sunk by *Leven*, January 1918. Oberleutnant K. Stoter killed.

UB36   Missing in Channel, June 1917. Oberleutnant von Keyserlinck killed.

UB38   Mined in Dover Strait, February 1918. Oberleutnant G. Bachmann killed.

UB40   Scuttled at Bruges, October 1918.

UB55   Mined in Dover Strait, April 1918. Oberleutnant Wenninger captured.

UB56   Mined in Dover Strait, December 1917. Oberleutnant H. Valentiner killed.

UB57   Mined off Zeebrugge, August 1918. Oberleutnant J. Losz killed.

UB58   Mined in Dover Strait, March 1918. Oberleutnant W. Lowe killed.

UB59   Scuttled at Bruges, October 1918.

UB103   Sunk by drifters, September 1918. Kapitänleutnant P. Hundius killed.

UB108   Mined in Dover Strait, July 1918. Kapitänleutnant W. Amberger killed.

UB109   Mined in Dover Strait, August 1918. Kapitänleutnant Ramien captured.

UB113   Mined in Dover Strait, September 1918. Oberleutnant U. Pilzeder killed.

UC1   Sunk by flying boat, July 1917. Oberleutnant O. Mildenstein killed.

UC4   Scuttled at Bruges, October 1918.

UC6   Sunk by flying boat, September 1917. Oberleutnant G. Reichenbach killed.

UC14   Mined off Zeebrugge, October 1917. Oberleutnant Fedderson killed.

UC19   Sunk by *Llewellyn*, December 1916. Oberleutnant A. Nitzsche killed.

UC21   Mined off North Foreland, September 1917. Oberleutnant von Zerboni di Sposetti killed.

UC26   Sunk by *Milne*, May 1916. Oberleutnant von Schmettow killed.

UC36   Sunk by flying boat, May 1917. Kapitänleutnant G. Buch killed.

UC46   Sunk by *Liberty*, February 1917. Oberleutnant F. Moecke killed.

UC50   Sunk by *Zubian*, February 1918. Kapitänleutnant R. Seuffer killed.

UC61   Destroyed off Cap Gris Nez, July 1917. Kapitänleutnant G. Gerth captured.

UC63   Torpedoed by *E52* Dover Strait, November 1917. Oberleutnant von Heydebrech killed.

UC64   Mined in Dover Strait, June 1918. Oberleutnant F. Schwartz killed.

UC65   Torpedoed by *C15* off Beachy Head, November 1917. Kapitänleutnant K. Lafrenz captured.

UC72   Sunk by flying boat, September 1917. Oberleutnant E. Voigt killed.

UC77   Sunk by trawler Dover Strait, July 1918. Oberleutnant J. Reis killed.

UC78   Sunk by drifter Dover Strait, May 1918. Kapitänleutnant H. Kukat killed.

UC79   Mined in Dover Strait, April 1918. Oberleutnant A. Krameyer killed.

Bibliography

The purpose of this book is to provide an account of events which occurred in the Dover Patrol during the First World War. Further reference to the bibliography will provide the reader with a selection of books which offer any amount of statistical data of a more specialist nature.

Aspinall-Oglander, Cecil. *Roger Keyes*, The Hogarth Press, 1951.

Bacon, Admiral Sir Reginald, KCB, KCVO, DSO. *The Dover Patrol 1915–1917*, vols 1, II, Hutchinson & Co., 1919.

Bennett, Geoffrey. *Naval Battles Of The First World War*, Batsford Ltd, 1968.

Carlile, J.C. *Folkestone During The War 1914–1919*, F.J. Parsons Ltd, 1919.

Carpenter, Captain A.F.B., VC, RN. *The Blocking of Zeebrugge*, H. Jenkins Ltd, 1921.

Chatterton, E.K. *The Auxiliary Patrol*, Sidgwick & Jackson Ltd, 1923.

Coxon, Lieutenant-Commander S.W., RNVR. *Dover During The Dark Days*, The Bodley Head, 1919.

Dittmar, F.J. and Colledge, J.J. *British Warships 1914–1919*, Ian Allen, 1972.

Dolby, James. *The Steel Navy*, Macdonald, 1962.

Dorling, Captain Taprell, DSO, FRHistS, RN. *Swept Channels*, Hodder & Stoughton Ltd, London, 1935.

Evans, Captain E.R.G.R., DSO, CB, RN. *Keeping The Seas*, Sampson Low, Marston and Co. Ltd, 1919.

Fleming, H.M. Le. *Warships Of World War 1*, Ian Allan Ltd, 1961.

Gilbert, Martin. *First World War*, Weidenfeld and Nicolson, 1994.

Gray, Edwyn A. *The U-Boat War 1914–1918*, Leo Cooper, 1972.

Keyes, Sir Roger. *The Naval Memoirs*, Thornton Butterworth Ltd, 1935.

Mowthorpe, Ces. *Battlebags*, Sutton Publishing Ltd, 1995.

Newbolt, H. *Naval Operations*, vols. iv, v, Longmans, 1928, 1931; Corbett, Sir Julian S. vols. i, ii, iii, Longmans, 1920.

Pound, Reginald. *Evans Of The Broke*, Oxford University Press, 1963.

Prendergast, M. and Gibson, R.H. *The German Submarine War 1914–1918*, Constable, 1931.

Roskill, Captain S.W., DSC, RN, MA. *The Naval Air Service, 1908–1918*, vol. 1, Navy Records Society, 1969.

Sturtivant, Ray and Page, Gordon. *Royal Navy Aircraft Serials And Units, 1911–1919*, Air Britain Publication, 1992.

Thomas, Lowell. *Raiders of the Deep*, William Heinemann Ltd, London, 1929.

Wells, Captain John. *The Royal Navy*, Alan Sutton Publishing Ltd, 1994.

Whitehouse, Arch. *The Zeppelin Fighters*, Robert Hale Ltd, 1968.

Williams, Geoffrey. *Wings Over Westgate*, Kent County Library, 1985.

Index

Lightfoot 87
Lightoller, Lt C.H. 109
Litchield-Speer, Captain
  F.S. 72
Llewellyn 92, 93
Lloyd George (Prime
  Minister) 88, 131, 146
Lombartzyde 21
London North West
  Railway Company 60
Lord Claud Hamilton 39,
  59, 81
Lord Charles Beresford 70,
  80
Lord Clive 46, 49, 52, 55,
  176
Lord Dunraven 62
Lord Leitrim 173
Lord Tredegar 62
Lord Warden Hotel 68
Losz, Oberleutnant J. 175
Lowe, Oberleutnant W.
  146
Lowestoft 9, 59
Loyal Friend 173
Loyal Star 104
Ludendorf, General 89,
  175
Lusitania (coaster) 69
Luisatania (liner) 61
Lynes, Commodore
  Hubert 107, 158, 167,
  168

Macedonia 70
Macfarlane 71
Mach, Flt Lt 79
Mackenzie, Flt Lt C.R. 80
Mackenzie, Flt Lt W.R.
  113
Magon 123, 147
Magor, Flt-Sub-Lt N.A.
  120, 121

Maloja 68
Majesty 128
Manning, Captain L. 60,
  61
Mansfield 157
Maori 11, 36, 39
Marcella 103
Marine Parade (Dover) 22,
  23, 119
Margate 49, 94, 100
Marksman 141
Marshal Ney 53, 54, 57, 94,
  100
Marshal Soult 75, 77, 114,
  122, 176
Mastiff 120
Maxwell, Lt Cmdr T.K. 39
Medea 37, 38, 69, 73
Melpomene 73, 74, 141
Melsom, Lt Cmdr A.P.
  139, 140
Mentor 98, 100, 105, 122
Mermaid 49, 87, 139
Meror 128
Mersey 13, 19, 22
Metz, Oberleutnant A. 73
Middlekerk 20, 54, 55
Middle Deep 46
Milne 73, 105
ML254 169
ML276 169
ML282 162
Miranda 105
Mitchell, Matron M.S. 61
Moorsom 122, 142
Morgan, Lt L. 64
Morris 147, 148
Morrish, Flt-Sub-Lt 106
Mohawk 1, 7, 11, 21, 23,
  58, 83
Muecke, Oberleutnant F.
  90, 91
Muloch, Flt Lt 67

Murray 73, 141
Myngs 93, 179
Myrmidon 56

Naiad 13
Nepaulin 90, 93
Newbury 141, 143
Newhaven 62
Nieuport 8, 45, 77, 103,
  124, 150, 181
Nieuport pier 19
Nieuport (aircraft) 65, 66,
  67, 80
Niger 24
Nimrod 113
North, Chief Skipper 127
North East Varne 130
North Foreland 8, 68, 70,
  87, 93, 94, 100, 143,
  175
North Hinder (light vessel)
  49, 69, 87, 105, 113
North Star 123, 157, 163,
  165
Nubian 11, 72, 83, 87, 89
Nugent 141

Ocean Crest 80, 81
Ocean Roamer 173
Oliphant, Cmdr H.G.L.
  50, 117
Ombra 81
Onward 181
Orvietto 72
Osta 72
Ostend 8, 9, 13, 14, 18,
  23, 39, 44, 51, 53, 77,
  79, 81, 84, 103, 104,
  107, 111, 114, 122, 123,
  133, 135, 136, 137, 148,
  149, 150, 151, 166, 172,
  181, 184
Ostrich 72